INTERNATIONAL
Home Cooking

fifty years ago...

The United Nations International School, (UNIS), was founded by a group of United Nations parents who wanted to provide their children with an education that fostered respect for their diverse backgrounds in the spirit of internationalism and global understanding.

From small beginnings—it started in 1947 as a nursery school for 20 children from 15 countries—UNIS has grown, so that it now has more than 1,500 students enrolled from kindergarten through grade 12, from more than 100 countries. The school continues to draw its multinational student body from United Nations families, but today more than half the students are from the local community and not related to the UN.

Located on two campuses in New York City, UNIS benefits in many ways from its special relationship with the United Nations. From an early age students learn about the ideals and principles embodied in the Charter of the United Nations and are taught to respect different values, traditions, cultures, languages, perceptions and aspirations. There are also more tangible links such as the outings for UNIS students to the UN Headquarters building, the annual graduation ceremony held in the impressive UN General Assembly hall, and the international government sponsorship of some faculty members.

Although English is the language of instruction, nine other languages— Arabic, Chinese, French, German, Greek, Italian, Japanese, Russian, and Spanish—are taught daily at the school by native speakers. The faculty represents 50 nations with most of the faculty members speaking at least one language in addition to English. The UNIS faculty has also played a major role in developing the International Baccalaureate, the innovative and rigorous high school curriculum and diploma that has now gained widespread acceptance as a credential of exceptional merit for entrance to universities and colleges in the United States and around the world.

One graduating student summed up her UNIS experience this way: "To be part of UNIS is to be part of a diverse and supportive global family....I can't imagine a more stimulating educational environment to have grown up in than that at UNIS. It helped shape me into who I am today...a citizen of the United States and of the world."

INTERNATIONAL
Home Cooking

The United Nations International School 50th Anniversary Cookbook

First published in the United States by the
United Nations International School Parents' Association
© 1997 The United Nations International School Parents' Association. All rights reserved.
No part of this book may be reproduced in
any form without written permission from the publisher.

For further information, please contact:
United Nations International School Parents' Association
24-50 Franklin D. Roosevelt Drive
New York, NY 10010-4046

All proceeds from the sale of this book are to be donated to UNIS by the UNIS Parents' Association.

Cataloging-in-Publication Data available from the Library of Congress
ISBN 0-9658603-1-0

Editor Nancy Melcher
Designer and illustrator Rita Lascaro
Photographer Elizabeth Watt

Printed and bound in the United States by Quebecor Printing; first printing, 1997

To all the members of the UNIS family,
far and wide, past and present,
who have come together to share learning and
friendship, pride in their cultures, and
their wonderfully varied cuisines,
we dedicate this book.

The UNIS Fiftieth Anniversary Cookbook Committee

contents

soups, salads & breads

entrées

contents

accompaniments

desserts

breakfast, brunch & afternoon tea

the UNIS fiftieth anniversary cookbook

coordinators

Mary Mallios
Anne Ferril McCaffrey
Nancy Melcher

Barbara Marsh
   (Queens Campus)

committee

Annette Becker
Sumie Tanaka-Bonet
Judy Boomer
Jonathan Brenner
Merle Brenner
Delia Cameo
Stephanie Cheah
Junghwa Choi
Yvette Duran
Honey Essman
Sara Evans
Douglas Fairchild
Sadica Garcia
Defne Halman
Sam Sabine Kaminitzer
Candy Karcher
Liz Kennedy
Mayumi Kasuga

Jan Kawamura Kay
Barbara Kolson
Rita Lascaro
Susan Gammie Leigh
Laurie Levin
Diana Lofti
Philip McCaffrey
Rebecca Murry
Suzanne Randolph
Susan Greenberg
   Schneider
Rajul Sheth
Olga Shumikhin
Dorothy Small
Suzanne Wasserman
Elizabeth Watt
Jay Weiser
Mary Ann Zimmer

special thanks

Jim Anderson
Elizabeth Arnold
Ellen Cash
Josseline Charas
Jessica Cunningham
W. H. Freeman and
   Company
Carin Goldberg
Gary Goldberg
Rose Grant
Katherine Greene
Richard Greene
Maia Holden
Susan Horton
Lara Hovanesian
Gail Kinn
Nicole Kunz
Susan Markham
Pentagram Design
Eric Rayman
Linda Readerman
David Rockwell
Allyson Siegel
Florie Sommers
Lyn Stallworth
Frederika Van
   Eyndhoven
Nach Waxman

foreword

welcome...

What could be more appropriate for the United Nations International School (UNIS) than an international cookbook?

UNIS was founded 50 years ago with a mission to serve primarily the international diplomatic and business communities. We now have 1,500 students of more than 100 nationalities and a staff representing 50 nationalities. At UNIS differences among students—whether nationality, ethnicity, or religion—are celebrated rather than tolerated. Our diversity is our greatest strength, and we are grateful for it.

All of us at UNIS look forward to tasting the delicious foods whose secrets lie among these pages.

Joseph J. Blaney
Director

introduction

sharing...

A simple exchange between two 6-year-olds—a quarter of a peanut butter and jelly sandwich for two pieces of sushi. An invitation to Thanksgiving dinner, a seder, a lunar New Year's feast, or a banquet at the end of Ramadan. For 50 years, the members of the UNIS community have been seated at a common table—sharing the foods we eat and our delight in the traditions and cuisines of our homelands. For 50 years, the members of our unique community have also shared our secret sources—the freshest Scotch bonnet peppers, the tangiest feta cheese, the most aromatic *garam masala*.

So what better way to commemorate our fiftieth anniversary than to publish a cookbook celebrating the joys of home cooking? The word went out, and more than 800 recipes poured in from all over the world—from alumni and former teachers and administrators, even one from a member of the first UNIS class! Still more came from the current UNIS parents, students, and staff.

Choosing some 300 recipes from this culinary bounty was a delicious challenge. We spent months reading and refining, testing and tasting. The yield? A cookbook filled with the best of traditional and contemporary home cooking from more than 50 United Nations member countries—proof that our culinary traditions, as mirrors of our respective histories and cultures, can indeed bring us together at a common table.

how this book is organized

Because this is so diverse a collection of recipes, we thought long and hard about how best to organize it and about how to express measurements and ingredients. Here, briefly, is what we decided.

The book is divided into six sections:

appetizers & beverages
soups, salads & breads
entrées
accompaniments
desserts
breakfast, brunch & afternoon tea.

Recipes in each section, except entrées, are organized alphabetically by country or region. Entrées are arranged in categories (for example, beef/lamb or vegetarian), and within each category the recipes are organized alphabetically by country or region. The names of most recipes are given in English followed by a national name. Familiar non-English names, such as *Baklava* and *Guacamole*, are given first; most are followed by a descriptive English name.

Because virtually all recipes submitted used the system of weights and measures common in the United States, we, too, have used that system. We have, however, included tables of equivalents (page 318) for those who cook more comfortably with either UK or metric weights and measures. The names used to describe foods and cooking processes are those typically used in the United States. Finally, because ingredients for some national cuisines are not readily available in supermarkets, we have also included a list of New York area suppliers (page 319), indicating those that can fill mail orders.

So…happy cooking. Come share the feast!

The UNIS Fiftieth Anniversary Cookbook Committee

appetizers & beverages

AUSTRIA

Cheese with Anchovies and Capers

Liptauer Käse

This recipe for a classic Austrian cheese spread was brought to the United States from Vienna 60 years ago by the great-grandmother of a UNIS student.

1. Mix cream cheese, onion, and anchovy paste or anchovies together with an electric mixer.

2. Add paprika until mixture turns pink.

3. Gently stir in capers. Serve with thinly sliced rye or pumpernickel bread or crackers.

servings: 1 cup

1 package (8 ounces) cream cheese

2 to 3 tablespoons finely chopped onion

1 tablespoon anchovy paste, or 3 teaspoons chopped anchovies with oil

½ teaspoon imported paprika, or to taste

2 teaspoons capers

Crab Claws Stuffed with Shrimp

Páng Xiè Xiā

---

servings: 10

1¼ pounds raw shrimp, peeled and deveined

2 teaspoons salt

10 blue crab claws

½ egg white

1 teaspoon chopped chives

⅛ teaspoon pepper

¼ teaspoon sugar

2 teaspoons cornstarch

1 teaspoon Asian sesame oil

1 cup fine dry bread crumbs

5 cups vegetable oil

Because Canton, a southern province of China, has over 1,000 miles of coastline, the sea has been a rich source for local cuisine, as this old Cantonese specialty reflects.

1. Toss shrimp with 1 teaspoon of the salt. Rinse under cold water and pat dry. Chop in food processor fitted with a steel blade. Set aside.

2. Bring 2 cups water to a boil in a medium saucepan. Place crab claws in a steamer and set over the water. Cover and steam crab claws for 10 minutes. Let cool.

3. Crack claws with a nutcracker. Carefully remove shell from base of claw, keeping meat at base and pincer shell intact. Set aside.

4. In a large mixing bowl, combine chopped shrimp, egg white, chives, remaining 1 teaspoon salt, pepper, sugar, 1 teaspoon cornstarch, and the sesame oil. Stir well.

5. Dust the crab claws with remaining 1 teaspoon cornstarch. Press some chopped shrimp around each crab claw, excluding the pincers (the uncoated pincers can serve as a handle). Place bread crumbs in a shallow dish; dredge claws in crumbs to coat completely, pressing firmly.

6. Heat oil in a large wok or deep frying pan until very hot. Slide in the stuffed claws and deep-fry until golden brown, about 5 minutes. Drain on paper towels.

CHINA

Salt and Pepper Shrimp

Yán Shuǐ Xiā

After black pepper was introduced to China during the Tang Dynasty, more than 1,100 years ago, its popularity among the wealthy was such that nearly every dish called for its use. This spicy, crunchy Cantonese dish, eaten with the shells, is redolent of garlic.

1. Marinate shrimp in salt, black pepper, and garlic powder for 1 to 2 hours.

2. Place cornstarch and shrimp in a plastic bag. Shake well to coat shrimp.

3. Heat 6 cups oil until very hot in a large, deep pan (350°F in deep fryer). Deep-fry shrimp until they turn red, about 3 minutes. Drain on paper towels. Arrange on serving platter atop a bed of shredded lettuce.

4. In a separate small frying pan, heat 2 tablespoons oil. Stir-fry chili pepper, scallion, and garlic for 2 to 3 minutes. Sprinkle over shrimp.

servings: 6 to 8

1½ pounds unshelled large raw shrimp, rinsed, deveined, legs removed, and patted dry

2 teaspoons salt

½ teaspoon black pepper

2 teaspoons garlic powder

2 tablespoons cornstarch

6 cups corn or vegetable oil for deep frying plus 2 tablespoons oil

½ green chili pepper, chopped

1 scallion, trimmed and chopped

4 to 5 garlic cloves, chopped

1 head Boston lettuce, shredded

CHINA

Boiled Five-Spice Eggs

Wǔ Xiang o Dàn

servings: 12

1 dozen eggs

5 tea bags (Orange Pekoe, China Black, or other black tea)

1 cup dark soy sauce

1 tablespoon five-spice powder*

Five-spice powder contains star anise, fennel seed, Szechuan pepper, clove, and cinnamon, which correspond to the five tastes: sweet, sour, bitter, pungent, and salty. These in turn represent the five elements: earth, wood, fire, metal, and water.

1. Place eggs in a pot with enough cold water to cover. Boil for 4 to 5 minutes. Lift one egg at a time out of the boiling water. Using a metal spoon, lightly crack each egg shell. Return eggs to pot.

2. Add tea, soy sauce, and five-spice powder to pot.

3. Simmer over low heat for 30 minutes.

4. Remove egg shells. Serve either hot or cold.

*Available at Asian food markets; see list of suppliers (page 319).

DENMARK

Danish Meatballs

Frikadeller

These meatballs are as Danish as the Dannebrog, the Danish flag. For all its simplicity, this dish provokes strong reactions, because each cook believes he or she holds the secret for preparing it in the proper way.

1. Preheat oven to 250°F. Place ground meat in a large bowl and add the flour or bread crumbs. Add onions, salt, pepper, thyme, and garlic.

2. Add eggs and blend well with a spoon. Add milk ¼ cup at a time, stirring, until the mixture reaches the consistency of uncooked meat loaf. Set aside for 30 minutes.

3. Shape into 1-inch balls.

4. Heat oil or butter in a large skillet. Cook over moderately high heat, turning occasionally, until meatballs are crispy and cooked through, about 10 minutes.

5. Transfer to serving platter and keep warm in oven while cooking the rest of the meatballs. Serve with rice, potatoes, or noodles.

servings: 6 to 8

1 pound each ground pork and ground veal or 2 pounds ground lamb

1 cup all-purpose flour or bread crumbs

2 medium onions, grated

2 teaspoons salt, or to taste

1 teaspoon pepper, or to taste

6 tablespoons fresh, chopped thyme or 2 tablespoons dried thyme

2 cloves garlic, minced

2 eggs (add 1 extra egg if using lamb)

1 cup milk (approximately)

¼ cup vegetable oil or butter for cooking

FRANCE

Roasted Peppers with Anchovies

Poivrons Grillés aux Anchois

servings: 6

4 large bell peppers, red and yellow, cut into ⅓-inch slices (8 to 10 strips each)

40 flat or rolled anchovies packed in oil (1 for each pepper strip)

3 tablespoons capers, drained and rinsed

1 to 2 tablespoons *herbes de Provence*

2 to 3 tablespoons olive oil

Bell peppers were first introduced to Europe in the early 16th century, a result of Christopher Columbus's explorations in America. They were soon adopted in sunny Provence, where roasted foods are often seasoned with herbes de Provence, *an aromatic combination of thyme, rosemary, bay leaf, basil, and savory.*

1. Preheat oven to 350°F. Place pepper slices in one layer on oiled roasting pan. Roast until soft and slightly brown on edges, about 15 to 20 minutes.

2. Transfer peppers to a serving platter. Arrange anchovies on pepper slices, one per slice. Sprinkle with capers and *herbes de Provence* and drizzle with olive oil.

3. Let stand for 2 to 3 hours. Serve at room temperature, accompanied by French bread.

FRANCE/VIETNAM

Smoked Turkey Spring Rolls

Paupiettes de Dinde Fumée

East meets West in this French-Vietnamese appetizer, which combines pasta with crunchy vegetables, aromatic herbs, and smoked turkey, all wrapped in soft rice paper and served with a fresh basil-mayonnaise dressing.

1. Combine egg, garlic, sugar, mustard, vinegar, and basil in a blender or food processor. Purée mixture.

2. With the motor running, slowly add the oil. Season with salt and pepper to taste and transfer to a container. Cover and refrigerate.

3. Cook pasta in a pot of boiling salted water for 2 minutes. Drain. Rinse with cold water and drain again.

4. Roll 2 slices of smoked turkey into a cigar shape. Repeat with remaining slices, to make 8 rolls.

5. In a large mixing bowl, combine pasta, carrots, cucumber, tomato, lettuce, basil, and bean sprouts.

6. In a large bowl of warm water, immerse one sheet of rice paper until it softens, about 30 seconds. Quickly remove and spread out flat on a dry work surface. Work with one sheet of rice paper at a time, keeping remaining sheets covered with a damp towel.

7. Place about ½ cup salad along bottom of the rice sheet, 2 inches away from the edges. Place 1 turkey roll on top of the salad. Roll rice paper halfway up, then fold both sides of the paper over the filling. Tuck in 3 or 4 sprigs of chives, and continue rolling the rice paper into a cylinder. Place seam-side down on a tray and cover with a damp towel. Continue with remaining sheets of rice paper. Serve with small individual bowls of dressing.

*Available at Asian food markets; see list of suppliers (page 319).

---

servings: 8 rolls

basil-mayonnaise dressing

- 1 large egg
- 1 teaspoon chopped garlic
- 1 teaspoon sugar
- 2 teaspoons Dijon mustard
- 2 tablespoons rice vinegar
- ¼ cup tightly packed basil leaves
- ½ cup vegetable oil
- Salt and freshly ground black pepper to taste

salad

- 4 ounces angel hair pasta (or rice noodles)
- 16 very thin slices smoked turkey breast (about 8 ounces)
- 2 large carrots, peeled and finely shredded (can be done in food processor)
- 1 medium cucumber, peeled, seeded, and finely shredded
- 1 large tomato, cored and diced
- 4 large Boston lettuce leaves, thick stem-ends removed, thinly sliced
- 3 cups fresh basil leaves, thinly sliced or whole
- 2 cups fresh bean sprouts
- 8 rounds rice paper *(banh trang),** 12½ inches in diameter
- 1 bunch fresh chives

Eggs in Mustard Sauce

Eier in Senfsosse

servings: 4

2 tablespoons butter

3 tablespoons all-purpose flour

½ cup half-and-half or light cream

1 cup chicken broth

2 to 3 tablespoons Dijon mustard

Salt to taste

8 hard-boiled eggs, peeled

These eggs, served whole in a golden mustard sauce, make a beautiful buffet offering. Keep warm in a chafing dish.

1. Preheat oven to 350°F. In a large skillet, melt butter over moderate heat. Gradually add flour, stirring with a whisk, to make a smooth paste. Slowly add half-and-half and chicken broth, stirring constantly. Add mustard and salt to taste.

2. Add eggs to sauce, stirring gently.

3. Place eggs and sauce in an ovenproof chafing dish. Bake for about 10 minutes, until slightly browned.

Cheese Roll

Käserolle

A tasty pinwheel of cheeses, meats, eggs, and herbs, this German appetizer is perfect for cocktail parties.

1. In the top half of a double boiler, melt cheese in one piece, 45 minutes to 1 hour.

2. While cheese is melting, mix cheese spread, butter, parsley, bell pepper, mustard, pickles, salt, pepper, and paprika until well combined. Set aside.

3. Place a 12 x 12-inch piece of plastic wrap on a cutting board. Slide melted cheese onto center of plastic wrap. Cover with another piece of plastic wrap of the same size. With a rolling pin, roll melted cheese into a square, approximately ½-inch thick. Remove top piece of plastic. Allow cheese to cool slightly.

4. While melted cheese is still warm, spread with prepared cheese-spread mixture. Sprinkle with chopped egg. Arrange meat slices to cover half of cheese-spread mixture. Beginning with meat side, using bottom piece of plastic wrap for help, roll to form a thick cylinder. Wrap tightly in foil. Chill at least 2 hours. Remove foil and cut roll into 1-inch slices. Remove plastic wrap and serve slices on French bread.

servings: 10 to 12

- 10-ounce piece Edam, Cheddar or Gouda cheese
- 16 ounces imported processed cheese spread
- 4 tablespoons (½ stick) butter, at room temperature
- 2 tablespoons chopped parsley or chives
- ¼ cup chopped red bell pepper
- 1 tablespoon prepared mustard
- 3 tablespoons chopped sour gherkin pickles
- ¼ teaspoon salt
- ¼ teaspoon pepper
- ¼ teaspoon paprika
- 1 hard-boiled egg, chopped
- 2 slices cold cuts, about 5 x 5-inches, such as ham, pastrami, or bologna

Greek Cheese Pastries

Tiropites

servings: about 60 pieces

- 8 ounces cottage cheese
- 8 ounces feta cheese, crumbled
- 3 eggs, beaten
- Salt and pepper to taste
- Flour (optional)
- 16 tablespoons (2 sticks) butter or margarine
- ¾ pound, about 20 sheets, phyllo dough*

Many popular Greek pastries, both savory and sweet, are made with the paper-thin dough called phyllo (or filo), which means "leaf" in Greek.

1. In a large bowl, beat cottage cheese, crumbled feta, and eggs. Mix well and add salt and pepper. If the mixture is very runny, add a little flour to thicken.

2. Melt butter in a small saucepan. Set aside.

3. Unfold phyllo dough and cut crosswise into 3 equal rectangles. (See diagram below.) Brush 1 rectangle with butter, using a pastry brush. Cover remaining dough with damp towel. Place 1 tablespoon of cheese mixture in lower-left corner of rectangle. Fold dough in half lengthwise. Then fold up a corner. Continue folding from side to side to form a triangle. As you are folding, periodically brush phyllo with the melted butter. Repeat with remaining rectangles.

4. Preheat oven to 425°F. Place finished triangles on baking sheets, brushing tops with melted butter.

5. Bake for 15 to 20 minutes, or until golden brown.

*Frozen phyllo should be thawed, unopened, in the refrigerator overnight. Unbaked phyllo dishes freeze well. To cook them, do not thaw; simply place directly into a preheated oven and increase baking time. Previously baked dishes can be reheated in a 350°F oven.

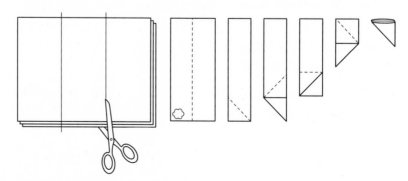

appetizers & beverages

GREECE

Greek Spinach Pie

Spanakopita

The Greek-American family of the contributor of this recipe enjoys this dish on holidays and special occasions. This spinach filling can also be used to make miniature phyllo appetizers. Scallions may be substituted for onions. See preceding page for tips on handling phyllo.

1. Preheat oven to 350°F. In a small frying pan, sauté onion in butter until soft. Set aside.

2. Cook spinach in the water clinging to its leaves over moderately high heat, covered, in a large pot until wilted, about 10 minutes. Press out excess liquid in colander. (Spinach may have to be added to pot in batches; as one batch wilts, add more spinach, stirring to evenly distribute over heat.)

3. In a large bowl, mix cooked onion, eggs, cottage cheese, feta cheese, dill, parsley, and wilted spinach. Season lightly with salt and pepper.

4. Lightly butter a 9 x 13 x 2-inch baking pan. Lay 1 sheet of phyllo in the pan and brush lightly with melted butter. Repeat with 9 more sheets in pan in the same manner. The edges of the phyllo will hang over sides of baking pan. Keep phyllo sheets covered with a damp cloth until you use them.

5. Pour in spinach mixture. Cover with remaining 10 phyllo sheets, brushing each lightly with melted butter. Trim overhanging edges of phyllo with scissors to an even length and roll up each edge decoratively, somewhat like a pie crust.

6. Bake pie for 40 to 50 minutes, or until it is piping hot throughout and golden brown on top.

---

servings: 12 to 16 pieces

- **1** medium onion, minced
- **3** tablespoons butter
- **3** pounds fresh spinach, well-rinsed, stemmed, and picked over
- **6** large eggs, lightly beaten
- **8** ounces cottage cheese
- **½** pound crumbled feta cheese
- **½** cup chopped fresh dill
- **½** cup minced flat-leaf parsley
  Salt and pepper to taste
- **¾** pound, about 20 sheets, phyllo dough
- **16** tablespoons (2 sticks) butter, melted

Mini Beef Patties

servings: 24 pieces

1 teaspoon vegetable oil

1 pound lean ground beef

1 medium onion, coarsely chopped

1 clove garlic

1 green bell pepper, coarsely chopped

1 red bell pepper, coarsely chopped

1 teaspoon each dried thyme, oregano, sage, and ground nutmeg

2 tablespoons tomato paste or barbecue sauce

Salt and pepper to taste

1 pound (4 cups) prepared refrigerated biscuit dough, puff pastry or homemade biscuit dough

Flaky, buttery little pastries containing meat, vegetables or cheese, are found in many Caribbean countries. However, this recipe is distinctly Grenadian, as it calls for a teaspoon of nutmeg. Though nutmeg was only introduced to Grenada in the mid-18th century, it is one of the country's principal exports, and Grenada is now responsible for a major part of the world's nutmeg supply.

1. Heat oil over moderate heat in large skillet. Add beef, stirring, until browned. Drain off excess fat.

2. In a food processor, combine onion, garlic, and bell peppers; pulse to finely chop. Add onion mixture, thyme, oregano, sage, nutmeg, tomato paste, salt, and pepper to beef. Over low heat, stirring constantly, cook until onions and peppers soften, about 10 minutes.

3. Preheat oven to 350°F. If using prepared biscuit dough, on a floured surface, roll to ⅛-inch thickness to yield three 3-inch rounds. If using puff pastry or homemade biscuit dough, on a floured surface, using a portion of the pastry at a time, roll to ⅛-inch thickness and cut into 3-inch rounds. Continue until all dough is used. Place rounds on an ungreased baking sheet.

4. Place 1 heaping teaspoon meat mixture on each round of dough and fold in half. Use fork to press edges together decoratively.

5. Bake for about 15 minutes or until patties are golden. Serve at room temperature.

Guyanese Split Pea Fritters

Poulourie

Many people in Guyana, on the Atlantic coast of South America, have roots in India. This dish, typical of East Indian cuisine, is often served at Hindu weddings and holidays, such as Diwali, *the Festival of Lights. Garam masala, the herb-and-spice blend used in these fritters, is composed of ground coriander, cumin, ginger, black pepper, cinnamon, pimiento, cardamom, bay leaves, and nutmeg.*

1. Mix garlic and pepper in a large bowl. Add ground peas, flour, baking powder, salt, turmeric, and *garam masala*. Stir and let stand for 30 minutes.

2. In a large skillet, heat oil until very hot. Add mixture to the oil by spoonfuls, and fry 2 to 3 minutes on each side. Cook in batches. Drain on paper towels. Serve hot.

*Available at Indian food markets; see list of suppliers (page 319).

servings: 4

4 cloves garlic, crushed

½ teaspoon pepper

2 cups dried split peas, soaked overnight in water, drained, and ground in food processor until smooth

2 tablespoons all-purpose flour

1 teaspoon baking powder

Salt to taste

½ teaspoon ground turmeric

½ teaspoon *garam masala**

2 cups vegetable oil, for frying

Sautéed Goat Cheese with Mint

Gvinat izim Metugenet im Naana

servings: 4

12-ounce goat cheese log, well-chilled

All-purpose flour for coating

1 egg, lightly beaten and seasoned with a pinch each of dried thyme and grated nutmeg

Vegetable oil for frying

1 clove garlic, cut in half

1 small onion, finely chopped

1 tablespoon olive oil

1 tablespoon red wine vinegar

Dash of Tabasco

8 heaping tablespoons chopped fresh mint

Watercress or lamb's lettuce (mâche) *can be substituted for the mint in this Israeli first course.*

1. Slice cheese into ½-inch rounds. Dip each round into flour, then into egg mixture, then into flour again. (This can be done ahead; refrigerate cheese, covered with plastic wrap, until ready to cook.)

2. Heat ¼-inch vegetable oil in a skillet until it is very hot. Gently place some of the cheese rounds in the skillet. Do not crowd. Cook on both sides until golden. Drain on paper towels.

3. Rub the inside of a bowl with the split garlic clove. Add chopped onion, olive oil, vinegar, Tabasco, and mint, and toss.

4. Spoon mixture onto four plates and top with cooked cheese slices.

Caponata

Eggplant Relish

Caponata *reveals the influence of Sicily's one-time Arab conquerors in its combination of vegetables, raisins, olives, and nuts in a single dish.*

1. In a large skillet heat the olive oil over moderately high heat. Cook eggplant in batches, turning to cook evenly. Drain on paper towels. In same skillet, sauté onion and garlic until translucent. Add tomatoes and cook until tender, about 10 minutes. As they cook, mash tomatoes with a wooden spoon.

2. Add olives, pine nuts, raisins, capers, celery, salt, and pepper. Cook uncovered for 20 minutes, or until celery is tender, stirring frequently.

3. Stir in sugar and vinegar and cook for 5 minutes. If there is a lot of liquid, reduce sauce by boiling for 5 additional minutes. Return eggplant to skillet and heat through.

4. Place in an airtight container. Serve hot as a vegetable dish or cold as a relish. *Caponata* keeps in the refrigerator for 1 week or in the freezer for up to 3 months.

servings: 20

¼ cup olive oil

2 eggplants, 1 pound each, peeled and cut into ½-inch cubes

1 small onion, chopped

1 clove garlic, chopped

12 large tomatoes, diced

1 jar (7 ounces) pitted green olives, drained and cut into quarters

1 cup pine nuts

1½ cups seedless golden raisins

½ cup capers, drained

6 stalks celery, chopped into ½-inch pieces

1 tablespoon salt

1 teaspoon freshly ground pepper

½ cup sugar

1 cup red wine vinegar

Garlic Toast with Tomatoes and Basil

Bruschetta

---

servings: 8

10 to 15 fresh, ripe plum tomatoes (about 2 pounds), cut into ¼-inch cubes

2 tablespoons minced garlic

2 tablespoons minced shallot

1 cup coarsely chopped fresh basil leaves

1 to 1½ teaspoons fresh lemon juice

Salt and freshly ground pepper to taste

⅔ cup extra-virgin olive oil

3 large cloves garlic, slivered

8 thick (¾-inch) slices of peasant bread, from an 8- to 10-inch round loaf

The flavors of the Mediterranean are embodied in this pungent and summery combination of tomatoes, basil, garlic, shallots, and lemon. Make this dish throughout the year if ripe, red tomatoes are available.

1. Mix tomatoes in a bowl with minced garlic and shallot. Add basil, lemon juice, salt, pepper, and ⅓ cup of the olive oil. Set aside. This can be prepared ahead and refrigerated up to 8 hours, but add the basil just before serving.

2. Heat remaining ⅓ cup olive oil in a small skillet and sauté slivered garlic until golden, about 4 minutes. Discard garlic and reserve oil.

3. Toast bread slices and cut each in half. Arrange a full slice on each of eight plates. Brush each with garlic-flavored oil; spoon tomato mixture over bread. Serve immediately.

JAPAN

Japanese Chicken Meatballs

Tsukune Dango

This popular Japanese dish is great as an appetizer or in soup.

1. Combine ground chicken, egg, onion, 1 tablespoon of the *sake*, 1 tablespoon of the soy sauce, and the cornstarch. Roll into 1-inch balls.

2. In a medium saucepan filled with boiling water, cook meatballs until they float, about 10 minutes.

3. In a small saucepan, combine the remaining 2 tablespoons *sake*, 2 tablespoons soy sauce, the *mirin*, and sugar and bring to a boil. Lower heat, add meatballs and sauté until browned. Remove meatballs and simmer sauce on low heat until it is reduced by half. Return meatballs to pot and coat them with sauce. Serve on bamboo skewers or with toothpicks.

   *Available at most liquor stores.

   **Available at Japanese food markets; see list of suppliers (page 319).

---

servings: 20 meatballs

½ **pound ground chicken**

1 **egg, beaten**

¼ **onion, minced**

3 **tablespoons Japanese rice wine (sake)***

3 **tablespoons soy sauce**

1 **tablespoon cornstarch**

2 **tablespoons Japanese sweet cooking wine (mirin)****

2 **teaspoons sugar**

MALAYSIA

Malaysian Shrimp Cocktail

Cocktail Udang

servings: 4

24 medium shrimp

cocktail sauce

3 tablespoons mayonnaise

½ teaspoon pepper

1 teaspoon salt

1 tablespoon tomato ketchup

Dash of Cognac

Dash of Worcestershire sauce

Dash of Tabasco

Juice of 2 lemons

1 head Boston lettuce (or other soft lettuce), finely sliced

1 ripe avocado, peeled, pitted, and sliced

1 lemon, cut into 4 wedges

4 quail eggs,* boiled, shelled, and cut in half

4 small sprigs coriander or parsley, for garnish

Not a run-of-the-mill shrimp cocktail, this Asian variation, served at elegant Malaysian hotels, has a Tabasco-and-Cognac–spiked sauce. The shrimp are elegantly garnished with quail eggs.

1. Poach shrimp in salted boiling water until they turn pink, 3 to 5 minutes. Drain and cool in cold water. Peel off shells but leave tails intact. Set aside.

2. For the sauce, whisk together mayonnaise, pepper, salt, ketchup, Cognac, Worcestershire sauce, Tabasco, and lemon juice.

3. Place lettuce strips on 4 individual serving plates and top each with 2 tablespoons of the cocktail sauce. On each plate, arrange 6 shrimp on the lettuce, alternating with avocado slices.

4. Place 1 lemon wedge on rim of each plate. Top shrimp and avocado with 2 tablespoons cocktail sauce and place a quail egg on top. Garnish with coriander or parsley.

Available at Asian food markets or specialty food markets; see list of suppliers (page 319).

Guacamole

Avocado Dip

A versatile Mexican appetizer. Serve with corn chips or as a garnish for grilled meat and tacos. Great with ice-cold Margaritas *(page 42).*

1. In a non-aluminum bowl, mix onion with 1 tablespoon of the lemon or lime juice and the salt. Let stand for 15 to 30 minutes.

2. Add avocados, tomatoes, and peppers. Add coriander and mix. Flavor with additional salt, pepper, garlic, and remaining lemon or lime juice. Mix well to fully incorporate juice.

3. Decorate platter with corn chips. *Guacamole* can be refrigerated for up to 3 hours but is best served immediately. To store, cover bowl of *guacamole* with plastic wrap pressed into it to prevent air from entering.

Note: When working with hot peppers, be sure to wash your hands thoroughly before touching your eyes.

*Available at Latin American and speciality food markets; see list of suppliers (page 319).

servings: 6

- 1 small sweet onion, finely chopped
- 3 tablespoons fresh lemon or lime juice
- Salt to taste
- 2 large or 3 small ripe avocados, peeled, pitted, and mashed
- 2 medium tomatoes, finely chopped, or 2 tomatillos,* outer brown husk removed, pulp puréed
- 4 serrano or jalapeño peppers, seeded and finely chopped (1 for mild heat; 4 for hot)
- ¼ cup fresh coriander, finely chopped
- Pepper to taste
- 1 mashed garlic clove (optional)

Baba Ghanouj

Smoky Eggplant Purée

servings: 5

2 medium eggplants, 1 pound each

½ cup fresh lemon juice

½ cup tahini* (sesame sauce)

2 tablespoons water

1 clove garlic, minced

½ teaspoon salt

3 tablespoons chopped fresh parsley

2 tablespoons olive oil

¼ cup plain yogurt (optional)

Eggplant is an integral part of all Middle Eastern cuisine, and this dip is popular throughout the region. Roasting gives eggplant a delicious, smoky flavor. Serve with scallions, olives, and pita bread for dipping. It is especially tasty when sprinkled with a small amount of olive oil.

1. Preheat oven to 400°F. Pierce eggplants with a fork. Place on oiled baking sheet and cook until skin blisters, turning once, about 30 minutes. Let cool.

2. Remove skin and seeds, and mash pulp in a large bowl.

3. Stir in lemon juice, tahini, 1 tablespoon of the water, the garlic and salt.

4. Stir in remaining 1 tablespoon water as mixture thickens. Mix in 2 tablespoons of the parsley, the olive oil, yogurt, and salt to taste. Garnish with remaining 1 tablespoon parsley.

Available at Middle Eastern food markets; see list of suppliers (page 319).

Leek and Potato Pie

This New Zealand recipe has ancestral resonance for the many New Zealanders who have roots in Wales, where the leek is the national vegetable.

1. Blanch leeks in boiling salted water for 10 minutes. Refresh under cold running water and drain.

2. In a saucepan, boil potatoes in salted water until just cooked, about 10 to 15 minutes. Drain, return potatoes to pan, and place over low heat for 5 minutes to dry. Mash potatoes until smooth, adding 1 tablespoon of the butter and the egg yolk. Set aside.

3. Place milk and studded onion in a medium saucepan and heat milk to just below boiling.

4. Preheat oven to 375°F. In a separate saucepan, melt the remaining 1 tablespoon of butter. Add flour and gently cook over moderate heat until mixture reaches a soft, sandy texture. Add warmed milk gradually, stirring constantly between each addition to prevent lumps. Lower heat and simmer 3 minutes. Season with salt, pepper, lemon juice, and nutmeg.

5. In an 8-inch round ovenproof casserole, toss leeks in sauce and mix in ⅔ cup of the blue cheese. Spread mashed potatoes on top, sprinkle with remaining ⅓ cup blue cheese, and bake for 30 minutes. Place casserole under broiler to brown just before serving.

servings: 8 to 10

- 1¼ pounds leeks, well-rinsed, trimmed, and cut into 1-inch-thick rounds
- 1 pound potatoes, peeled
- 2 tablespoons butter
- 1 egg yolk
- 1¾ cups milk
- 1 onion studded with 6 cloves and ½ bay leaf
- 1 tablespoon all-purpose flour
- Salt and pepper to taste
- 3 drops fresh lemon juice
- Pinch of ground nutmeg
- ⅔ cup blue-veined cheese, such as Stilton, crumbled, plus ⅓ cup for topping

PERU

Scallops Marinated in Lime Juice

Ceviche

servings: 4

1 pound bay scallops

marinade

⅓ cup fresh lime juice

2 tablespoons olive oil

½ red bell pepper, seeded and cut into thin strips

¼ cup thinly sliced red onion

¼ teaspoon red pepper flakes

⅛ teaspoon ground cloves

1 tablespoon chopped fresh coriander

Salt and pepper to taste

vinaigrette

¼ cup red wine or cider vinegar

1 teaspoon dry mustard

1 teaspoon Dijon mustard

Salt and pepper to taste

¾ cup olive oil

salad

1 medium ripe avocado, peeled, pitted, and diced

1 medium grapefruit, peeled, and membranes removed, cut into sections

3 cups mesclun or mixed salad greens

This simple method of marinating scallops originated in Peru and has become popular throughout Latin America. If scallops are not available, any firm, white fish will work.

1. In a medium bowl, mix scallops with marinade ingredients. Cover and refrigerate for 3 to 10 hours. *Ceviche* is ready to eat when the scallops turn white throughout.

2. For the vinaigrette, in a small bowl, whisk together vinegar, dry and Dijon mustards, salt, and pepper. Gradually whisk in oil. Set aside.

3. Shortly before serving, in a medium bowl, mix together avocado, grapefruit, and mesclun. Pour vinaigrette over salad and toss gently.

4. To serve, divide salad among four plates. Drain scallops and arrange on top of salad.

PHILIPPINES

Deep Fried Cheese Rolls

Lumpia

Although cheese is not common in Filipino cuisine, these cheese rolls, served piping hot from the oven, are a popular finger food, especially at celebrations.

1. Place each cheese stick on the lower end of a spring roll wrapper.

2. Roll cheese in wrapper to the center, fold sides of wrapper in over cheese. Brush top edge of wrapper with beaten egg, continue rolling and press top edge to seal closed.

3. Heat oil over moderately high heat and deep-fry the cheese rolls until golden brown, about 4 minutes. Drain on paper towels. Serve immediately.

servings: 20 pieces

1 pound hard cheese, such as Gruyère, Swiss or sharp Cheddar, cut into 4 x ½-inch sticks

20 sheets spring roll wrappers or wonton wrappers, 6 x 6-inches

2 eggs, beaten

1 quart vegetable oil, for frying

Chicken *Empanadas*

These crispy half-moon–shaped chicken-and-vegetable pastries, are part of the culinary legacy of the Spanish colonizers.

servings: 50 pieces

dough

3 cups plus 2 tablespoons all-purpose flour

1½ teaspoons baking powder

½ cup sugar

12 tablespoons (1½ sticks) butter or margarine, softened

½ cup water

filling

1 pound skinless, boneless chicken breasts

3 tablespoons vegetable oil

2 cloves garlic, minced

1 small onion, diced

¼ red bell pepper, minced (optional)

¼ green bell pepper, minced (optional)

1 celery stalk, finely chopped

Salt to taste

2 medium potatoes, boiled, cooled, and diced

½ cup golden raisins

2 eggs, hard-boiled, and finely chopped

glaze

2 egg yolks, lightly beaten

1. For the dough, sift together flour, baking powder, and sugar.

2. With a pastry cutter, or in the bowl of a food processor fitted with a steel blade, or with two kitchen knives, cut butter into flour until mixture resembles fine bread crumbs.

3. Add the ½ cup water and knead or pulse dough to form a ball. If necessary, add more water, 1 tablespoon at a time, until dough comes together. Wrap tightly and refrigerate until ready to roll out.

4. Cover chicken with water and simmer 12 to 15 minutes or until firm when pierced with a fork. Remove from water and let cool.

5. Chop chicken into ¼-inch pieces. (This can be done by pulsing in a food processor.)

6. In a large skillet, heat oil over moderate heat and sauté garlic, onion, bell peppers, and celery until soft, about 7 minutes. Stir in salt and add chicken, potatoes, raisins, and chopped eggs.

7. Remove dough from refrigerator. Let warm slightly. On a lightly floured surface roll to ⅛-inch thickness.

8. Preheat oven to 350°F.

9. With a 3-inch cookie cutter cut dough into rounds. Place 1 tablespoon filling on lower half of each round and fold top half over to form half-moon shape. Seal by pressing edges or crimping with the points of a fork. Brush tops with egg yolk.

10. Sprinkle flour on baking pan or baking sheet. Arrange *empanadas* on pan and bake for 35 minutes, or until golden brown.

PHILIPPINES

Mushroom Orientale

An original recipe from a noted Filipino chef, these mushrooms are an easy-to-prepare appetizer or a side dish.

1. In a large saucepan or casserole, combine all ingredients and bring to a boil over high heat.

2. Reduce heat to moderate and cook for 5 to 8 minutes, half-covered. Liquid should be reduced to just coat the mushrooms. Serve hot.

servings: 4

1¼ pounds fresh whole mushrooms, cleaned and stems trimmed

½ cup olive oil

¼ cup white or cider vinegar

2 tablespoons soy sauce

3 tablespoons minced garlic

1 bay leaf

1 teaspoon chili sauce (optional)

Singapore Savory Bread

Roti Babi

servings: 8 to 10

- ½ **pound fresh fish paste***
- ½ **pound small shrimp, peeled and minced**
- ½ **pound ground pork**
- 1 **can (6 ounces) crabmeat, drained**
- 3 **tablespoons light soy sauce**
- 2 **teaspoons Asian sesame oil**
  Pepper to taste
- 2 **large eggs, lightly beaten**
- 1¼-**pound loaf white bread, sliced, with or without crusts**
- 1 **quart vegetable oil for frying**

The multicultural, multiracial population of Singapore is mirrored in its cuisine, which mixes Chinese, Malay, and Indian ingredients and cooking techniques, as this recipe demonstrates. Roti is a collective name in India for a wide variety of breads, and ground seafood and pork are traditional Chinese ingredients.

1. Combine fish paste, shrimp, pork, crabmeat, soy sauce, sesame oil, pepper, and eggs in a medium bowl. Beat together with a spoon to thoroughly blend.

2. Spread mixture evenly on each slice of bread. Cut each slice into 6 small rectangles, or bite-size pieces.

3. In a deep pan, heat vegetable oil until hot. Fry bread pieces until they are golden brown, about 7 minutes.

4. Drain pieces on paper towels. Let cool before serving.

Available at Asian food markets; see list of suppliers (page 319).

Spanish Potato Omelet

Tortilla Española

With the discovery of the Americas, Spain was introduced to the potato in the 16th century. Since then, potatoes have been a staple of Spanish cooking, served with almost every main course. These crisp potato-and-egg wedges, eaten warm or at room temperature, are a popular Spanish tapas, assorted appetizers that may accompany a glass of port, sherry, or wine.

1. Heat 2 tablespoons of the oil in a large skillet. Add potatoes and onion and sauté until soft but not brown. Drain oil from potato mixture. In a large bowl, combine potatoes, onion, and eggs. Season with salt and pepper and stir.

2. Heat remaining 1 tablespoon oil in same skillet over moderately high heat, and return potato-and-egg mixture to skillet. Cook until crisp and golden on one side. Place a platter over skillet, and invert omelet onto a plate. Return omelet to pan and cook other side until golden. Cut into wedges and serve warm or at room temperature.

servings: 4

3 tablespoons olive oil

4 to 5 russet potatoes, peeled and grated

1 medium onion, chopped

6 eggs, beaten

Salt and freshly ground pepper to taste

1 teaspoon dried rosemary (optional)

THAILAND

Grilled Chicken on Skewers

Gai Satay

servings: 4

- 1 small onion, peeled and coarsely chopped
- 1 clove garlic, peeled
- 2 tablespoons Thai fish sauce (nam pla)*
- 2 tablespoons brown sugar
- 1 tablespoon lemon or lime juice
- 1 pound boneless chicken breasts
- 3 tablespoons peanut oil
- ½ cup chunky peanut butter
- ¾ cup cream of coconut*
- 2 tablespoons Thai sweet chili sauce*
- 1 teaspoon lemongrass powder*

The satay, a ribbon of meat grilled on a bamboo skewer, is a much-loved snack in many parts of Southeast Asia. This version reflects its Thai origins in the marinade and spicy dipping sauce. If using bamboo skewers, which are more traditional, soak skewers in water at least 30 minutes before using and oil lightly with vegetable oil before threading.

1. In a food processor, pulse onion, garlic, Thai fish sauce, and 1 tablespoon of the brown sugar to a thin paste. Add the lemon or lime juice.

2. Place chicken breasts on work surface. Using a mallet, pound each chicken breast to even, ½-inch thickness. Slice each breast across the grain into ½-inch-wide strips.

3. Thread chicken strips onto bamboo or metal skewers. Place skewers flat in a glass dish.

4. Pour onion-garlic mixture over chicken. Cover with plastic wrap and refrigerate for at least 3 hours.

5. To make spicy peanut sauce, mix remaining 1 tablespoon brown sugar, the peanut oil, peanut butter, cream of coconut, chili sauce, and lemongrass powder into a paste. Pour into a small bowl for serving.

6. Preheat grill or broiler. Place skewers on grill, or 4 inches from the heating element of a broiler, for 5 to 7 minutes, or until evenly cooked. Turn several times to ensure they are evenly done. Serve satays warm with spicy peanut sauce for dipping.

Available at Asian food markets; see list of suppliers (page 319).

TURKEY

Turkish Meat Pastries

Kiymali Tepsi Böregi

This is just one of dozens of filled or stuffed Turkish pastries, generally known as borek. *They come large and small, sweet and savory, baked and fried. Small savory* boreks, *such as these, are highly popular as part of a* mezze, *an assortment of small tasty dishes and salads that together form a first course.*

1. Preheat oven to 375°F. In a large skillet, heat 1 tablespoon of the oil and sauté onions until soft, about 5 minutes, stirring often. Add ground meat, pepper, salt, and cumin. Stir until meat is no longer pink, about 7 minutes.

2. Place 1 puff pastry sheet in a lightly greased 8 x 8-inch or 6 x 10-inch baking pan and spread pastry to fit. Spread ground meat over pastry.

3. Mix egg, ⅓ cup milk, and remaining 1 tablespoon oil in a medium bowl. Pour evenly over meat mixture.

6. Place second pastry sheet on top. Trim or roll edges decoratively. Make diagonal slits across the top and lightly brush with milk. Bake for 30 to 45 minutes, or until nicely puffed and golden brown. Cut into squares and serve hot.

servings: 10

2 tablespoons vegetable oil

1 onion, finely chopped

1 pound ground beef or lamb

    Black pepper to taste

    Salt to taste

1 tablespoon ground cumin, or to taste

½ pound puff pastry, thawed, rolled ⅛-inch thick, and cut into 2 pieces

1 egg

⅓ cup milk, plus more for brushing pastry

Fresh Vegetable Tart with Cheese

servings: 6 to 10

- **1 pound prepared refrigerated dinner-roll pastry**
- **1 package (8 ounces) cream cheese or goat cheese, at room temperature**
- **½ medium onion, minced**
- **4 tomatoes, cored, seeded, and diced**
- **1 small head broccoli, rinsed and broken into tiny florets**
- **3 carrots, peeled and grated**
- **⅓ cup grated Parmesan cheese**

Crisp and colorful vegetables and two types of cheese atop rich pastry make this an ideal appetizer or first course.

1. Preheat oven to 350°F. Remove pastry from package and arrange pieces with edges touching on a 10 x 15-inch baking sheet. Press edges together to form one piece. Prick surface all over with a fork. Bake 20 to 25 minutes, until golden brown. Let cool.

2. Mix cheese and onion and spread over the dough.

3. Distribute tomatoes over the cheese, then sprinkle with broccoli florets and carrots.

4. Top with Parmesan cheese and cut into small squares. This recipe can be made a day in advance and refrigerated, covered with plastic wrap.

UNITED STATES

Cheddar Cheese Shortbreads

Savory, not sweet, these shortbreads have a wonderful, dense texture. The inclusion of pecans and cayenne pepper reveals this recipe's origin in the South. These shortbreads are equally delicious if Swiss cheese is substituted for Cheddar, and walnuts for pecans. They make a lovely accompaniment to a full-bodied red wine.

1. Preheat oven to 350°F. Mix all ingredients well. If baking immediately, roll into marble-size balls. Place on cookie sheet and flatten with fork. Or, for later use, dough may be shaped into a cylinder 1 inch in diameter, wrapped and frozen for up to 1 month. If frozen, defrost until soft before proceeding.

2. Bake for 15 minutes. Place on brown paper or paper towels until cool.

servings: 30

14 tablespoons (1¾ sticks) unsalted butter

2½ cups flour

2 cups grated sharp Cheddar cheese, about ¾ pound

1½ teaspoons salt

½ teaspoon cayenne pepper

1 cup chopped pecans

Salmon Mousse

servings: 6 to 12

1 envelope unflavored gelatin

¼ cup cold water

½ cup boiling water

½ cup mayonnaise

1 tablespoon lemon juice

Dash of Tabasco

¼ teaspoon paprika

1 teaspoon salt

2 teaspoons fresh dill, minced, plus sprigs for garnish

2 cups finely flaked cooked fresh salmon, or 1 can (14.5 ounces) salmon, drained, bones and skin discarded

1 cup heavy cream

Unlike many dishes containing gelatin, this salmon mousse can be frozen because it contains cream and mayonnaise. A luxurious appetizer, it is very attractive molded in a fish shape.

1. In a large bowl, soften the gelatin in the cold water for 2 minutes. Stir in the boiling water and whisk until gelatin is dissolved. Cool to room temperature.

2. Whisk in mayonnaise, lemon juice, Tabasco, paprika, salt, and dill. Refrigerate for 20 minutes.

3. Remove from refrigerator and fold in crumbled salmon.

4. In a small bowl, whip cream until peaks form. Fold into salmon mixture.

5. Pour mixture into a lightly oiled 5- to 6-cup mold, preferably fish-shaped. Chill at least 4 hours to let gelatin set fully.

6. To serve, dip mold in hot water for a few seconds to release mousse. Invert immediately onto a platter, garnish with sprigs of dill, and serve with assorted crackers or small, thin slices of rye or pumpernickel bread.

Note: Mousse can be made ahead and frozen in an airtight container for up to 1 month.

Phyllo Pastries with Pistachios and Roquefort Cheese

Years back, a doctor who practiced medicine in southern New Jersey often received food or other gifts instead of money for his services. The large round of Roquefort and the 20-pound bag of shelled pistachios he received were the inspiration for this family recipe.

1. Cream both cheeses until well combined. Add eggs, one at a time, stirring well after each addition. Stir in pistachios. Season with nutmeg and pepper to taste.

2. Unfold phyllo, cut sheets in half lengthwise, and work individually with a half sheet at a time. Cover remaining dough with a damp towel.

3. Preheat oven to 350°F. Brush a half sheet of phyllo with melted butter. Place 1 heaping teaspoon of the filling on the lower left-hand corner. Fold dough in half lengthwise. Then fold up a corner. Continue folding from side to side to form a triangle (see diagram on page 12). As you are folding, periodically brush phyllo with the melted butter. (This recipe can be made ahead to this point, refrigerated for up to 8 hours or frozen for up to 3 months. Leave unopened in the refrigerator overnight. Do not thaw at room temperature.)

4. Place on baking sheets and bake 10 to 15 minutes, until golden.

servings: 60 pieces

filling

- ¾ **pound Roquefort cheese, at room temperature**
- 8 **ounces cream cheese, at room temperature**
- 2 **large eggs**
- 1½ **cups shelled, chopped natural pistachio nuts**
- ¼ **teaspoon ground or freshly grated nutmeg**
- **White pepper to taste**

pastries

- 1 **pound phyllo dough**
- 12 **tablespoons (1½ sticks) butter, melted**

Grampy's Stuffed Clams

servings: 4

12 Quahogs, or other clams, like cherrystones

¼ cup cornmeal

1 cup water

½ teaspoon salt

⅛ teaspoon pepper

1 teaspoon Bell's Seasoning (a blend of thyme, rosemary, and sage)

4 cups dried seasoned bread crumbs

2 tablespoons vegetable oil

3 ounces salt pork, thinly sliced

For its contributor, this recipe evokes childhood memories of bright summer days spent clamming with her family from her grandfather's skiff on Long Island Sound. The children used their toes to dig the clams from the sandy bottom near the shore.

1. In a large bowl, soak clams with the cornmeal in cold water to cover for 30 minutes. Drain clams and rinse thoroughly.

2. In a large pot, steam clams in the water until they open, about 10 to 15 minutes. Transfer clams to a bowl, reserving cooking liquid. Discard any unopened clams.

3. Preheat oven to 350°F. Remove clam meat from the shells and finely chop in a food processor or grinder. Add salt, pepper, and Bell's seasoning. Add reserved cooking liquid and bread crumbs. Mix well.

4. Grease the insides of the shells with the oil. Stuff shells with clam mixture. Top each stuffed clam with a slice of salt pork and bake for 30 minutes, or until browned.

VIETNAM

Vietnamese Spring Rolls

Cha Giò

Cha Gio *is considered the national dish of Vietnam. Because of its preparation time, it is usually served for special occasions, such as the Vietnamese New Year and weddings. The dipping sauce uses Vietnamese fish sauce, nuoc mam, instead of the soy sauce used in other Southeast Asian cuisines. The rolls can be fully cooked weeks in advance, frozen, thawed, and reheated in a 350°F oven.*

1. In a large bowl, combine the crabmeat, pork, carrots, onion, mushrooms, cellophane noodles, eggs, pepper, and garlic. Set aside.

2. Fill a large bowl with warm water. Immerse one sheet of rice paper in the water until it becomes soft. Keep remaining rice papers covered with a damp towel. Arrange rice paper on work surface and place 3 or 4 tablespoons of the crab-pork mixture in the center of the rice paper. Fold edges in tightly and roll up. Place on a platter and cover with a damp towel. Continue filling rice papers until all mixture is used, placing rolls under damp towel.

3. In a large wok or fryer, heat oil over moderate heat. Fry spring rolls until golden on both sides, about 5 minutes. Drain on paper towels and place on a platter.

4. In a small bowl, mix fish sauce, sugar, water, and lime juice or vinegar and serve as a dipping sauce with spring rolls.

*Available at Asian food markets; see list of suppliers (page 319).

servings: 20 rolls

- 1 cup crabmeat, picked over and cartilage discarded
- ¼ pound ground pork
- 2 cups shredded carrots
- 1 medium onion, chopped
- ⅓ cup tree ear mushrooms,* soaked in warm water, rinsed and finely chopped
- 2 ounces cellophane noodles (clear vermicelli),* soaked in warm water 10 minutes and cut into ¼-inch lengths
- 2 eggs
- 1 teaspoon black or white pepper
- 2 tablespoons chopped garlic
- 1 package large rounds of rice paper*
  Vegetable oil for deep frying

dipping sauce
- ¼ cup Vietnamese fish sauce *(nuoc mam)**
- ¼ cup sugar
- ½ cup water
- 2 tablespoons lime juice or white vinegar

BRAZIL

Little Peasant Girl Cocktail

Caipirinha

---

servings: 1

1 lime, quartered

2 tablespoons sugar

2 ounces *cachaça**

   Ice cubes, crushed

This popular Brazilian cocktail is made with cachaça, *a potent spirit distilled from sugar cane. For best results, make one drink at a time.*

1. Mash lime quarters in a cocktail glass with a muddler or wooden pestle. Do not remove the pieces of crushed lime.

2. Add sugar and *cachaça*. Stir to blend.

3. Fill the glass with crushed ice, stir once and serve.

   *Available at some liquor stores.

ITALY

Americano

Campari and Vermouth Cocktail

Campari, a somewhat bitter extract of herbs and distilled spirits, is a popular aperitif in Italy. Sweet vermouth mixed with Campari makes a light drink that balances the sweet and bitter tastes.

1. Divide the Campari and vermouth between two short cocktail glasses filled with ice cubes.

2. Add club soda and stir. Garnish each with a twist of lemon.

servings: 2

2 ounces Campari

1 ounce sweet Italian vermouth

8 ounces club soda, chilled

2 lemon twists

Bellini

Champagne Peach Cocktail

---

servings: 8

6 large ripe peaches, peeled and pitted

¼ to ½ cup superfine sugar

½ cup peach schnapps

2 bottles brut Champagne, chilled

According to legend, this delightful drink originated at the famous Harry's Bar in Venice, one of Ernest Hemingway's favorite watering holes. Fresh peaches, schnapps, and Champagne make for a heavenly libation.

1. Purée peaches and sugar in a blender. Add peach schnapps and 1 bottle of the Champagne.

2. Place mixture in ice cube trays and freeze for 2 to 6 hours until hardened.

3. Place a few cubes in each of 8 Champagne flutes or glasses and top with remaining bottle of chilled Champagne.

Special Rum Punch

Fruit punches laced with rum are popular throughout the entire Caribbean region. The subtle flavors of this Jamaican rum punch are enhanced by the addition of bay leaves during its preparation.

1. In a bowl, dissolve the sugar in the citrus juices. Set aside.

2. In a large bowl, combine ginger ale, rum, claret, bay leaves, and soda water. Stir in egg white and beat until frothy.

3. Slowly add sugar-citrus mixture. Add grenadine and bitters. Mix ingredients well. Remove bay leaves.

4. Serve in punch glasses filled with crushed ice. Add a dusting of grated nutmeg. Twist a piece of orange rind over each glass and drop it in.

servings: 12

- 2 ounces sugar
- Juice of 1 large lime or lemon
- Juice of 2 oranges
- 4 cups ginger ale, lemon soda, orange juice, or water
- 1½ cups dark rum
- 12 ounces claret (red Bordeaux wine)
- 3 to 4 bay leaves
- 6 ounces soda water
- 1 egg white
- 1 tablespoon grenadine syrup
- ½ teaspoon bitters, such as Angostura
- 8 cups ice, crushed
- Pinch of grated nutmeg, for garnish
- 12 thin strips of orange rind, for garnish

MEXICO

Margarita

Tequila and Lime Cocktail

servings: 4

4 limes, cut in half

½ cup coarse or kosher salt

¼ cup sugar

1 cup tequila

¼ cup Cointreau

¼ cup Grand Marnier

1 cup crushed ice

   Lime slices, for garnish

There is an amusing tale told about the origins of this well-known cocktail. A Mexican bartender took pity on a poor soul who was unable to tolerate fiery straight tequila, a spirit made from the juice of a maguey plant that grows only around the town of Tequila. This bracing sweet-and-sour drink was the result. Fermented with sugar, tequila can be drunk after just four months. But seven-year old tequila is better—and, like well-aged Scotch, much more expensive.

1. Juice the limes. Retain one of the halves and rub around lips of 4 martini glasses.

2. Place salt in a small bowl. Dip glass rims in salt to coat.

3. In a separate small bowl, mix lime juice with sugar and stir well.

4. In a cocktail shaker combine tequila, Cointreau, Grand Marnier, the sweetened lime juice, and crushed ice. Shake vigorously and pour into glasses. Garnish each with a lime slice.

Dragon's Eyes Drink

Longan Sui

Tropical fruits and flavorful seeds and leaves combine to make an ethereal drink that is often served to welcome the lunar New Year because of its many symbolic ingredients. The longan fruit represents happiness and union, sweet winter melon stands for the sweetness of life, and lotus seeds symbolize continuity and the hope for many happy children. Served ice cold, this drink is very refreshing in a hot climate such as that in Singapore, where it is sold by street vendors.

1. In a medium saucepan, bring to a boil the longan, red dates, candied winter melon strips, and pandan leaves in the water, cooking until longan fluffs out and melon is transparent.

2. If using, soak the white fungus in cold water to cover for about 10 minutes. Drain well and detach and discard core of fungus.

3. Add white fungus and lotus seeds to longan mixture and boil for 10 minutes.

4. Add sugar to taste. Serve hot or very cold.

Available at Asian food markets; see list of suppliers (page 319).

servings: 6 to 8

4 ounces dried longan*

10 dried red dates*

4 ounces sweet candied winter melon strips*

3 pandan leaves,* knotted

10 cups water

2 clumps of dried white fungus* (optional)

1 cup boiled lotus seeds,* drained of syrup and rinsed

Sugar to taste

Glögg

Swedish Mulled Wine

servings: 10

2 bottles dry red wine

⅓ cup raisins

6 cloves

1 cinnamon stick

½-inch piece fresh gingerroot

6 cardamom seeds

½ cup sugar

½ cup brandy

20 whole blanched almonds

A hot, Swedish Yuletide punch named for the sound made when drinking it. Glögg is guaranteed to warm both body and spirit on the coldest winter day.

1. Combine 1 bottle red wine, the raisins, cloves, cinnamon stick, gingerroot, and cardamom seeds in an enamel, glass, or stainless-steel container. Cover and let stand overnight.

2. Transfer mixture to a large pot and add the remaining bottle of wine, the sugar and brandy. Bring to a boil. Discard gingerroot, cloves, and cinnamon stick.

3. Pour *glögg* into a serving pot and set over a low chafing dish flame. Ladle into mugs and garnish each drink with 2 almonds.

UNITED STATES

Assam Iced Tea

The northeastern Indian state of Assam produces some of the world's finest teas, which are grown in thousands of tea gardens along the banks of the Brahmaputra River. This recipe for spicy, dark iced tea was discovered in an American women's magazine published more than 50 years ago.

1. Bring 1 quart of the water to a boil in a large covered pot. As soon as the water boils, turn off the heat and add the tea. Let the tea steep in covered pot for 5 minutes.

2. While the tea is steeping, mix sugar with the remaining 1 quart cold water in a large bowl.

3. Pour hot tea through a strainer into the bowl of sweetened water. Stir until sugar dissolves and let tea cool. Refrigerate.

Note: For very sweet tea, increase the amount of sugar up to 1 cup. The sugar may also be decreased, but not to less than ¼ cup.

Available at specialty food markets; see list of suppliers (page 319).

servings: 8 to 12

2 quarts cold water
  Scant ¼ cup loose Assam tea*
  Scant ½ cup sugar

appetizers & beverages   **45**

UNITED STATES

Chocolate Phosphate

servings: 1

3 tablespoons chocolate syrup, or to taste

8 ounces cold seltzer or carbonated water

A drink from the American heartland from the late 1800s, chocolate phosphate is a Midwestern version of the famous New York egg cream, minus the milk or cream. The sign of the Main Street drugstore in Disneyland near Paris features phosphates because Walt Disney himself was raised in Missouri at the turn of the century.

1. Place chocolate syrup in a tall glass. Add 1 or 2 ounces of seltzer water and stir until well blended.

2. Add remaining seltzer and stir until just blended.

UNIS Lemonade

Made by parents for UNIS's annual International Book, Crafts, and Food Festival, this delicious, all-natural lemonade is sold by first-graders. Each batch makes 1 gallon, just perfect for a picnic.

1. Squeeze juice from lemons into a 1-quart container. This should yield about 2 cups of juice with pulp. (At this point, lemon juice may be strained to remove seeds and pulp. The lemonade is tastier with pulp, but this requires picking out the seeds.)

2. Add sugar and stir until dissolved. This will make 3 to 3 ½ cups of concentrate. At this point, the concentrate may be refrigerated for up to 2 days or frozen.

3. Combine concentrate with ice water. The exact amount of water depends on the intensity of flavor desired.

4. If serving in a punch bowl, float lemon slices or sprigs of mint on top.

Note: A thoroughly washed plastic 1-gallon milk jug is ideal for mixing the concentrate and water and for storing at home or transporting to a picnic or party.

servings: 20 6-ounce cups

12 lemons
1 pound sugar
3 to 4 quarts ice water

soups, salads & breads

CHINA

Velvet Chicken Corn Soup

Yù Mǐ Jī Tāng

Corn reached China some 400 years ago, brought by Spanish and Portuguese explorers. This soup was originally prepared with field corn (not sweet table corn), which is available and succulent only for a short time at the height of summer, and thus considered a great treat.

1. Bring chicken broth to a boil in a medium saucepan.

2. In a bowl, mix sesame oil and soy sauce with ground chicken.

3. Whisk chicken mixture into boiling broth, separating the chicken so it does not form clumps.

4. Return broth to a boil and add beaten eggs; stir until well mixed.

5. Add corn and stir. Simmer for 1 to 2 minutes.

6. When ready to serve, add pepper and salt.

Note: For a heartier soup, place 2 to 3 tablespoons cooked white rice and ½ cup rinsed and chopped raw spinach in each bowl.

servings: 4

2 cups chicken broth

¼ teaspoon Asian sesame oil, or to taste

¼ teaspoon soy sauce, or to taste

½ pound ground chicken

2 eggs, beaten

1 can (15 ounces) cream-style corn

⅛ teaspoon white pepper

Salt to taste

FRANCE

Potato Leek Soup

Potage Parmentier

---

servings: 4 to 6

4 Idaho potatoes, peeled and diced

4 tablespoons butter

1 large onion, peeled and diced

3 medium leeks, cleaned and chopped

1 bay leaf

2 tablespoons chopped fresh parsley, or 2 teaspoons dried

1 tablespoon chopped fresh thyme, or 1 teaspoon dried

Salt and freshly ground pepper to taste

4 cups chicken broth

1 cup heavy cream

1 bunch chopped fresh chives, for garnish

This soup is named in honor of the late 18th-century French pharmacist and agronomer Antoine Augustin Parmentier, who devoted much of his energy to popularizing the nutritional qualities of the potato. In France, potatoes had been previously considered unwholesome and indigestible.

1. In a medium saucepan, cook potatoes in boiling salted water for about 10 minutes. Remove from heat, drain, and set aside.

2. In a large pot over moderate heat, melt butter. Sauté onions and leeks for 5 to 7 minutes, stirring occasionally, until soft.

3. Add potatoes, bay leaf, parsley, thyme, salt, pepper, and chicken broth. Bring to a boil, lower heat, and simmer, uncovered, for 15 minutes, or until potatoes are soft. Remove bay leaf. Stir in cream.

4. In a blender or food processor, purée the soup in batches. Adjust seasoning to taste. Return soup to pot and simmer over moderate heat for about 5 minutes. Ladle soup into bowls and sprinkle with chives.

FRANCE

Onion Soup

Soupe à l'Oignon

Onions have been a mainstay of French cooking since the Middle Ages. Onion soup prepared in this manner is quintessentially French.

1. In a large pot, heat oil and cook onions over moderate heat until golden, about 5 to 8 minutes. Stir often.

2. Add bay leaf, thyme, peppercorns, and wine.

3. Add broth to pot and bring to a boil. Add salt and pepper. Cook, covered, for 30 minutes. Add brandy and stir.

4. Preheat the broiler. Pour the soup into 6 individual ovenproof serving bowls, top with toasted bread, and sprinkle with grated cheese. Place bowls under the broiler until cheese melts.

servings: 6

3 tablespoons olive oil

4 large onions, peeled and thinly sliced

1 bay leaf

½ teaspoon dried thyme

1 teaspoon black peppercorns

½ cup dry white or red wine or a combination of both

4 cups chicken or beef broth

Salt and pepper to taste

¼ cup brandy

6 slices sourdough bread, brushed with olive oil, rubbed with garlic, then toasted

½ cup or more grated Gruyère and Parmesan cheeses, for topping

FRANCE

Pistou Soup

Soupe au Pistou

servings: 5 to 6

1 can (9 ounces) white beans, drained, or ½ cup dried white beans

6 cups water

2 medium potatoes, cut into small cubes

1 can (9 ounces) red beans, drained, or ½ cup dried red beans

9 ounces flat, wide green beans, (broad beans) cut in ¼-inch lengths

1 cup elbow macaroni

2 carrots, peeled and cut into ¼-inch dice

2 medium whole tomatoes, rinsed and cored

2 medium zucchini, cut into small cubes

1 bunch fresh basil, rinsed and chopped

2 cloves garlic, minced

3 tablespoons olive oil

Salt to taste

Grated Parmesan cheese, for garnish (optional)

This Provençal vegetable soup gets its name from pistou, *a condiment made from fresh basil crushed with garlic and olive oil. Serve with a loaf of crusty French peasant bread.*

1. If using dried beans, place beans in a medium saucepan, cover with water and soak for 2 hours. Then boil for 1 to 2 hours, until tender, before proceeding with recipe.

2. Bring the 6 cups water to boil in a large pot and cook the potatoes for 10 minutes. Add all the beans, the macaroni, carrots, and tomatoes. Boil another 5 minutes. Remove tomatoes and add zucchini.

3. Remove tomato skins and discard. Purée the tomatoes in a blender with the basil, garlic, and olive oil. Add to soup and simmer for 5 minutes. Add salt. Serve soup hot, sprinkled with grated Parmesan cheese (optional).

Potato Soup

Krumpli Leves

This recipe traveled from Hungary to the United States with a young bride whose cooking equipment consisted of a single kerosene burner. She cooked this one-pot meal, relishing the taste of home in her new land.

1. In a large pot, cover sausage with the 8 cups water. Add onions and bring to a boil. Lower heat and simmer for 1½ hours.

2. Add potatoes to the pot and cook until soft. Transfer the sausage to a plate and slice thinly.

3. Melt butter in a saucepan. Add salt, then flour. Cook, stirring over low heat, until flour mixture reaches a paste-like consistency. Brown slowly over very low heat 15 minutes or more. Slowly add 2 cups of the liquid from the pot to the flour mixture, stirring continuously to prevent lumps. Add this mixture to pot and stir to blend.

4. Over moderate heat, simmer soup until thickened, stirring occasionally.

5. Add sausage slices to the soup and stir. Garnish with parsley.

servings: 6

1 pound kosher beef garlic ring or kielbasa sausage

8 cups water

2 large onions, peeled and chopped

6 medium potatoes, peeled and cut into ½-inch slices

4 tablespoons (½ stick) butter

Salt to taste

1 to 2 tablespoons flour

Parsley, for garnish

MEXICO

Lime Soup

Sopa de Lima

servings: 4

- 1 (3-pound) chicken, cut into 8 pieces, plus 2 extra legs
- 1 medium yellow onion, peeled and quartered
- 5 to 10 whole peppercorns, or to taste
- ½ cup vegetable oil
- 5 fresh corn tortillas, cut into strips
- 3 plum tomatoes, diced, for garnish
- 1 medium avocado, peeled and diced, for garnish
- ½ cup finely chopped coriander, for garnish
- 2 limes, quartered
- 1 fresh or dried habanero or Scotch bonnet chili pepper*
- Salt to taste

Limes are abundant in Mexico's Yucatán Peninsula, home of the ancient Mayan civilization. Mexican limes have a distinctive, sweet-and-sour flavor, rather like that of Key limes grown in Florida. But even if specialty varieties are not available, the juice of common limes lends a sprightly note to this soup.

1. Place chicken in a large pot and fill with water to cover. Add onion and peppercorns. Bring to boil over high heat, lower heat and simmer, covered, for 1½ hours.

2. While the soup is cooking, heat the oil in a small frying pan and fry tortilla strips until crisp. Set aside to drain on paper towels.

3. Remove the soup from the heat. Remove the skin from chicken, shred chicken-breast meat, and set aside. Remove the remaining chicken from the broth, and refrigerate or freeze for another use.

4. Strain the broth through a sieve. Return strained broth to the pot and warm over low heat. Skim off fat.

5. To serve, ladle broth into four individual bowls. Evenly distribute shredded chicken among bowls. Garnish each with tomato, avocado, coriander, and lime wedge. Squeeze remaining lime wedges, one per bowl, over each bowl. Sprinkle fried tortilla strips on top. Dip chili pepper in each bowl of soup until desired heat is achieved, and remove from the bowl.

Note: Tortilla strips may be fried using flavored oils, such as garlic oil. For a more substantial meal, add cooked rice to the broth before serving.

Available at specialty food markets and some supermarkets; see list of suppliers (page 319).

Creamed Corn Soup

Sopang Mais

This soup reflects the Filipino fondness for dishes that are both rich and sweet.

1. Purée corn kernels and water in a blender. Strain through a sieve, pressing with a large spoon, to extract cream. Discard contents of sieve.

2. Heat vegetable oil and sauté garlic until light brown, stirring. Add corn cream, crabmeat, if using, and broth.

3. Cook over low heat, stirring constantly to prevent burning.

4. Season with salt and pepper and remove from heat. Garnish with parsley or coriander.

servings: 6 to 8

4 cups whole corn kernels, fresh, canned or frozen

8 cups water (2 cups milk may be substituted for 4 cups of the water)

1 tablespoon vegetable oil

3 cloves garlic, crushed

1 cup crabmeat (about ½ pound lump), picked over to remove bits of shell and membrane (optional)

2 tablespoons vegetable or chicken broth

Salt and pepper to taste

3 sprigs parsley or coriander, chopped, for garnish

Mushroom Barley Soup

Gribnoy Sup

servings: 4

3 tablespoons butter or margarine

3 cups white mushrooms, sliced

2 scallions, trimmed and chopped

1 large onion, chopped

2 carrots, diced

2 stalks celery, diced

3 tablespoons chopped parsley

3½ cups water

3 vegetable bouillon cubes

½ cup regular pearl barley

2 teaspoons Worcestershire sauce

½ teaspoon pepper

1 cup milk

1 tablespoon dry sherry (optional)

Salt to taste

A noted food writer once described mushroom barley soup as the Jewish triumph "over the agricultural limitations of the Russian empire."

1. In a 4-quart saucepan or Dutch oven, melt butter or margarine. Sauté mushrooms, scallions, onion, carrots, and celery. Add parsley and set aside.

2. In a medium saucepan, bring water, bouillon cubes, barley, Worcestershire sauce and pepper to a boil. Reduce heat, cover and simmer, stirring occasionally, for 40 to 55 minutes, or until barley is tender. Add mushroom-mixture and milk. Heat thoroughly. Remove from heat. Stir in sherry and salt to taste.

Note: For a thicker soup, combine ½ cup milk and ¼ cup flour. Mix until well blended. Gradually stir into soup, bring to a boil, lower heat and simmer for 5 minutes.

SPAIN

Gazpacho

Chilled Fresh Tomato and Vegetable Soup

This well-known Spanish chilled soup of Arab origin can be made in minutes. In Andalusia, it is sometimes also made with green tomatoes, while in other regions it may include fresh ground almonds and grapes.

1. Combine all ingredients in a blender or food processor and chop. Do not purée. The soup should have a thick texture.

2. Chill about 2 hours and serve.

servings: 6 cups

4 medium fresh ripe tomatoes, peeled and chopped

½ medium onion, finely chopped

1 medium cucumber, peeled, seeded, and diced

½ medium green bell pepper, chopped

3 tablespoons chopped fresh parsley

2 tablespoons chopped fresh chives

2 cups tomato juice

⅓ cup wine vinegar

¼ cup olive oil

¼ teaspoon cayenne pepper

1 teaspoon salt, or to taste

THAILAND

Chicken and Coconut Milk Soup

Tom Kha Gai

---

servings: 4

2 kaffir lime leaves* or lemongrass,* outer leaves removed, 3 inches of stem end finely chopped

2 cups coconut milk*

1½ cups chicken broth

3-inch piece gingerroot, peeled and minced

½ pound boneless chicken breast, cut into bite-size pieces

1 fresh hot red chili pepper

2 tablespoons Thai fish sauce (nam pla)*

12 ounces fresh or canned straw mushrooms*

1½ tablespoons fresh lime juice

2 tablespoons finely chopped fresh mint or coriander, for garnish

---

Soup is an essential part of a Thai meal, during which diners refresh their palates with sips between tastes of other dishes. Chicken and coconut milk soup is an aromatic ensemble of distinctive flavors. For a heartier version, soak 3 ounces cellophane noodles in warm water for 15 minutes, drain, and add to the simmering soup 5 minutes before serving.

1. In a large pot, combine lime leaves or lemongrass, the coconut milk, chicken broth, and gingerroot. Cover and bring to a boil. Reduce heat and simmer for 5 minutes.

2. Add chicken, chili pepper, fish sauce, mushrooms, and lime juice. Cook 3 to 5 minutes until chicken is no longer pink.

3. Just before serving, garnish with mint or coriander.

Available at Asian food markets; see list of suppliers (page 319).

Iowa Corn Chowder

It is fitting that this chowder is identified with the state of Iowa, since Iowa ranks first in the United States in corn production. This heartland soup is so substantial that it can be a complete meal. For best results, use fresh corn.

1. In a large pot, heat oil and sauté chicken, onion, and celery over moderate heat for 6 to 8 minutes, or until tender, stirring frequently.

2. In a blender, combine 1 cup of chicken broth and 2 cups of the corn. Blend on high speed until smooth.

3. Add corn mixture to pot, along with remaining 2 cups corn kernels, the potatoes, the remaining 3 cups chicken broth, and salt. Bring to a boil over high heat. Reduce heat to low and simmer, partially covered, for 40 minutes, or until potatoes are tender.

4. Stir in half-and-half or cream, cayenne, and white pepper and simmer 2 to 3 minutes. Ladle soup into 6 bowls and sprinkle with crumbled bacon and coriander.

servings: 6

- 2 tablespoons vegetable oil
- 1 pound boneless, skinless chicken breast, cut into ½-inch cubes
- 1 medium onion, finely chopped
- 2 celery stalks, finely chopped
- 4 cups chicken broth
- 4 cups whole corn kernels, fresh, canned, or frozen and thawed
- 3 medium red potatoes, diced, skin left on
- ½ teaspoon salt, or to taste
- 1 cup half-and-half or heavy cream
  Pinch cayenne pepper
- ⅛ teaspoon white pepper, or to taste
- 6 slices crisp-cooked bacon, crumbled
  Chopped fresh coriander, for garnish

Vegetable Meatball Soup

servings: 4 to 6

meatballs

½ **pound ground beef**

½ **cup cracker or bread crumbs**

1 **small onion, chopped**

1 **large egg**

½ **teaspoon salt**

½ **teaspoon pepper**

1 **tablespoon finely chopped fresh parsley**

soup

2 **tablespoons butter or margarine**

2 **large stalks celery with leaves, chopped**

2 **large carrots, sliced**

8 **ounces mushrooms, sliced**

8 **cups water**

3 to 4 **beef bouillon cubes**

1 **cup pasta such as orzo, macaroni or barley**

1 **pound fresh string beans, cut into 1-inch pieces, or frozen string beans, thawed**

1 **cup loosely-packed fresh spinach, rinsed well**

This recipe originated as a nourishing dinner for children before they donned costumes and masks to "trick-or-treat" for candy on Halloween.

1. For the meatballs, mix together ground beef, crumbs, onion, egg, salt, ¼ teaspoon of the pepper, and the parsley. Shape into small balls, simmer gently for 10 minutes in salted water. Drain and set aside.

2. For the soup, in a 4-quart saucepan or deep pot, melt butter. Sauté celery, carrots, and mushrooms for 10 minutes. Stir frequently. Add the 8 cups water and bouillon cubes; heat to combine.

3. Add pasta, remaining ¼ teaspoon pepper, and the string beans. Heat to boiling. Reduce heat and simmer for 15 to 20 minutes. Add cooked meatballs and spinach. Heat and serve.

UNITED STATES

Cucumber Soup

A refreshing creamy soup, easy to prepare and wonderful on a hot summer day.

1. In a blender, mix all ingredients and refrigerate for 1 hour. Serve soup chilled, garnished with additional fresh dill.

2. Soup may be refrigerated for 2 to 3 days.

servings: 2 to 3

- 2 large cucumbers or 4 Kirby cucumbers, peeled, seeded, and chopped
- 1 cup plain yogurt
- ½ cup sour cream, or to taste
- 2 teaspoons fresh dill, plus additional for garnish
- 2 cloves garlic, peeled
- Salt to taste

CHINA

Chinese Chicken Salad

Shā Là Jī

servings: 4

dressing

2 tablespoons soy sauce

½ cup vegetable oil

2 tablespoons Asian sesame oil

3 tablespoons rice wine vinegar

½ teaspoon dry mustard

2 tablespoons sugar

1½ teaspoons pepper

1 tablespoon ground ginger

salad

1½ tablespoons sesame seeds

1 pound cooked chicken breasts, diced

10 ounces spinach, rinsed, trimmed, and torn into bite-size pieces

1 bunch scallions, trimmed and thinly sliced on the diagonal

3 tablespoons slivered almonds or pine nuts, toasted

8 ounces mushrooms, thinly sliced

2 ounces rice sticks *(saifun)**

Handed down over many generations, this recipe is great for either brunch or lunch. Crispy rice sticks, slivered almonds, and toasted sesame seeds add a delightful crunchiness.

1. Blend soy sauce, ¼ cup of the vegetable oil, the sesame oil, vinegar, mustard, sugar, pepper, and ginger. Set aside.

2. In a dry skillet, over moderate heat, stir sesame seeds until golden brown. Set aside.

3. Combine chicken, spinach, scallions, almonds or pine nuts, and mushrooms in a salad bowl. Pour dressing over salad and mix.

4. Heat remaining ¼ cup vegetable oil in a large skillet and fry rice sticks until crisp, about 2 minutes, stirring often. Drain on paper towels. Add to salad and toss gently. Sprinkle on the sesame seeds.

*Available at Asian food markets; see list of suppliers (page 319).

INDIA

Gujarati Carrot Salad

Gajar ka Kachumbar

A tangy vegetable salad that goes as well with roast chicken or beef as with traditional Indian fare.

1. In a large bowl, toss grated carrots with salt.

2. In a small pan, heat oil over moderate heat until hot. Add mustard seeds. When mustard seeds begin to pop, about 2 to 3 seconds, remove pan from heat and pour oil and seeds over carrots.

3. Add lemon juice and raisins, if using, and mix. Salad may be served cold or at room temperature.

*Available at Indian food markets; see list of suppliers (page 319).

servings: 4

5 carrots, peeled and coarsely grated

¼ teaspoon salt

2 tablespoons vegetable oil

2 tablespoons whole black mustard seeds*

2 teaspoons lemon juice

2 tablespoons golden raisins, soaked in hot water for 2 hours (optional)

Cabbage with Pomegranate Seeds

Patta Gobi Anardane Ke-Sath

---

servings: 4

....

½ **medium head cabbage, about ¾ pound, finely chopped**

1 **teaspoon salt**

2 **tablespoons fresh pomegranate seeds**

¼ **green bell pepper, chopped (optional)**

1 **tablespoon grated carrot**

Salt to taste

½ **teaspoon fresh lemon juice**

Pomegranate season usually runs from October through January in the United States. For fresh pomegranate seeds, slice a pomegranate in half with the tip of a paring knife and carefully loosen the red seeds from the pulpy membrane, taking care not to tear the juice sacs.

1. Sprinkle cabbage with the salt. Mix well and let sit for 5 to 7 minutes. Squeeze out liquid between the palms of hands.

2. Place cabbage in serving bowl and toss with pomegranate seeds, bell pepper, carrot, salt, and lemon juice. Chill and serve.

JAPAN

Wonton and Tofu Salad

Wantan Sarada

When the mother of UNIS student was growing up in Japan, her mother used to prepare this unusual salad.

1. Deep-fry wonton skins in the oil until crisp. Drain on paper towels.

2. In a small bowl, mix together soy sauce, sugar, vinegar, and mustard.

3. Combine tofu, lettuce, carrots, radishes, and snow peas in a large serving bowl. Add dressing and toss, scattering fried wonton pieces on top.

*Available at Japanese food markets; see list of suppliers (page 319).

servings: 4 to 6

1 package wonton skins,* cut into thin strips

2 cups vegetable oil, for frying

dressing

1 cup soy sauce

2 tablespoons sugar

2 teaspoons white vinegar

1 teaspoon prepared hot mustard

salad

1 package firm tofu *(momen)*, water drained, cut into small cubes

½ head lettuce, shredded

2 carrots, peeled, sliced, and cut into thin strips (optional)

5 radishes, sliced and cut into thin strips (optional)

20 snow peas, blanched for 30 seconds, then dropped into ice water (optional)

LEBANON

Lebanese Salad with Pita

Fattoush

servings: 4 to 6

- **3** medium ripe tomatoes, cut into ¼-inch dice

- **2** large cucumbers, peeled, seeded, and cut into ¼-inch dice

- **1** large green bell pepper, cored, seeded, and cut into ¼-inch dice

- **10** scallions, trimmed and thinly sliced

- **¼** cup finely chopped parsley

- **¼** cup finely chopped mint leaves

- **½** cup olive oil

- **¼** cup lemon juice

  Salt to taste

- **1** medium-size pita (Arab pocket bread), toasted and broken into bite-size pieces

During Ramadan, the ninth month of the Muslim calendar, the daily sunrise-to-sunset fast is broken with the evening meal. Fattoush, traditionally served during this meal, is refreshing after a long day of fasting.

1. Combine tomatoes, cucumbers, green pepper, and scallions in a large salad bowl. Add parsley and mint and toss. Add olive oil, lemon juice, and salt and toss until all vegetables are coated.

2. Refrigerate for 1 hour before serving. A few minutes before serving, add the toasted pita bread pieces and toss until bread is well coated with dressing.

MIDDLE EAST

Tomato Salad with Walnut Sauce

Sharkasiyak

Chopped nuts are a characteristic element of many Middle Eastern dishes—from desserts to salads—such as this one, which comes from the area around the West Bank city of Nablus.

1. Purée walnuts in a food processor or blender with lemon juice and oil.

2. In a small bowl, soak bread in the ½ cup water. Squeeze out excess water, and add bread to walnut mixture. Blend well.

3. In a large bowl, combine tomatoes, bell pepper, and scallion. Pour walnut sauce over salad.

4. Add mint, salt, and pepper, and garnish with olives.

servings: 5

½ cup shelled walnuts

½ cup fresh lemon juice

2 tablespoons olive oil

2 slices stale white bread, crusts removed

½ cup water

6 tomatoes, coarsely chopped

1 medium green bell pepper, seeded and coarsely chopped

3 scallions, trimmed and chopped

½ cup chopped fresh mint leaves

Salt and pepper to taste

½ cup pitted black or green olives

Hussar Salad

Huzaresalade

servings: 6

- 2 cups cooked roast beef, cut into small cubes
- 4 medium potatoes, peeled, boiled, and cut into small cubes
- 2 tablespoons vinegar
- 2 hard-boiled eggs, mashed, plus 2 hard-boiled eggs sliced for garnish (optional)
- ¾ cup mayonnaise, plus more for garnish (optional)
- 4 cups mixed vegetables (cooked peas and carrots and green beans, cut into ¼-inch pieces)
- 3 medium apples, such as Golden Delicious or Granny Smith, peeled, cored, and cut into small cubes
- 1 medium onion, minced
- 2 cups cooked beets, cut into ¼-inch cubes
- ½ cup chopped bread-and-butter pickle chips
- Salt and pepper to taste
- Lettuce leaves, for garnish
- Small onions for garnish (optional)
- Gherkin pickles, for garnish (optional)
- Chopped parsley, for garnish (optional)

This colorful salad was inspired by the brilliantly colored uniforms of the Hussar cavalrymen. The beets represent their red jackets, the strips of meat their swords, the potatoes their high hats, and the beans and gherkins their guns and ammunition.

1. In large bowl, combine beef, potatoes, vinegar, 2 mashed eggs, and the mayonnaise.

2. Add mixed vegetables, apples, onion, beets, and pickle chips; mix well. Season with salt and pepper.

3. Line a serving platter with lettuce leaves. Spoon salad on top.

4. Garnish, if desired, with additional mayonnaise, small onions, gherkin pickles, 2 sliced hard-boiled eggs, and parsley.

Note: Cooked ham or turkey can be used instead of beef.

Eggplant Salad

Baigan ka Bharata

This cold salad is popular in Pakistan and neighboring countries. The eggplant, or aubergine, originated in the Indian subcontinent, where it was cultivated for centuries before it was known in Europe.

1. Preheat oven to 450°F. Bake eggplant slices on greased baking sheet until golden brown, about 20 minutes. Let cool.

2. In a bowl, mix yogurt, cumin, sugar, cayenne pepper, black pepper, and salt. Add eggplant, and garnish with coriander.

3. Serve well chilled.

servings: 6

1½ pounds eggplant, cut into ½-inch slices

3 cups plain yogurt

2 teaspoons ground cumin

1 teaspoon sugar

Cayenne pepper, black pepper, and salt to taste

Finely chopped fresh coriander, for garnish

Turkish-Style *Tabbouleh*

Kisir

---

servings: 15

4 medium onions, finely chopped

½ cup olive oil

16 ounces fine cracked wheat (bulgur), rinsed twice, drained in colander lined with cheesecloth

1 teaspoon salt

5 tablespoons red hot pepper paste (harissa)*

2 bunches scallions, trimmed and finely chopped

1 bunch fresh mint, finely chopped

1 bunch parsley, finely chopped

Juice of 5 fresh lemons

1 head romaine lettuce, leaves rinsed and dried

Cracked wheat is a staple throughout the Middle East and commonly appears in a salad. This Turkish version is associated with holidays and festive times.

1. In a large skillet, sauté onions in olive oil until golden brown.

2. Add cracked wheat, salt, and red hot pepper paste, and mix thoroughly. Let cool for 10 minutes.

3. Add scallions, mint, parsley and juice of 4 of the lemons. Mix well.

4. Toss romaine lettuce leaves with juice of remaining lemon. Place leaves on serving platter and arrange salad on top.

*Harissa, *a spicy sauce of hot red peppers, garlic, spices, and salt, is sold in tubes, already mixed. Available in Indian and Middle Eastern food markets; see list of suppliers (page 319).*

Avocado Salad with Stilton and Grapes

This salad is a wonderful example of the contemporary cuisine of England: a once-unknown ingredient, the avocado, has been artfully combined with a classic, the Stilton cheese. Finely chopped toasted walnuts can be used instead of bread crumbs.

1. Scoop flesh from avocados, chop and mix with lemon juice. Reserve avocado shells.

2. In a bowl, mix cheese, grapes, pepper, and sour cream and add to chopped avocado.

3. Spoon avocado mixture back into shells. Sprinkle with bread crumbs.

4. Serve with lettuce and garnish with whole grapes.

servings: 4

2 ripe avocados, halved and pits removed

Juice of ½ lemon

¼ pound Stilton cheese, crumbled

2 cups black seedless grapes, halved

Freshly ground pepper to taste

3 tablespoons sour cream

½ cup toasted fresh bread crumbs

Lettuce and grapes, for garnish

Wild and White Rice Salad

servings: 6

¾ cup wild rice

¾ cup long-grain white rice

¼ cup raisins

1 clove garlic, minced

2 scallions, chopped

3 tablespoons orange juice

3 tablespoons balsamic vinegar

2 tablespoons olive oil

1 carrot, diced

3 asparagus spears, sliced

2 stalks celery, chopped

1 small red onion, chopped

Wild rice is the common, but misleading, name for an aquatic grass distantly related to common cultivated rice. It grows wild in swamps in the state of Minnesota, which produces 80 percent of the world's supply. Traditionally, commercial wild rice has been harvested by Native Americans, who pull the grains directly from the wild plants while sitting in canoes or boats.

1. In a medium saucepan, bring 3 cups of water to a boil. Add wild rice, return to the boil, reduce heat and simmer, covered, for about 45 minutes or until rice is open and fluffy. Drain. Rinse in cold water and drain again.

2. In a medium saucepan, bring 1½ cups of water to a boil. Add white rice, return to the boil, reduce heat and simmer, covered, for about 20 minutes. Rinse in cold water and drain.

3. While the rice is cooking, combine raisins, garlic, scallions, orange juice, vinegar, and olive oil.

4. Steam carrot and asparagus in a vegetable steamer over boiling water until cooked but still crunchy, about 4 minutes. Rinse in cold water and drain. If asparagus is out of season, omit or substitute another green vegetable, such as broccoli.

5. Combine rice, cooked vegetables, celery, and onion in a large bowl.

6. Add dressing and toss until rice is coated. Refrigerate for at least 2 hours before serving.

Cucumber Salad

A simpler recipe doesn't exist. Even non-cooks can make it. Great for a barbecue or picnic.

1. Combine cucumbers and onions in a bowl.

2. Mix sugar, water, and vinegar and pour over salad. Cover bowl with plastic wrap and marinate overnight in the refrigerator. Adjust sugar to taste. Serve chilled.

servings: 6 to 8

3 to 4 medium cucumbers, peeled and thinly sliced

2 onions, peeled and thinly sliced

4 tablespoons sugar

1 cup water

1 cup cider vinegar

Pasta Salad with Fresh Tomatoes and Mozzarella

servings: 4

2 medium ripe tomatoes, chopped

1 medium red onion, minced

¼ to ½ pounds mozzarella cheese, shredded

⅓ cup olive oil

2 tablespoons balsamic vinegar

5 large fresh basil leaves, chopped

Salt and pepper to taste

½ pound bowtie or rotelle pasta

A simple pasta salad, bursting with flavor. It's best when vine-ripened summer tomatoes and freshly made mozzarella cheese are available.

1. In a medium bowl, mix together tomatoes, onion, mozzarella, olive oil, vinegar, basil, salt and pepper. Marinate mixture at room temperature for at least 2 hours.

2. Cook pasta in boiling salted water until *al dente* (firm to the bite). Drain.

3. Toss tomato mixture with pasta and serve immediately. This dish can also be served cold.

Mixed Green Salad with Herbs and Oranges

In recent years, Americans have embraced fresh herbs with enthusiasm, as with this distinctive and refreshing combination of mint, chives, and Italian parsley.

1. Using a sharp knife, carefully separate orange flesh from membrane. Discard membrane and seeds. Set segments aside.

2. In a large salad bowl, toss lettuces, mint, parsley, and chives.

3. In a small bowl, combine shallots, vinegars, and mustard. Whisk in olive oil gradually. Add salt and pepper and whisk again.

4. Pour half the dressing over the greens and toss.

5. Add orange segments and remaining dressing, and lightly toss again. Serve immediately.

servings: 8 to 10

- 2 navel oranges, peeled, with white pith removed
- 10 to 12 cups mixed baby lettuce leaves (Bibb, Boston or other tender small greens), rinsed and well-drained
- 1 cup loosely packed fresh mint leaves, rinsed and patted dry with paper towels
- 1 cup loosely packed flat-leaf Italian parsley leaves, rinsed and patted dry with paper towels
- 1 bunch chives, cut into 1½-inch lengths
- 1 tablespoon minced shallots
- 1 tablespoon apple cider vinegar
- 1 teaspoon balsamic vinegar
- 1 tablespoon honey mustard
- 5 tablespoons extra-virgin olive oil
- Salt and freshly ground pepper to taste

Mexican Corn Salad

servings: 8

4 **ears fresh uncooked corn, husks removed**

2 **medium ripe beefsteak tomatoes, seeded and chopped**

2 **stalks celery, diced**

2 **medium carrots, peeled and chopped**

1 **red pepper, seeded and chopped**

1 **poblano pepper, seeded and chopped**

1 **jalapeño pepper, seeded and chopped**

4 **scallions, trimmed and chopped**

2 **tablespoons ground cumin**

2 **tablespoons ground coriander**

2 **tablespoons chili powder, or to taste**

4 **tablespoons olive oil**

4 **tablespoons red wine vinegar, or to taste**

2 **cloves garlic**

Salt and pepper to taste

1 **bunch coriander, rinsed and chopped**

This colorful vegetable salad is a fiesta in a bowl. Because it travels well, it makes a good dish for summer barbecues and picnics.

1. Cut corn kernels off cobs. In a serving bowl, mix corn with tomatoes, celery, carrots, peppers, and scallions.

2. Toast cumin, coriander, and chili powder in a dry frying pan over moderate heat, stirring constantly for 4 minutes, or until fragrant. Let spices cool.

3. In a small bowl, whisk together oil, vinegar, garlic, salt, and pepper. Add toasted spice mixture and fresh coriander and toss with vegetables.

INDIA

Whole-Wheat Indian Bread

Bhakari

This whole-wheat bread from the Gujarat region of western India can be served as a snack or as an accompaniment to an Indian meal.

1. Combine flour, salt, and oil in a medium bowl. Add milk and the water. Mix with fingertips or wooden spoon, adding water, 1 tablespoon at a time, as needed to form dough into a ball.

2. With lightly oiled hands, knead dough for 10 minutes. Dough should be somewhat firm. Return dough to a bowl and let stand 15 minutes.

3. Remove dough from bowl and divide into 4 or 5 pieces. Roll each piece into a ¼-inch-thick round.

4. Heat a flat griddle or large skillet. Cook dough, 1 piece at a time, occasionally pressing down lightly to cook evenly. Carefully turn dough and cook on other side. Repeat process with remaining dough pieces. Bread will balloon a little while cooking. Lightly spread butter on bread and serve.

servings: 4 to 5

2 cups whole-wheat flour

1 teaspoon salt

1½ to 2 tablespoons vegetable oil

¼ cup milk, at room temperature

½ cup water

Butter to spread on cooked bread

Irish Soda Bread

servings: 1 large loaf

- 4 cups all-purpose flour
- 1 teaspoon salt
- ½ cup sugar
- 2 heaping teaspoons baking powder
- ½ teaspoon baking soda
- 8 tablespoons (1 stick) butter, cut into ¼-inch pieces
- 2 cups buttermilk
- 1 teaspoon caraway seeds
- 1 cup raisins

Irish soda bread is served in virtually every household in Ireland, and every family has its own recipe. Another common version, evocative of harder times, uses whole-wheat flour, is unsweetened, and omits raisins and caraway seeds. In days past, soda breads were "baked" in an iron kettle over a peat fire.

1. Preheat oven to 400°F. Heavily grease a 10-inch round baking pan. Combine flour, salt, sugar, baking powder, and baking soda in a large bowl.

2. Add butter using fingertips to rub it into the flour, or cut in using two kitchen knives, until mixture resembles fine bread crumbs. (This can also be done in a food processor fitted with a steel blade. Remove from processor to a mixing bowl before proceeding.) Add buttermilk and stir well.

3. Stir in caraway seeds and raisins. Stir until dough comes together in a ball. Do not overmix.

4. Shape dough in pan and bake for 1 hour, or until knife inserted in the center comes out clean. Dough can also be divided in half and formed into two loaves, baked on a greased baking sheet for 45 minutes.

Note: For scones, cut batter into 4 pieces, then cut each piece into 6 to 8 pieces and place in heavily greased pan. Bake 20 to 25 minutes at 400°F. Some dough can be frozen if not using all at once.

RUSSIA

Challah

Braided Egg Bread

Loaves of challah *are a traditional part of the Friday evening meal at the start of the Jewish Sabbath. This recipe is the result of efforts to re-create a beloved grandmother's special bread.*

1. In a large bowl, dissolve the yeast in the water. Add salt, oil, sugar, vanilla, and eggs.

2. Mix in flour, 1 cup at a time, until dough is sticky. Add more flour if needed.

3. Place dough on a lightly floured board and knead until smooth.

4. Return dough to bowl and cover with a clean cloth. Let rise for 1½ hours.

5. Punch dough down with fist and turn out onto floured board again. Knead for 8 to 10 minutes. Divide dough in half and divide each half into either 3 or 6 balls.

6. Roll balls of dough into long strips. Braid into two loaves, using 3 or 6 braids each.

7. Place on greased baking sheet for 1 hour, covered with a cloth.

8. Preheat oven to 350°F. Brush tops with reserved egg. Bake for 30 minutes, or until golden brown.

---

servings: 10 to 12

1 package (¼ ounce) dry yeast

1 cup warm water

2 teaspoons salt

½ cup corn or vegetable oil

½ cup sugar

1 teaspoon vanilla extract

2 large eggs, beaten (reserve a little for glaze)

5 cups all-purpose flour

Court's Zucchini Bread

servings: 6

- 3 eggs
- 1½ cups sugar
- 1 cup vegetable oil
- 1 tablespoon vanilla extract
- 2 cups grated unpeeled, rinsed zucchini
- 3 cups all-purpose flour
- 1 teaspoon salt
- 1 teaspoon baking soda
- ½ teaspoon baking powder
- 3 teaspoons cinnamon
- ½ cup chopped walnuts

A Connecticut grandmother's vegetable garden produced an enormous crop of zucchini each summer. To deal with the abundance, she created this bread for her son, Court, after whom the recipe was named.

1. Preheat oven to 325°F. Grease a 9 x 5 x 3½-inch pan. With an electric mixer, beat eggs with sugar, oil, and vanilla in a large bowl until creamy.

2. Add zucchini, flour, salt, baking soda, baking powder, cinnamon, and walnuts; stir well. Transfer to prepared pan.

3. Bake for 1 hour, or until toothpick inserted in center comes out clean.

UNITED STATES

California Corn Bread

Corn bread, an American classic, originated in the South. As its popularity has spread, many variations have developed. This one reveals its California connection by the addition of chili peppers and Monterey Jack cheese. Corn bread goes well with chili or ham. It can also be used for stuffing a chicken or turkey, or for breakfast with ham and eggs.

1. Preheat oven to 350°F. Grease an 8-inch square pan. Combine cornmeal, flour, baking powder, and sugar in a bowl.

2. In a separate bowl, cream eggs and butter until fluffy. Add corn, chili peppers, milk, and cheese. Add dry ingredients and stir to blend.

3. Pour into pan and bake for 60 to 70 minutes, or until a knife inserted in center of bread comes out clean. Remove from pan and cut into squares.

servings: 10 to 12

1 cup yellow cornmeal

½ cup all-purpose flour

1 teaspoon baking powder

¼ cup sugar

2 large eggs

8 tablespoons (1 stick) butter, sliced

1 can (15¾ ounces) creamed corn

1 can (8 ounces) green chili peppers, drained and diced

½ cup milk

½ cup diced or grated Monterey Jack cheese, Cheddar cheese, or a combination of both

entrées

Beef Stew with Noodles

Goulash und Spätzle

This recipe is the legacy of a family who escaped Vienna just before World War II. Allowed only two crates of belongings, the mother of the family threw the breadboards that she used for making pastry and spaetzle into one at the last minute. When the border guards opened this crate, they saw the old breadboards on top and assumed the other crate also contained nothing of value. But inside it were bars of yellow soap that hid the pieces of gold that paid for the family's passage to safety. The breadboards—and the recipe—are still treasured by this UNIS family.

1. For the goulash, in a large pot, heat oil or margarine over moderately high heat. Add onions, stirring often, until browned, about 5 minutes.

2. Season beef with salt and paprika and add to pot. Cook, uncovered, about 15 minutes, stirring occasionally, until meat is browned.

3. Add water to pot, cover, reduce heat to low and cook for 1½ hours, stirring occasionally. Add additional water, if needed, to keep beef moist.

4. For the spaetzle, in a large bowl, sift flour, salt, and nutmeg. In a separate bowl, lightly beat eggs with the water and add to flour mixture. Beat with a spoon until dough is thick and smooth.

5. Fill a large pot halfway with water and bring to a boil.

6. Dampen a small cutting board or breadboard with water. Place one-third of the dough on the board. With a wet metal spatula, flatten dough into a sheet about ¼ inch thick. Cut dough into 2 x ¼-inch strips and slip into boiling water. Boil for 3 to 4 minutes, or until firm. Remove spaetzle with a slotted spoon and drain in a colander. Repeat process with remaining strips.

7. Transfer spaetzle to a warm serving bowl. Toss with melted butter. Serve goulash in separate serving bowl.

servings: 8 to 10

goulash

- 3 tablespoons oil or margarine
- 3 medium onions, sliced
- 3 pounds stewing beef, cut into 1½-inch pieces
- 2 teaspoons salt
- 1 tablespoon sweet paprika
- 3 cups water

spaetzle

- 3 cups sifted flour
- 1 teaspoon salt
- ⅛ teaspoon nutmeg
- 4 eggs
- ¾ cup water
- ½ cup melted butter

Carpetbag Steak

Steak Stuffed with Oysters

servings: 4

marinade

2 cloves garlic, minced

1-inch piece of gingerroot, minced

½ teaspoon Colman's English mustard powder

4 ounces pineapple juice

6 ounces teriyaki sauce

¼ cup sesame seeds

meat

4 filet mignon steaks, each 8 ounces (1½ to 2 inches thick)

12 small oysters

A staple at Australian barbecues, this dish is served with snags (sausages), prawns and Sydney Rock Oysters, a sweet, small variety found only in New South Wales. This combo is great with an icy cold Australian lager or wine.

1. Mix together garlic, ginger, and mustard powder to a paste in a large bowl. Add pineapple juice and teriyaki sauce in a slow stream. Mix in sesame seeds.

2. Create a pocket in each steak by making a horizontal incision halfway through. Insert 3 oysters into each steak. Place steaks in marinade and let stand 2 hours in the refrigerator.

3. Heat broiler or barbecue grill until hot. Broil or grill meat, about 4 inches from heat, 3 minutes on each side for rare and 5 minutes for medium-rare.

BELGIUM

Birds' Nests

Vogelnestjes

Hard-boiled eggs nestled in ground beef crusted with bread crumbs actually resemble birds' nests. The Madeira sauce gives this Belgian specialty a sophisticated touch.

1. In a large bowl, mix salt, pepper, and taragon or thyme with ground meat.

2. Roll eggs in flour, then cover each completely with a layer of meat. Roll balls in lightly beaten egg whites and then in bread crumbs until completely covered.

3. Heat oil in a deep frying pan over moderately high heat. Fry the balls until crisp, turning to brown evenly. Cover with lid to keep warm.

4. For the sauce, melt butter and add flour, stirring constantly over moderately low heat for 3 minutes. Slowly add milk, whisking constantly. When mixture is smooth, stir in tomato paste, mushrooms, and Madeira or port. Simmer for 3 minutes.

5. Cut each ball in half and arrange on a serving platter. Sprinkle with parsley and pour Madeira sauce on top. Serve with mashed potatoes.

---

servings: 8

- 1½ teaspoons salt
- ½ teaspoon ground pepper
- 2 tablespoons fresh tarragon or thyme
- 1¾ pounds ground meat (beef or beef and pork mixture)
- 8 eggs, boiled for 10 minutes, cooled and peeled
- ½ cup all-purpose flour
- 2 egg whites
- 1 cup bread crumbs
- 4 tablespoons vegetable oil

Madeira sauce

- 4 tablespoons butter
- 1½ tablespoons all-purpose flour
- 1½ cups milk
- 4 tablespoons tomato paste
- 5 mushrooms, sliced thin
- 3 tablespoons Madeira or port wine
- Fresh chopped parsley, for garnish

Flemish Beef Stew

Vlaamse Karbonnaden

servings: 4

2 tablespoons butter

1½ pounds beef stew meat (preferably chuck), cut into 1½-inch pieces

2 carrots, peeled and cut into thin rounds

2 tablespoons chopped onion

Salt and pepper to taste

1 bay leaf

1 teaspoon dried thyme, crumbled

1 bottle Belgian Trappist beer (Monastery or Duvel beer), or other full-bodied dark beer or stout

4 tablespoons raisins or prunes

2 tablespoons Dijon mustard

1 slice white bread, crust removed

1 cup chicken broth

Many Belgian recipes call for beer, not surprising in a country where there are more than 300 specialty brews.

1. In a large, heavy skillet, melt butter over moderately high heat and sauté beef cubes in batches, turning to brown all sides, about 5 minutes.

2. Stir in carrots, onion, salt, pepper, bay leaf, and thyme.

3. Add beer and bring to a boil. Add raisins.

4. Spread mustard on bread and add to stew. Reduce heat to low, slowly pour in the chicken broth, and cover.

5. Simmer the stew, stirring occasionally, until bread dissolves and meat is tender, about 1½ hours. (Add water as necessary, if stew seems dry.) Serve with applesauce, fried carrots or French fries, and garnish with *cornichons* (pickled gherkins) and baby pickled onions.

Note: The flavor of the stew improves if prepared a day ahead, refrigerated overnight, and reheated before serving.

BRAZIL

Black Bean Stew

Feijoada

Feijoada *is the national dish of Brazil, one in which each cook takes personal pride. It was originally created by slaves to make use of the leftover bits of meat that could go a long way with black beans. Even today, when unexpected guests arrive, there is a saying: "Add more water to the* feijoada."

1. Place beans in a large heavy kettle or pot with cold water to cover by 2 inches, about 3 ½ quarts. Bring to a boil over moderate heat.

2. Add meat. Lower the heat and simmer, covered, for 3 hours, stirring occasionally.

3. In a small skillet, heat olive oil and sauté onions and garlic until onions are tender, about 5 minutes, stirring often. Stir into the bean mixture. Add bay leaf and parsley.

4. Simmer the mixture, covered, for 30 minutes, or until the sauce has become thick and creamy. (Although the meats used to flavor the beans are usually discarded at this point having given up most of their flavor to the sauce, they may be cubed and returned to the pot.)

5. Season with salt and pepper. Serve over rice, accompanied by collard greens, *Farofa* (page 197), and sliced oranges. This dish tastes best when refrigerated overnight and reheated before serving.

Note: As an alternative to soaking beans overnight, cover dried beans with water and bring to a boil. Turn off heat and let stand 1 hour. Drain and use fresh water to cook according to recipe.

*Available at Brazilian food markets; see list of suppliers (page 319).

servings: 12

4 cups dried black beans, rinsed, picked over, soaked overnight in water, and drained

1 pound salted dried beef *(carne seca)*,* rinsed, soaked overnight in water and drained, or smoked ham, smoked pork, sausage, or ham hocks

2 tablespoons olive oil

2 medium onions, chopped

2 cloves garlic, minced

1 large bay leaf

Bunch of fresh parsley, chopped (about 1 cup)

Salt and freshly ground pepper to taste

Beef with Broccoli

Gì Lun Ni

servings: 2 to 4

½ to ¾ pounds flank steak, thinly sliced on the diagonal against the grain

1 tablespoon cornstarch

2 to 3 tablespoons soy sauce

1 tablespoon Asian sesame oil (optional)

1 tablespoon cooking wine

2 cloves garlic, finely chopped

2 teaspoons salt

6 tablespoons vegetable oil

1 pound broccoli, stalks cut into thin slices and florets cut into bite-size pieces

2 tablespoons water

Broccoli was introduced to China in the 16th century and rapidly gained popularity. The contributor of this easy-to-prepare recipe learned it from her mother, who was born in Shanghai. Onions, green peppers, or tomatoes can be substituted for the broccoli.

1. In a large bowl, marinate beef for 2 hours in a mixture of cornstarch, soy sauce, sesame oil (if using), wine, garlic, and salt.

2. Heat 3 tablespoons of the vegetable oil in large frying pan or wok over high heat until hot. Stir-fry broccoli 1 minute. Add 2 tablespoons water and cook 2 more minutes. Remove from pan and set aside.

3. Heat remaining 3 tablespoons vegetable oil in frying pan until hot and stir-fry beef mixture for 2 minutes. Add broccoli and stir-fry for 2 minutes more. Serve with rice.

Groundnut Stew

Nketie Wonu

The groundnut, or peanut, brought to West Africa in the late 1500s from Brazil, is an essential element in West African cooking, including this stew.

1. Heat oil in a large saucepan over moderately high heat. Add beef and brown on all sides.

2. Add onions and sauté until translucent. Add chili peppers, if using.

3. Add tomato paste and peanut butter and stir for 30 seconds. Add water and bouillon cubes and bring to a boil. Reduce heat to a simmer and add potatoes, carrots, salt and pepper.

4. Simmer, covered, for 1 hour, or until meat is tender and sauce has thickened. Serve with white rice.

Note: This stew develops a more intense flavor if prepared a day ahead and reheated. Chicken, mutton, or goat may be substituted for the beef.

---

servings: 2 to 4

2 to 3 tablespoons vegetable oil

1 pound stewing beef, cut into 1-inch cubes

2 medium onions, diced

1 to 2 chili peppers (optional)

1 can (6 ounces) tomato paste

5 tablespoons creamy peanut butter, preferably unsalted and unsweetened

3 cups water

2 beef bouillon cubes

2 potatoes, peeled and coarsely diced

3 carrots, coarsely diced

1 teaspoon salt

½ teaspoon black pepper

GREECE

Lamb and Spinach Stew

Arni Yahni me Spanaki

servings: 4 to 6

¼ cup olive oil

5 pounds lamb neck cut into about 24 pieces

3 medium onions, chopped

2 cloves garlic, chopped

1 tablespoon tomato paste, diluted in 1 cup water

½ cup chopped fresh parsley

2 tablespoons chopped fresh thyme or ½ teaspoon dried thyme

1 can (35 ounces) plum tomatoes, coarsely chopped or 2 cans (18 ounces each)

⅛ teaspoon red pepper flakes

Salt and pepper to taste

2 pounds fresh spinach, rinsed well, stems removed

This recipe from Northern Greece originated in times when money was scarce, meat was a luxury, and the cheapest cuts had to be used to best effect. Serve with hearty peasant bread for dipping in the irresistible sauce.

1. In a large pot, heat olive oil over moderately high heat. Add meat and brown on all sides. Remove meat and set aside.

2. Over moderate heat, sauté onions in same pot until golden, stirring to loosen meat particles.

3. Add garlic and cook for 30 seconds.

4. Add meat and all remaining ingredients except spinach. The sauce should almost cover the meat. Loosely cover and simmer for 1½ hours.

5. Place spinach on top of stew, cover tightly, and cook for 10 minutes, or until spinach is wilted.

6. Uncover and stir in spinach. Simmer for 1 hour.

7. Serve with boiled red potatoes tossed with a dressing of olive oil and lemon juice.

Grandma Tessie's Hungarian Goulash

Gulyás Leves

The herdsmen and cowboys of the Puszta, the Great Plains of Hungary, prepared this meal over a campfire. When Tessie Ungar, whose surname means "Hungarian," emigrated in 1910, she took with her this recipe for Hungary's national dish.

1. In a large frying pan, heat 2 tablespoons of the bacon drippings over moderate heat and sauté onions and garlic until lightly browned.

2. Add salt, bell pepper, celery, parsley, and mushrooms. Sauté, stirring, for 4 or 5 minutes, until almost soft. Set aside.

3. In a large casserole or Dutch oven, heat remaining bacon drippings, and brown meat on all sides.

4. Add the sautéed vegetables, tomato paste, and the 2 cups water. Cook, covered, over low heat for 1¼ hours. (Add a little water as needed during cooking if goulash seems too dry.) Add potatoes and cook for 30 minutes. Add carrots and cook an additional 15 minutes, or until meat is tender when pierced with a fork. Add peas and cook a few minutes more until peas are warmed through.

5. Add additional salt, pepper, and paprika to taste.

servings: 6

4 tablespoons bacon drippings or butter

3 medium onions, diced

12 garlic cloves, chopped

Salt to taste

1 medium green bell pepper, diced

3 large celery stalks, diced

½ cup Italian parsley, chopped

1 pound mushrooms, diced

2 pounds beef chuck steak (or stewing lamb, veal, chicken or fresh pork shoulder), cubed

1 can (6 ounces) tomato paste

2 cups water

3 large potatoes, peeled and quartered

3 medium carrots, cut into 1-inch slices

1 package (10 ounces) frozen peas

Pepper to taste

1 teaspoon to 1 tablespoon imported hot paprika, or to taste

Stuffed Cabbage

Töltött Káposzta

servings: 6

1 medium head green cabbage

1½ pounds ground beef

1 small onion, minced

2 eggs, beaten

1 cup tomato juice

1 teaspoon salt

⅛ teaspoon pepper

½ cup white rice

sauce

1 small onion, minced

1 can (28 ounces) whole tomatoes

Juice of 2 lemons

1 teaspoon salt, or to taste

¾ cup brown sugar

½ cup golden raisins

Contributed by the grandfather of a UNIS student, this recipe is the re-creation of one of the best-loved dishes remembered from his mother's kitchen.

1. Fill a large pot about two-thirds full with water and bring to a boil over high heat.

2. Using a sharp knife cut the core out of the cabbage. Place cabbage in boiling water to cover until cabbage leaves can be loosened, about 10 to 15 minutes. Drain and rinse under cold water. Separate cabbage leaves. Shred tough outer leaves into pieces and set aside.

3. In a large bowl, mix together ground beef, onion, eggs, tomato juice, salt, pepper, and rice.

4. Place 1 tablespoon of the stuffing mixture in the center of a cabbage leaf. Fold sides in first, then starting with stem end, roll up. Repeat until all stuffing mixture has been used. Line a heavy pot with shredded cabbage leaves.

5. For the sauce, sauté onion in a large skillet over moderate heat, until translucent, about 5 minutes. Add tomatoes, lemon juice, salt, brown sugar, and raisins. Stir, lower heat, and simmer about 20 minutes.

6. Preheat oven to 375°F. Arrange cabbage rolls in layers, seam-side down, on shredded cabbage. Cover with sauce.

7. Bake, covered, for 1 hour. Serve 3 or 4 stuffed cabbage leaves with sauce per person.

Braised Beef and Potatoes

Nikujaga

The secret of this dish is to cook it thoroughly until the potatoes have absorbed the flavor of the meat. The dashi *in this recipe is a basic ingredient in Japanese cooking. A combination of dried kelp* (kombu) *and dried flaked bonito (a variety of tuna),* dashi *is mixed with water and used as the stock for many Japanese soups.*

1. Place oil in a heavy skillet over high heat. Add beef and sauté, turning to brown evenly, about 3 minutes.

2. Reduce heat to moderate, add onions and sauté lightly, stirring often.

3. Add potatoes and carrots. Stir.

4. When meat and vegetables have absorbed the oil, add the water and *dashi* and stir.

5. Add the *sake*, sugar, *mirin*, and soy sauce. Raise heat to bring mixture to a boil, then reduce heat slightly. Skim off any surface particles, cover and cook for 20 to 25 minutes.

6. Stir occasionally as stock reduces to coat meat and vegetables evenly. When almost all the stock has been absorbed, remove pan from heat and transfer stew to a serving dish. Sprinkle with green peas. Serve with rice in individual bowls.

*Available at Japanese food markets; see list of suppliers (page 319).

**Available at most liquor stores.

servings: 5 to 6

1½ teaspoons vegetable oil

¾ pound thickly sliced, well-marbled beef (top round or sirloin), with any fat left on, cut into 2- to 2½-inch lengths

¾ pound onions, peeled, cut lengthwise in half and into ½-inch slices

1¾ pounds potatoes, peeled, quartered, rinsed, and drained

2 carrots, cut into 1-inch slices

3 cups water

1 teaspoon instant *dashi**

3 tablespoons Japanese rice wine *(sake)***

6 tablespoons sugar

2 tablespoons sweet Japanese cooking wine *(mirin)**

5 tablespoons soy sauce

2 tablespoons cooked green peas, for garnish

Shabu-Shabu

Japanese Hot Pot

---

servings: 4

4 cups water

1 piece dried kelp *(kombu)*,*
4 x 1½ inches

1¼ pounds filet or tender, well-
marbled beef, sliced paper thin

1 firm tofu cake, cut into 1 x 2-inch
rectangles

1 bunch watercress, rinsed

5 leaves Japanese bok choy, cut into
bite-size pieces

10 dried shiitake mushrooms, soaked
in warm water for 30 minutes,
drained, and sliced

Soy and lemon sauce (*ponzu*
sauce),* for dipping

2 cups Japanese noodles*

In this Japanese version of Mongolian "fire pot" or hot pot, diners cook their own meals at the table, putting meat and vegetables into simmering broth. The name comes from the swishing sound made when the food is gently stirred with chopsticks. At formal Japanese dinners, shabu-shabu is cooked by the hostess for the guests.

1. In a large pot, boil the water, then lower heat to simmer. Snip *kombu* in 4 or 5 places and add to pot with a pinch of salt. Simmer for 15 minutes. Remove from heat and set aside for 30 minutes.

2. Remove *kombu* and pour broth into a *shabu-shabu* pot, mongolian hot pot, fondue pot, or any pot than can be set on a heating element at the table. Bring the pot to the table and place on heating element. Continue to simmer broth.

3. Drop some beef slices in the broth along with some tofu, watercress, bok choy, and mushroom and swirl with chopsticks to cook. The beef will cook in a few seconds; the vegetables take a bit longer. Remove beef and vegetables with chopsticks and place in small individual bowls. Add *ponzu* sauce and mix.

5. When all the beef and vegetables have been cooked, add Japanese noodles to the broth, which is traditionally served in individual bowls after the meat and vegetables have been eaten.

Note: To more easily slice beef very thinly, place meat in freezer for 1 hour or until just firm enough to cut.

*Available at Japanese or Asian food markets; see list of suppliers (page 319).

JAPAN

Cold *Shabu-Shabu*

Hiyashi Shabu-Shabu

This contemporary, chilled version of classic shabu-shabu *is a perfect meal in hot weather.*

1. Boil the 4 cups water in a large pot. Cook beef slices individually. Remove beef with tongs as soon as the color of the meat changes, about 30 seconds. Let cool in refrigerator.

2. Mix lemon juice with 3 tablespoons of the soy sauce in a small bowl. Sprinkle with half the scallions.

3. In a separate bowl, combine peanut butter, mayonnaise, the remaining 1 tablespoon soy sauce, and the garlic. Sprinkle with the remaining scallions.

4. Arrange chilled beef on a large platter. Garnish with watercress, daikon sprouts, *kaiware* or mustard cress, and celery. Place the sauces next to platter for dipping beef.

*Available at Japanese food markets (see list of suppliers, page 319) and at health food stores.

servings: 4

4 cups water

1¼ pounds filet or tender, well-marbled beef, sliced paper thin

Juice from 1 lemon

4 tablespoons soy sauce

1 to 2 scallions, trimmed and chopped

2 tablespoons smooth peanut butter

1 tablespoon mayonnaise

1 small clove garlic, finely minced

3½ ounces watercress, cut into bite-size pieces, for garnish

3½ ounces daikon sprouts (*kaiware* or mustard cress),* rinsed and roots removed, for garnish

1 stick celery, cut into 2- to 3-inch pieces, for garnish

Korean Barbecue Beef

Bulgogi

servings: 2

1½ teaspoons sesame seeds

2 tablespoons sugar

1 tablespoon Asian rice wine* or sherry

2 tablespoons soy sauce

2 cloves garlic, thinly sliced

3 tablespoons chopped scallions

2 tablespoons Asian sesame oil

½ medium-size Asian pear, peeled and chopped

¼ teaspoon black pepper

1 pound top round or tenderloin of beef, sliced thinly against the grain, and cut into bite-size pieces

1 cup cooked rice

Red leaf lettuce leaves, rinsed and patted dry

Bulgogi is a favorite beef dish in Korea, where beef is the most popular meat. This dish is often served on special occasions such as birthdays or Chuseuck, a September festival in which ancestors are thanked for a good harvest. Asian pears are juicier than European pears and contain an enzyme that helps to tenderize the meat, but if they are not available, the more common European type can be substituted.

1. Place sesame seeds in a small skillet over medium heat and cook, stirring, until golden brown, about 5 minutes.

2. In a large bowl, mix together sesame seeds, sugar, rice wine, soy sauce, garlic, scallions, sesame oil, pear, and pepper.

3. Add beef to bowl, stir, and marinate about 1 hour. Meanwhile, take each lettuce leaf and place a small spoonful of rice in the center. Fold the lettuce leaf around the rice to create a loose packet.

4. Heat grill or broiler, drain beef and cook for 30 seconds to 1 minute on each side.

5. Serve hot beef slices over packets of rice wrapped in lettuce.

Available at Asian food markets; see list of suppliers (page 319).

KOREA

Korean Cabbage Rolls

Yangbaechoo Mandoo

Served alone or in soup, these cabbage rolls are a popular family dish. On New Year's Day they are served in broth, along with a special rice cake, doku, a symbol of long life. Pork may be substituted for beef.

1. Mix carrot, bell peppers, ground beef or pork, bean sprouts, egg, scallions, garlic, rice wine, soy sauce, sesame oil, sugar, sesame seeds, salt, and pepper. Shape mixture into oval meatballs about 2 inches long. Place cornstarch on a large plate. Gently roll each meatball in cornstarch.

2. Dip inner surface of each cabbage square in cornstarch. Place meatballs in cabbage leaves and fold edges of leaves around meat to form small bundles.

3. Heat water in a steamer to boiling. Arrange bundles, seam-side down, in the upper part of steamer. Steam for 15 minutes. Garnish with parsley.

*Available at Asian food markets; see list of suppliers (page 319).

servings: 4

½ **carrot, cut into ¼-inch cubes**

2 **green bell peppers, cored, seeded, cut into ¼-inch cubes**

1 **pound ground beef or pork**

2 **ounces mung bean sprouts, scalded briefly in boiling water, drained, rinsed under cold water, and finely chopped**

½ **egg, beaten**

2 **scallions, chopped**

2 **cloves garlic, chopped**

1 **tablespoon Asian rice wine***

2 **tablespoons soy sauce**

1 **teaspoon Asian sesame oil**

1 **tablespoon sugar**

1 **tablespoon sesame seeds**

1 **teaspoon salt**

Black pepper to taste

½ **cup cornstarch**

6 **cabbage leaves, cut into 4-inch squares, scalded briefly in boiling water, and rinsed under cold water**

Chopped parsley, for garnish

MIDDLE EAST

Lamb Pilaf

Lahm Pilav

servings: 6

- 3 tablespoons vegetable oil or butter
- 1 large onion, peeled and finely chopped
- 1 pound boneless lean lamb, cut into small pieces
- ½ cup pine nuts, plus ¼ cup for garnish
- 4 tablespoons seedless white raisins
- Salt to taste
- Freshly ground black pepper to taste
- 1-inch piece cinnamon stick
- 3 tablespoons finely chopped fresh parsley
- 3 tablespoons tomato paste
- 3 cups beef broth
- 2½ cups long-grain rice
- 4 cups water
- ½ bunch fresh coriander leaves, for garnish

Lamb and rice appear in many savory combinations throughout the Middle East. This recipe, of Palestinian origin, also includes raisins and cinnamon, which have been used in Middle Eastern cooking since ancient times. Serve this dish with slightly warmed plain yogurt, or with cold plain yogurt mixed with grated cucumber.

1. Heat oil or melt butter in a large, heavy saucepan over moderate heat. Add onion and sauté until soft, stirring often.

2. Add lamb and brown on all sides.

3. Add ½ cup of the pine nuts and brown, stirring constantly.

4. Stir in raisins, salt, pepper, cinnamon, parsley, and tomato paste. Cover with broth and stir.

5. Bring to a boil, cover, then lower heat and simmer for at least 45 minutes, or until meat is very tender.

6. Place rice in a medium saucepan. Add water to cover. Add 1 to 2 teaspoons salt and stir. Simmer, covered and undisturbed, for 20 minutes or until rice is cooked and all the water has been absorbed. Meanwhile, place the remaining ¼ cup pine nuts in a skillet and toast, over medium heat, until pine nuts begin to turn golden brown. Set aside.

7. Place rice on a platter and mound meat mixture on top. Decoratively arrange coriander sprigs around pilaf. Sprinkle toasted pine nuts over top. Serve hot.

MOROCCO

Beef Meatball Stew

Tajine Kefta

The word tajine *describes a range of North African stews prepared with vegetables, lamb, veal, chicken, and even fruit, that are cooked slowly in a flavored sauce. It is also the name of the distinctive glazed-earthenware dish with a conical top that fits flush with the rim, in which the food is cooked. Serve with couscous or rice.*

1. In a large bowl, combine 1 teaspoon of the salt, 1½ teaspoons of the cumin, 1 tablespoon of the paprika, 1 tablespoon of the parsley, and 1 tablespoon of the coriander with the ground beef. Form tablespoon-size meatballs.

2. Sauté onions and garlic in the olive oil in a large frying pan over moderately high heat for about 4 minutes, stirring frequently. Lower heat, add tomatoes, and cook for 5 to 10 minutes, stirring frequently. Add tomato paste, the water, the remaining salt, paprika, cumin, parsley, and coriander and cook for 5 minutes over low heat.

3. Add meatballs, cover pan, and cook for 25 minutes over moderately low heat, stirring occasionally.

servings: 4 to 6

2 teaspoons salt, or to taste

3 teaspoons ground cumin, or to taste

2 tablespoons paprika

2 tablespoons minced fresh parsley

2 tablespoons minced fresh coriander

2 pounds ground beef

3 medium onions, finely chopped

2 cloves garlic, minced

2 tablespoons olive oil

2 large tomatoes, chopped

1 can (6 ounces) tomato paste

1¼ cups water

MOROCCO

Stuffed Artichokes

Kournit Ma'amer

---

servings: 4 to 6

1 teaspoon salt

1 teaspoon fresh lemon juice, plus 1 tablespoon

6 large artichokes

1 cup ground lamb, cooked and drained of fat

½ cup minced onion

2 tablespoons finely chopped blanched almonds (about 6 whole almonds)

2 tablespoons chopped parsley

1 egg, beaten

⅛ teaspoon grated nutmeg, or to taste

Salt and pepper to taste

6 slices tomato

Although stuffed vegetables are not often found in Morocco, this inventive recipe comes from Rabat, a royal city and the capital of Morocco. The use of almonds in a dish with lamb is typical of Moroccan cooking.

1. Fill a very large pot with 2 inches of water and 1 teaspoon each salt and lemon juice. Heat to a boil. Meanwhile, cut off the stem of each artichoke flush with the bottom leaves, so the artichoke will stand upright. Cut off about 1 inch of the top of each artichoke.

2. Place artichokes on steamer rack fitted into pot. Cover and cook over medium heat for about 45 minutes or until tough outer leaves pull off easily, or are tender when pierced with a fork. Let cool.

3. While artichokes are cooking, combine lamb, onion, almonds, parsley, egg, nutmeg, salt, and pepper.

4. When artichokes are cool, pull off tough outer leaves. Spread center leaves until the light-colored cone of young leaves appears. Grasp and pull out with one tug. Remove fuzzy center by gently scraping with a spoon.

5. Preheat oven to 350°F. Gently spread artichoke leaves apart. Push lamb mixture into center and between the leaves. Sprinkle with the remaining 1 tablespoon lemon juice. Place 1 tomato slice on top of each artichoke.

6. Place artichokes in a baking dish with a little water. Bake for 5 to 10 minutes, or until warmed through.

SINGAPORE

Beef Curry with String Beans

Assam Beef

This fragrant curry is reflective of the mingling of Chinese and Malay cultures that took place in Singapore during the 19th century, when Chinese men who had been imported to work as laborers married Malay women. The resulting distinctive style of cooking, called Nonya, mixes Chinese ingredients, like pork, with Malay spices. Serve this curry hot over rice.

1. Pound together (or purée in food processor) lemongrass, fresh turmeric, shrimp paste, chili peppers, shallots, garlic, candlenuts, and sugar.

2. In a large nonstick pan, heat oil. Stir-fry the puréed mixture and the turmeric leaves until fragrant, about 3 minutes.

3. In a separate pan, cook bacon pieces for about 3 minutes, until partially cooked. Add to spice mixture.

4. Add beef slices and stir-fry 1 to 2 minutes. Pour in tamarind mixture and stir well.

5. Add string beans and cook an additional 3 to 5 minutes, until beef is cooked but string beans are still crisp. Add salt to taste.

*Available at Asian food markets; see list of suppliers (page 319).

servings: 4 to 6

2 stalks lemongrass,* outer leaves removed, lower 6 inches of stalk finely sliced

1-inch piece fresh turmeric,* minced

2 tablespoons shrimp paste*

15 dried chili peppers, minced, or to taste

20 shallots, peeled and minced

2 cloves garlic, minced

5 candlenuts* (optional)

Pinch of sugar

2 tablespoons vegetable oil

2 turmeric leaves* (optional)

8 slices bacon, cut into 2-inch lengths

2 pounds rump steak, cut into thin slices

2 tablespoons soaked and strained tamarind pulp* or tamarind concentrate,* mixed with ½ cup water

20 to 25 string beans or 10 Chinese long beans, cut into 1½- to 2-inch lengths

Salt to taste

South African Meat Curry

Bobotee

servings: 4

- 1 teaspoon butter or vegetable oil, plus more for baking dish
- 2 medium onions, chopped
- 1 large slice white bread
- 1 cup milk
- 2 pounds ground beef or lamb
- 2 teaspoons salt
- ½ teaspoon pepper
- 2 teaspoons curry powder, or to taste
- 1 tablespoon brown sugar
- Juice of 1 medium lemon
- 8 to 10 almonds, chopped, plus more for garnish
- ½ cup golden raisins or 1 cup chopped Granny Smith or other sour apple, or a combination of raisins and apples
- 3 eggs
- 3 bay leaves or lemon leaves (*kaffir lime leaves*)*
- 1 medium onion, sliced and rings separated, for garnish

This popular South African dish, has roots in the Malaysian community, which came to Capetown during the late 17th century with the Dutch East India Company. As a child, the contributor of this recipe accompanied her mother to the spice markets to buy spices for this and other dishes originating from Southeast Asia.

1. Preheat oven to 250°F and grease a 3-quart baking dish or casserole with butter. Fry onions in 1 teaspoon of the butter or vegetable oil in a medium skillet over moderate heat, until softened, about 5 minutes.

2. Soak bread in the milk in a small bowl. Lightly squeeze milk from bread. Reserve milk.

3. Combine onions, bread, meat, 1½ teaspoons salt, pepper, curry powder, brown sugar, lemon juice, chopped almonds, raisins, and 1 egg in a large bowl.

4. Place mixture in baking dish and bake, uncovered, for 30 minutes.

5. Mix together the remaining 2 eggs, reserved milk, bay or lemon leaves, and the remaining ½ teaspoon of salt. Pour over casserole. Decorate with onion rings and extra almonds. Raise oven temperature to 350°F and bake an additional 45 minutes. Serve with rice and chutney.

Available at Asian food markets; see list of suppliers (page 319).

TURKEY

Stuffed Squash

Kabak Dolmasi

Stuffed vegetables—squash, peppers, and grape leaves—are enjoyed throughout the Middle East. This version originates in the southeastern section of Turkey near Syria, between the Tigris and Euphrates Rivers, known since ancient times as the Fertile Crescent. Like many other Turkish recipes, this dish is tangy rather than spicy. Pita bread and yogurt are ideal accompaniments.

1. Heat olive oil in a large skillet over moderately high heat, and sauté onion and half of the minced garlic. Add ground meat and brown. Stir often.

2. Stir in tomato paste, salt, pepper, 1½ teaspoons of the oregano, and 3 teaspoons of the mint. Add rice, raisins, and pine nuts and mix. Set aside.

3. Cut squash in half lengthwise. Scoop out seeds and fibers from center cavities. Fill both cavities loosely with meat and rice mixture. Do not overstuff.

4. Preheat oven to 300°F. Place squash in a large, deep baking dish filled with enough hot water to reach halfway up the sides of the squash. Mix lemon juice with the remaining 1½ teaspoon oregano, the remaining 1½ teaspoon mint, and the remaining minced garlic. Pour over squash and cover baking dish with foil. Cook for 1 hour.

5. Remove squash from water bath. Place in an oiled ovenproof dish, raise oven to 350°F and bake, uncovered, another 20 minutes, or until brown on top.

---

servings: 4

2 tablespoons olive oil

2 cloves garlic, minced

½ cup chopped onion

1 pound ground lamb or beef

3 tablespoons tomato paste

Salt and pepper to taste

3 teaspoons oregano

4½ teaspoons chopped mint

1 cup cooked white rice or Arborio rice

½ cup golden raisins (optional)

½ cup pine nuts (optional)

1 large squash, such as acorn, spaghetti or butternut, about 1½ to 2 pounds

½ cup fresh lemon juice

Welsh Leg of Lamb

servings: 10 to 12

- 1 whole leg of lamb (approximately 8 pounds)
- 3 cloves garlic, slivered
  Salt and pepper to taste
- 2 tablespoons mustard, preferably grainy
- ½ cup water
  Juice of 1 lemon
  Mint sauce or jelly (optional)

Tender young lamb is the traditional specialty of this mountainous land. A quick, hot glaze of mustard, lemon juice, and herbs seals in the flavor of the meat when poured over the garlic-studded roast.

1. Preheat oven to 350°F. Make tiny incisions with the tip of a paring knife all over the lamb and insert thin slivers of garlic. Rub lamb with salt and pepper.

2. In a saucepan, bring mustard, the water, and lemon juice to a boil. Pour over lamb.

3. Roast lamb on rack for 16 minutes per pound. Let meat rest for 15 minutes. Slice and serve with mint sauce.

Cincinnati Chili

Chili is an all-American dish, finding its inspiration in the Southwest, where meat is combined with a spicy sauce and eaten from a bowl with a big spoon. Beyond that, generalizing about chili is difficult, as spices and other ingredients vary widely, and each version has passionate proponents. This recipe, with its origins in a chili-loving town, has a secret ingredient—bitter chocolate. Variations abound: among them are "Cincinnati Chili: 3 Ways," with chili, spaghetti, and grated Cheddar cheese, and "Cincinnati Chili: 4 Ways," with chopped onions as well.

1. Heat the water in a large pot and slowly simmer ground beef for 30 minutes.

2. Add remaining ingredients. Simmer uncovered for 3 hours. Let cool, and refrigerate overnight.

3. Skim fat from the top of the pot. Reheat slowly over low heat until chili is hot. Serve over spaghetti, with chopped raw onions and grated Cheddar cheese.

Note: This version may be prepared with ground turkey or a combination of beef and turkey. If using turkey, increase the chili powder to taste.

servings: 5 to 6

- 4 cups water
- 2 pounds ground beef
- 2 medium onions, chopped
- 1 pound tomato sauce
- 5 whole allspice berries
- ½ teaspoon cayenne pepper
- 1 teaspoon ground cumin
- 4 tablespoons chili powder
- ½ ounce bitter chocolate
- 4 cloves garlic, minced
- 2 tablespoons vinegar
- 1 large bay leaf
- 5 whole cloves
- 2 teaspoons Worcestershire sauce
- 1½ teaspoons salt
- 1 teaspoon cinnamon

Lamb and White Bean Chili

servings: 6

- 1 cup dried white beans (such as great northern or navy)
- 4 ounces (¼ pound) smoked slab bacon
- 3 quarts plus ¾ cup water
- 4 large dried New Mexico red chili peppers
- 1 large chipotle chili pepper
- 3 cups hot water
- 1½ pound trimmed boneless lamb shoulder, cut into 1-inch cubes
- Salt and pepper to taste
- 3 tablespoons olive oil
- 1 medium onion, finely chopped
- 3 cloves garlic, minced
- 4½ teaspoons ground cumin
- 2 tablespoons coarsely chopped fresh thyme, or 1 tablespoon dried
- 1 tablespoon coarsely chopped fresh oregano, or 1 tablespoon dried
- 1 can (28 ounces) crushed tomatoes
- 1 can (6 ounces) tomato paste
- 2 tablespoons sugar
- 3 bay leaves

The annual spring ritual of sheep shearing on the Elizabeth Islands, off Martha's Vineyard in Massachusetts, inspired this unusual and incendiary chili. Reducing the chili peppers by half results in a dish that is merely hot.

1. Place beans in a medium saucepan with 6 cups of the water and boil for 3 minutes. Remove from heat and let stand, covered, for 1 hour. Drain beans, return to pan. Add bacon and additional 6 cups of water. Simmer until beans are tender, about 1 hour. Coarsely chop bacon and return to mixture. (The beans can be frozen, or the chili can be prepared up to 3 days in advance, covered and refrigerated. Re-warm over moderate heat.)

2. Soak chili peppers in the hot water in a medium bowl for about 20 minutes. Pour off liquid, reserving 1 cup. Stem and seed chili peppers and purée in a food processor or blender with the reserved liquid until smooth. Reserve.

3. Season lamb with salt and pepper. Heat 2 tablespoons of the oil in a large casserole. Over high heat cook lamb in batches until all cubes are browned. Remove lamb and set aside.

4. Heat the remaining 1 tablespoon oil, add onions and garlic, and cook until onions are translucent, about 4 minutes. Stir in cumin, thyme, and oregano and cook until fragrant, about 2 minutes.

5. Return lamb to casserole. Add chili peppers, tomatoes, tomato paste, sugar, bay leaves, and remaining ¾ cup water. Bring to a boil over moderately high heat. Lower heat, partially cover, and simmer gently until meat is very tender, about 1½ hours. Discard bay leaves. Mix lamb with beans and serve over hot rice.

Caucasian Pilaf

Plof

A UNIS parent who lived in Russia for several years was introduced to this tasty pilaf at Uzbek restaurants in Moscow and St. Petersburg. It is typically accompanied by salads, such as grated carrots with garlic, black pepper, honey, and chopped coriander, or chopped tomato with cucumber, and dill.

1. Brown lamb in 2 tablespoons of the oil in a large skillet over moderately high heat. Remove lamb and set aside.

2. In the same skillet, sauté onion and garlic over low heat, until translucent, about 6 minutes. Stir often.

3. Stir-fry rice in the remaining 2 or 3 tablespoons oil in a large pot, at high heat for 2 minutes, stirring constantly. Add carrots and continue stirring 1 to 2 minutes. Add lamb, sautéed onions, and garlic and stir 30 seconds.

4. Add bouillon mixture and stir well. Bring to a boil and reduce to a simmer. Add raisins and cover pan. Simmer 25 to 30 minutes or until rice is tender. Stir in *garam masala* and serve.

Garam masala, a blend of ground coriander, cumin, ginger, black pepper, cinnamon, pimiento, cardamom, bay leaves, and nutmeg, is available at Indian food markets; see list of suppliers (page 319).

servings: 2 to 4

2 pounds ground lamb

4 to 5 tablespoons olive oil or vegetable oil

1 medium onion, finely chopped

2 cloves garlic, finely chopped

2 cups long-grain rice

2 carrots, slivered

2 vegetable bouillon cubes, dissolved in 4 cups water

½ cup raisins

¼ teaspoon *garam masala**

Chicken in Black Bean Sauce

Dòu Chǐ Jī

servings: 6

4 teaspoons soy sauce

2½ teaspoons Asian sesame oil

2 teaspoons cornstarch

6 boneless chicken breasts (about 2 pounds), cut into bite-size chunks

4 tablespoons vegetable oil

1 red bell pepper, diced

1 medium onion, diced

3 tablespoons black bean sauce*

Black bean sauce has been used in Chinese cooking since ancient times. Prepared with chicken (or beef), this dish has been embraced by Chinese food lovers the world over. Before black bean sauce was commercially available, cleaning the beans and salting them to make the sauce was a laborious process.

1. Mix soy sauce, sesame oil, and cornstarch in a large bowl. Add chicken pieces and marinate at least 6 hours.

2. Heat 2 tablespoons of the vegetable oil in a wok or large skillet over high heat. Sauté pepper and onion, stirring often. Remove from pan when softened, about 5 minutes.

3. Heat 1 tablespoon of the oil in the wok or skillet until almost smoking. Add chicken pieces and lower heat to moderate. Brown chicken on all sides, but do not overcook. Remove chicken and set aside.

4. Heat the remaining 1 tablespoon of oil and add black bean sauce. Stir for 2 to 3 minutes. Return chicken, pepper, and onion to skillet. Mix well. Serve with rice.

*Available at Asian food markets and some supermarkets; see list of suppliers (page 319).

FRANCE

Chicken Provençal

Poulet Provençal

The generous mix of herbs, preferably fresh, evokes sun-drenched Provence, with its vineyards and fields of lavender. Serve with rice, a salad, and a chilled French white or rosé wine.

1. Dredge chicken pieces in the flour seasoned with the salt and pepper.

2. Heat the oil in a large skillet over moderate heat and add half the chicken pieces, skin-side down. Cook 4 to 5 minutes until golden brown. Turn and cook on other side, about 3 minutes. Drain on paper towels. Brown the second batch and drain. Pour off fat from skillet.

3. Return chicken pieces to skillet. Add wine, thyme, rosemary, oregano, garlic cloves, and bay leaf. Scrape bottom of skillet and stir briefly. Boil until liquid is reduced by half, about 7 minutes. Cover, lower heat, and cook another 15 minutes.

4. Add chicken broth and simmer uncovered, about 10 minutes, or until sauce is reduced by half and garlic cloves are tender.

5. Remove chicken to a warmed serving plate.

6. Remove bay leaf from the sauce remaining in skillet. Add butter, stir until melted, and pour sauce over chicken. Sprinkle with chervil or parsley. Serve several garlic cloves with each portion.

servings: 4

- 1 chicken (3½ pounds), cut into 6 to 8 pieces
- ½ cup all-purpose flour
- 2 teaspoons salt, or to taste
- 1 teaspoon pepper, or to taste
- 2 tablespoons olive oil
- ½ cup dry white wine
- 3 teaspoons fresh chopped thyme, or 1 teaspoon dried thyme
- 3 teaspoons fresh chopped rosemary, or 1 teaspoon dried rosemary
- 1½ teaspoons fresh chopped oregano, or ½ teaspoon dried oregano
- 12 cloves garlic, peeled
- 1 bay leaf
- ½ cup chicken broth
- 2 tablespoons butter
- ¼ cup fresh chopped chervil or parsley, for garnish

Jollof Rice

servings: 4

8 pieces chicken (thighs, drumsticks, wings), skin removed

¼ cup fresh lemon juice

Salt and freshly ground pepper to taste

3 large cloves garlic, crushed

1 cup vegetable oil

3 large onions, peeled and chopped in blender until mushy

2 bunches scallions, finely chopped

3 large tomatoes, cut into chunks and blended to a pulp

2 large chicken bouillon cubes

3 bay leaves

1 can (6 ounces) tomato paste

3 cups water

2 cups short-grain rice, rinsed and drained

5 carrots, diced

Named for the Wollof ethnic group, this dish is one of the finest offerings of West Africa. It is often served at weddings in Gambia and neighboring Senegal. It was served at the wedding feast of the UNIS parent who contributed this recipe.

1. Place chicken in a large bowl and season with lemon juice, salt, pepper, and garlic. Marinate in refrigerator for 2 to 3 hours.

2. Reserve marinade. Heat oil in a large skillet, and sauté chicken on both sides over moderately high heat, until golden brown, about 10 minutes. Remove and set aside.

3. Pour the oil from the skillet into a large pot. Add the onions, scallions, tomatoes, bouillon cubes, bay leaves, tomato paste, the water, and marinade. Add chicken and bring to a boil over high heat. Lower heat and simmer for 30 minutes.

4. Add rice to the pot. (The chicken can be removed before the rice is added or can continue cooking with the rice.) Add carrots. Cover tightly and cook over low heat until rice is done, about 20 minutes.

Chicken Paprikash

Paprikás Csirke

A recipe for chicken paprikash appeared in the first "modern" Hungarian cookbook, published in 1829, and has remained popular in Hungary and throughout the world ever since. Serve with noodles and cucumber salad.

1. Melt butter in a large saucepan over moderately high heat. Add chicken pieces and sauté until golden brown on one side. Turn chicken pieces over, add onions and sauté until chicken is golden and onions are wilted, about 10 minutes, stirring often.

2. Add tomato, paprika, vinegar, salt, and broth or water. Cook about 20 minutes, then remove chicken pieces. Set aside.

3. Add flour to the pan and cook briefly, stirring, until sauce thickens. Add sour cream and blend well. Return chicken pieces to pan, turn pieces to coat with sauce, and heat through.

servings: 4

2 tablespoons butter

1 frying chicken, (3½- to 4-pounds), skinned and cut into 8 pieces

2 medium onions, coarsely chopped

1 large ripe tomato, coarsely chopped

1 teaspoon paprika, or more to taste

1 tablespoon vinegar

Salt to taste

1 cup chicken broth or water

1 tablespoon all-purpose flour

2 tablespoons sour cream

INDIA

Senhor Teodosio's Chicken Curry

Murg Masala

servings: 4 to 6

curry paste

- 2 medium onions, finely chopped
- 1-inch piece ginger, chopped
- 2 teaspoons ground cumin
- 2 teaspoons ground coriander
- ½ teaspoon ground turmeric
- 1 teaspoon cayenne pepper
- 2 teaspoons salt
- 2 tablespoons water

chicken

- 4 tablespoons extra-virgin olive oil
- 1-inch piece cinnamon stick
- 2½ pounds boneless chicken breasts, trimmed of fat and quartered
- Juice of 1 lemon
- 1 cup chicken broth
- 3 peppercorns
- Sprigs of coriander, for garnish

Sometime during the monsoon of 1933, Senhor Teodosio Rodrigues, noted music teacher and reputed big-game hunter, promised Dona Elena da Penha Fonseca, the wealthy widow he was courting, that he would cook a bokkem (grey paddy heron) for her birthday. Because his aim with a shotgun was even worse than his eyesight, he shot her rooster instead. No matter—the curry was sensational, and the recipe, updated for our times, follows.

1. Put curry ingredients in a blender and reduce to a moist paste.

2. Heat oil in a wide-bottomed saucepan over moderate heat. Add paste mixture and cinnamon stick. Stir-fry until mixture bubbles, no more than 9 minutes.

3. Add chicken pieces and stir until coated. Add lemon juice, chicken broth, and peppercorns. Bring to a boil.

4. Lower heat and simmer, covered, for 20 minutes. Uncover, raise heat, and boil off some of the liquid.

5. Garnish with coriander sprigs and serve with Dona Elena's Never-Fail Festive Rice Pilaf (page 211).

Note: Senhor Teodosio and the widow Dona Elena are fictional characters in Victor Rangel-Ribeiro's novel about the mythical Goan village of Tivolem.

Chicken with Porcini Mushrooms

Pollo ai Funghi Porcini

The name of these "porky" mushrooms was inspired by their bulbous shape. An autumn delicacy from Northern Italy, their meaty flavor is intensified by drying. This fragrant dish tastes wonderful served over pasta.

1. Place mushrooms in a small bowl with the 2 cups warm water for 20 minutes. Strain soaking liquid through a paper towel lining the strainer and reserve. Rinse mushrooms with cold water.

2. Combine flour, salt, and pepper in a shallow dish. Dredge chicken pieces in flour.

3. Heat ¼ cup of the oil over moderately high heat in a large, heavy-bottomed pot.

4. Sauté chicken until golden brown, approximately 5 minutes on each side. This can be done in several batches; add a little oil to the pot if needed. Remove chicken and set aside.

5. Place onion and garlic in the pot, reduce heat to moderately low, adding more oil if necessary. Sauté until onion is translucent, about 5 minutes, stirring to loosen meat particles.

6. Add mushrooms, 1 cup of the mushroom soaking liquid, the tomatoes, wine, bay leaf, and chicken. Simmer, covered, for 1½ hours. Correct seasoning, adding more salt and pepper, if needed.

---

servings: 6

- 1 cup dried porcini mushrooms, chopped
- 2 cups warm water
- 2 cups all-purpose flour
- 2 teaspoons salt
- 1 teaspoon pepper, or to taste
- 2 small chickens (about 3 pounds each), each cut into 10 pieces
- ½ cup olive oil
- 1½ cups chopped onion
- 3 cloves garlic, minced
- 1 can (28 ounces) crushed tomatoes
- ½ cup white wine
- 1 bay leaf

KOREA

Korean Fried Chicken

Dak Doritang

---

servings: 2

....

3 tablespoons soy sauce

1 teaspoon ground ginger

1 tablespoon chopped scallion (about ¼ scallion)

1½ tablespoons sugar

1 teaspoon finely chopped garlic

1 tablespoon vegetable oil

¼ pound carrots, sliced (about 4 thin carrots)

1 pound chicken pieces, preferably drumsticks

1 cup water

In Korea, mothers prepare this dish for their childrens' birthday parties. Because of the sweetness of the dish, children everywhere find it appealing. For a more "adult" taste, add thin strips of green hot pepper or Korean red pepper. Serve with thin Asian noodles or rice.

1. Combine soy sauce, ginger, scallion, sugar, and garlic in a small bowl. Set aside.

2. Heat oil in a large skillet over moderately high heat and stir-fry carrot slices for about 3 minutes. Remove carrots and set aside.

3. Fry the chicken in the same skillet until golden brown, about 5 minutes per side. Add carrots, the 1 cup water, and half of soy sauce mixture. Cover pan and boil for 10 minutes. Reduce heat and cook, uncovered, until almost no liquid remains. Pour in remaining sauce and stir gently. The recipe may be multiplied to serve more people.

MALAYSIA

Ginger Chicken

Ayam Masak Halia

In many Asian countries, ginger is thought to have healthful properties. Perhaps that is the reason that in Malaysia this dish is often eaten after the birth of a baby. In any event, this pungent and delicious chicken will appeal to ginger lovers.

1. Heat sesame oil and cooking oil, if using, in a large skillet over moderately high heat. Add ginger slices and stir-fry until soft, about 2 minutes. Add chicken, pepper, and soy sauce. Stir-fry over high heat until chicken begins to brown, about 5 minutes.

2. When chicken is almost cooked, add wine or brandy and the 1 cup water. Bring sauce to a boil, about 2 minutes. Lower heat and simmer, covered, until chicken is tender, about 30 minutes. Add salt.

Note: This dish can be made into a soup by doubling the wine and adding 6 cups water.

Available at Asian food markets; see list of suppliers (page 319).

servings: 8

4 tablespoons Asian sesame oil

2 tablespoons cooking oil (optional)

½ pound gingerroot, peeled and sliced (about 1 cup)

1 chicken (about 3½ pounds), cut into 20 pieces and seasoned with salt

1 teaspoon white pepper

1 teaspoon thick black soy sauce*

5 to 10 tablespoons Chinese rice wine or brandy

1 cup water

1 teaspoon salt, or to taste

Moroccan Couscous with Chicken and Vegetables

Seksu Bedjaj wa Lkhodra

---

servings: 4

- **4 merguez* or other spicy sausage, cut into 2-inch pieces**
- **6 boneless chicken thighs**
- **4 tablespoons olive oil**
- **1 medium onion, chopped**
- **2 cloves garlic, minced**
- **1 tablespoon minced fresh gingerroot**
- **1 tablespoon ground cumin**
- **Several sprigs each fresh coriander and parsley, tied together with thread**
- **1 tablespoon ground cinnamon**
- **1 teaspoon salt**
- **1 sweet potato, peeled and cubed**
- **3 carrots, peeled and diced**
- **2 zucchini, diced**
- **1 can (16 ounces) chickpeas, drained**
- **1½ cups tomato sauce (12-ounce can)**
- **1¾ cups chicken stock (14-ounce can)**
- **½ cup raisins**
- **1 box (10 ounces) couscous****
- **1 tube (6 ounces) *harissa******

Couscous is one of the truly great dishes of Morocco. Called seksu *by most Moroccans, the dish originated with the Berbers, Morocco's indigenous people. Couscous refers to the entire dish as well as to the tiny grains of semolina. This version, which consists of the semolina grain, chicken, sausage, and assorted vegetables, has been adapted for the contemporary kitchen. Couscous, the grain, may also be served as a side dish with meat, shellfish, or vegetable entrées.*

1. Brown sausage and chicken in 2 tablespoons of the oil in a large pot or deep skillet over moderate high heat. Remove meats from pan and cut chicken into chunks. Set aside.

2. Add the remaining 2 tablespoons oil and sauté onion, garlic, and ginger over moderate heat for 15 minutes. Stir in cumin, coriander, parsley, cinnamon, and salt.

3. Add sausage, chicken, and all remaining ingredients except the couscous to the pot. Bring the mixture to a boil, lower heat, and simmer, covered, for 45 minutes.

4. Cook couscous according to instructions on the package.

5. Spread couscous on a large serving platter. Spoon chicken and vegetables on top. Put remaining broth in a bowl or sauceboat. Mix a bit of *harissa* with broth, to taste, and spoon some over the couscous. Serve couscous accompanied by extra broth and *harissa*.

*Merguez, a spicy lamb sausage, is available at specialty food markets; see list of suppliers (page 319).

**Available at Middle Eastern food markets and many supermarkets; see list of suppliers.

***Harissa, a spicy sauce of hot red peppers, garlic, spices, and salt, is sold in tubes, already mixed. Available at Indian or Middle Eastern food markets; see list of suppliers.

Chicken With Peanut Sauce

Carapulcra

This dish, like others that originated in the Peruvian Andes, is based on potatoes and seasoned with a hot chili called ají-panca. Traditionally, this dish was made with dried potatoes, toasted in the oven and pounded into tiny bits before being mixed with lard. This recipe has been adapted for modern convenience.

1. Grind peanuts and chili pepper in a blender.

2. Sauté the chicken in 3 tablespoons of the olive oil in a large skillet, over moderate heat, about 3 minutes on each side. Remove chicken from pan and set aside.

3. Add remaining 1 tablespoon oil and sauté the garlic and onion, stirring often.

4. When onion is golden, return chicken to pan, and add the water and potatoes. Cover and cook over moderate heat until potatoes are soft, about 20 minutes. About 5 to 10 minutes before potatoes are soft, add peanut-chili mixture, the paprika, pepper, and salt. Add additional water, if necessary. Serve with white rice.

*Available at Latin American food markets, see list of suppliers (page 319).

servings: 4

½ cup ground peanuts

1 dried red chili pepper, or
  1 *ají-panca**

2 chicken breasts, finely diced

4 tablespoons olive oil

2 cloves garlic, chopped

½ medium onion, chopped

2 cups water

5 medium potatoes, peeled and
  finely diced

3 tablespoons paprika

½ teaspoon pepper

1½ tablespoons salt, or to taste

PHILIPPINES

Stuffed Boned Roast Chicken

Rellenong Manok

servings: 4 to 6

2 roasting chickens (3½ pounds each), boned

3 tablespoons soy sauce

2 teaspoons lemon juice

1 pound ground pork

4 canned Vienna sausages

¼ cup sweet pickle relish

½ cup Cheddar or Parmesan cheese, grated

3 eggs

½ cup raisins

10 green olives, pitted and chopped

2 tablespoons tomato ketchup

Salt and pepper to taste

2 hard-boiled eggs, quartered

4 tablespoons (½ stick) butter, melted

sauce

Chicken liver, gizzard, and heart

2 cups water

¾ cup pan drippings

3 tablespoons flour

2 cups chicken broth

Salt to taste

¼ teaspoon pepper

Three-hundred years of Spanish rule left their mark on Filipino cuisine, as seen in this elegant roast chicken, filled with cheese, olives, and raisins from the European larder.

1. Marinate chickens in soy sauce and lemon juice for 30 minutes. Set aside.

2. Mix ground pork, Vienna sausages, sweet relish, cheese, eggs, raisins, olives, ketchup, salt, and pepper.

3. Preheat oven to 350°F. Place stuffing mixture in cavity of each chicken, placing 1 hard-boiled egg in the center of each. Pull edges together and sew up openings with heavy thread or tie with string. Wrap chickens in aluminum foil.

4. In a roasting pan, bake chickens for 1½ hours. Midway through cooking, loosen foil and baste with butter. Rewrap and continue baking.

5. Boil chicken liver, heart, and gizzard in water until tender, about 30 minutes. Remove from broth, chop and set aside. Reserve broth.

6. Remove foil from chicken and continue baking until skin is brown, about 30 minutes.

7. Remove chicken from oven and let stand for 15 minutes on a cutting board before slicing. While chicken rests, make the sauce.

8. Blend flour in the roasting pan with the pan drippings and brown slightly over moderate heat. Add chopped giblets and broth, stirring constantly. Cook until thick. Add salt and pepper. Slice chicken, arrange on serving platter and serve with sauce.

Chicken in Red Sauce with Potatoes and Peppers

Apritadang Manok

The Spanish legacy in Filipino cooking is deliciously represented in this dish by the tomatoes and potatoes, both introduced to Spain from the Americas before making their way to the Philippines. The multicolored peppers are a contemporary addition.

1. Heat oil in a large skillet and sauté onion and garlic over moderately high heat.

2. Add chicken and brown, turning, about 5 minutes per side.

3. Season with salt and pepper and add bay leaves.

4. Pour in tomato sauce, stirring to coat chicken pieces.

5. Cover and simmer over low-to-moderate heat for 15 minutes, turning chicken pieces once.

6. Add potatoes and simmer for 20 to 30 minutes, until tender.

7. Add bell peppers, cook for 2 minutes, and serve.

servings: 4

- 2 tablespoons vegetable oil
- 1 small onion, chopped
- 3 cloves garlic, chopped
- 4 chicken legs, cut apart into thigh and drumstick, (about 2½ pounds)
- 1 teaspoon salt, or to taste
- ½ teaspoon freshly ground black pepper, or to taste
- 2 whole bay leaves
- 1 can (8 ounces) tomato sauce
- 2 large potatoes, peeled and cut into large cubes
- ½ medium red bell pepper, diced
- ½ green bell pepper, diced
- ½ yellow bell pepper, diced

Spicy Roasted Chicken

servings: 8

1 cup Chinese barbecue sauce*

4 teaspoons salt

6 teaspoons sugar

¼ teaspoon each black pepper and white pepper

4 teaspoons dark soy sauce

2 teaspoons rice wine vinegar*

2 cloves garlic, chopped

2 chickens, 5 to 6 pounds each

A visit to Tahiti inspired a Chinese-born member of the UNIS community to re-create this tasty dish for her family. The sauce is equally good on barbecued or oven-baked chicken pieces. Make extra sauce and freeze it for the next time you make this entrée.

1. Preheat oven to 400°F.

2. Combine barbecue sauce, salt, sugar, peppers, soy sauce, vinegar, and garlic and pour over chickens, coating well.

3. Place chickens in large baking dish lined with aluminum foil. Place in oven. Immediately lower oven temperature to 350°F. Roast for 1¼ to 1½ hours, basting occasionally. Cut into pieces and serve with rice.

Available at Asian markets; see list of suppliers (page 319).

SPAIN

Chicken in Almond Sauce

Gallina en Pepitoria

The centuries-old influence of the Arabs who once ruled Spain is seen in many Spanish dishes, including the ground almonds in this fragrant entrée.

1. In a saucepan, warm chicken broth, add saffron and set aside. Saffron will infuse the broth.

2. Place flour, salt, pepper, and chicken pieces in a large plastic bag. Close bag and shake until chicken is well coated with flour mixture.

3. In a large, heavy-bottomed pot, heat oil over moderately high heat and sauté chicken pieces, turning often, until all sides are golden, 10 to 12 minutes. Remove chicken, drain on paper towels, and set aside. Sauté garlic cloves until golden, remove and set aside.

4. Fry onion in the same pot, adding more oil if necessary, until onion is soft. Return chicken to pot and stir. Add sherry. When sherry comes to a boil, add 2 cups of the chicken broth, the parsley, and bay leaf. Lower heat and simmer, covered, until chicken is tender, stirring occasionally, about 30 to 35 minutes.

5. Blend egg yolks, ground almonds, and garlic cloves with remaining ¼ cup stock in a blender. Add mixture to chicken and cook for another 20 minutes over moderately low heat. The sauce should be the consistency of thick cream. If it is too thick, add additional broth.

---

servings: 4

2¼ cups chicken broth
  Pinch of saffron
⅓ cup all-purpose flour
  Salt and pepper to taste
1 chicken (3½ to 4 pounds), skinned and cut into 8 pieces
⅓ cup olive oil
2 whole large cloves garlic, peeled
1 medium onion, chopped
1 cup dry sherry
1 bunch parsley, coarsely chopped
1 bay leaf
  Yolks of 2 hard-boiled eggs
2 tablespoons ground almonds

Chicken, Rice, and Vegetable Casserole

Arroz con Pollo

servings: 8 to 10

- 2 roasting chickens (2½-pounds each), each cut into 6 pieces
- 2 teaspoons dried oregano
- ½ teaspoon pepper
- 4 teaspoons salt
- ½ cup olive oil
- 2 cups chopped onions
- 1 clove garlic, peeled and chopped
- 1 medium green bell pepper, cut into ¼-inch-wide strips
- 1 bay leaf
- ⅛ teaspoon crushed red pepper flakes, or to taste
- 1 teaspoon saffron threads, crushed
- 2 cups raw white rice
- 1 can (1 pound 12 ounces) tomatoes, with juice
- 1¾ cups chicken broth
- ½ cup water
- 5 ounces frozen green peas, thawed
- ½ cup pimiento-stuffed green olives
- 4 ounces pimientos, drained and cut into ¼-inch strips

This classic, saffron-infused Spanish dish has become an international favorite. It was through the Arabs that Spain became acquainted with saffron, the best of which is cultivated around Valencia, the home of this casserole and of most Spanish rice dishes.

1. Sprinkle chicken pieces with oregano, pepper, and 2 teaspoons of the salt. Let stand for 10 minutes.

2. Heat olive oil in a 6-quart ovenproof pot, casserole, or Dutch oven over moderately high heat. Sauté chicken, 4 to 6 pieces at a time, about 5 minutes per side, until golden brown. Remove and repeat with remaining chicken.

3. Using same pot, add onions, garlic, bell pepper, bay leaf, and red pepper flakes. Sauté, stirring, over moderate heat, about 5 minutes.

4. Preheat oven to 350°F. Add saffron threads, the remaining 2 teaspoons salt, and the rice to the pot. Cook, stirring, until rice is lightly browned, about 10 minutes.

5. Add tomatoes with juice and chicken broth.

6. Arrange browned chicken pieces over rice mixture. Bring just to a boil, uncovered.

7. Cover and bake in oven for 1 hour.

8. Remove pot from oven and sprinkle the ½ cup water over surface but do not stir. Sprinkle on peas, olives, and pimiento strips. Serve immediately.

Broiled Chicken with Olive-Coriander Sauce

Gai Phat Chee

This full-flavored recipe mixes Thai and European cuisine. Coriander, cinnamon, and fresh ginger are characteristic of Thai cooking; olives and olive oil are European. Serve with rice.

1. Preheat broiler. Season chicken with salt and pepper and 1 teaspoon of the olive oil. Place on baking sheet with sides and broil chicken about 4 inches from heat, 10 minutes on each side.

2. While chicken is cooking, heat remaining 1 teaspoon olive oil in a medium-size saucepan over low heat. Add shallots, gingerroot, garlic, saffron, and the cinnamon stick. Stir often, until soft, about 5 minutes.

3. Add chicken broth and bring to a boil. Reduce to simmer and cook 20 minutes. Remove cinnamon stick. Add olives and coriander. Spoon sauce over chicken breasts.

servings: 4

4 chicken breasts, bone in
   Salt and pepper to taste

2 teaspoons olive oil

3 shallots, peeled and chopped

1-inch piece gingerroot, peeled and
   cut into very fine sticks

2 cloves garlic, minced

5 saffron threads or ¼ teaspoon
   turmeric

2-inch piece cinnamon stick

1 cup chicken broth

2 tablespoons green olives, pitted and
   minced

1 tablespoon chopped fresh
   coriander

Thai Chicken in Coconut Milk

Gai Satay

servings: 3 to 4

spice paste

2 teaspoons Chinese chili-garlic sauce,* or 2 to 4 small dried red chili peppers

1 teaspoon pepper

1 teaspoon ground cumin

1 teaspoon ground coriander

1 teaspoon ground ginger

2 tablespoons grated lemon or lime peel

½ small onion, chopped

1 clove garlic

2 tablespoons smooth peanut butter

1 tablespoon vegetable oil

chicken

½ teaspoon salt, or to taste

¼ teaspoon pepper, or to taste

2 pounds chicken breasts, bone in, cut into thirds, or 3-pound frying chicken, cut into 6 pieces

2 tablespoons vegetable oil

1 can (13 ounces) unsweetened coconut milk*

2 large tomatoes, diced

1 can (12 to 14 ounces) whole corn kernels

1 cup green peas, or 1½ cups chopped green bell peppers

½ red bell pepper, cut into ¼-inch strips

The creation of a European-born cook who has lived in several Asian countries, this recipe combines some favorite aspects of Thai and Malaysian cooking. It has been adapted to the availability of vegetables and herbs in Europe and the United States. One or two strands of lemongrass may be substituted for lemon peel.

1. To make spice paste, in a food processor or blender, combine chili-garlic sauce, pepper, cumin, coriander, ginger, lemon or lime peel, onion, garlic, peanut butter, and oil. Blend to create a paste. Set aside.

2. Sprinkle salt and pepper over chicken pieces. In a medium skillet or wok, over moderately high heat, heat oil and sauté chicken until lightly browned, about 5 minutes on each side. Cook chicken in 2 batches. Remove from skillet and set aside.

3. Pour the coconut milk into skillet and bring to a boil over high heat. Reduce heat to low and add chicken pieces. Regulate heat so that liquid barely bubbles, then cover and cook about 15 to 20 minutes until meat is no longer pink near the bone. Remove chicken from skillet.

4. Stir spice paste into reduced cooking liquid and boil for 3 to 5 minutes. Add tomatoes, corn, peas or green bell peppers, and red bell pepper to sauce. Season, if desired, with salt and pepper, and return chicken to sauce. Reduce heat and simmer for 10 to 15 minutes. Serve with rice.

Available at Asian food markets; see list of suppliers (page 319).

Taunton Chicken

The lovely county of Somerset in the west of England is the source of this recipe. It is made with scrumpy, the local hard cider, which tastes innocent, but actually has a high alcohol content.

1. Roll chicken in flour and season with salt and pepper.

2. Heat 4 tablespoons of the butter in a large, heavy-bottomed skillet over moderately high heat. Sauté chicken until golden, about 10 minutes, turning often.

3. Stir in cider and bring to a boil. Reduce heat. Add the onion and simmer for 45 minutes, uncovered.

4. Sauté apple slices in remaining 4 tablespoons butter in another large skillet, over medium heat, about 10 minutes. Set aside.

5. Remove onion from skillet containing chicken and discard. Stir in cream, and cook over low heat for 5 to 10 minutes.

6. Arrange chicken pieces on a warmed serving dish and pour on the sauce. Garnish with sautéed apples, parsley, and lemon slices.

Note: This dish can also be made with boneless chicken breasts; reduce initial cooking time from 45 minutes to 20 minutes.

servings: 6

- 6 skinless chicken breasts on the bone
- ¼ cup all-purpose flour
- Salt and pepper, to taste
- 8 tablespoons (1 stick) butter
- 2½ cups fermented apple cider
- 1 onion, peeled and quartered
- ⅔ cup heavy cream
- 2 to 3 unpeeled green apples, cored and sliced
- Parsley, for garnish
- Lemon slices, for garnish

Fried Chicken with Buttermilk

An American classic, this toothsome version of Southern fried chicken is much lighter than many others. Serve with mashed potatoes, gravy, and creamed peas for a true old-time meal.

servings: 6

3 cups self-rising flour

1 tablespoon cinnamon

1 tablespoon pepper

1 chicken (5 pounds), cut into 10 to 12 pieces

1 quart buttermilk

Vegetable oil for frying

1. In a medium bowl, mix flour, cinnamon, and pepper. Dip chicken pieces in flour, then in buttermilk. Re-dip in flour.

2. Pour oil ¼ inch deep in a large skillet and heat over moderately high heat. Fry chicken, turning to brown all sides. Lower heat and fry, covered, at least 20 minutes or until cooked. Drain briefly on paper towels before serving.

UNITED STATES

Chicken in Cider

First enjoyed at an evening musicale, this dish and the music were equally memorable. Serve with rice, tossed salad, and bread.

1. Slice sausages and brown in heavy skillet over moderately high heat. Transfer sausage slices to a large pot, but leave the drippings in skillet.

2. Season chicken pieces with salt and pepper and brown, in sausage drippings, over moderately high heat about 5 minutes per side. Add a little butter or olive oil if needed. Transfer chicken to the pot containing sausage.

3. Add onions, garlic, mushrooms, and bell pepper to skillet and sauté in the drippings. When onions are translucent and mushrooms and peppers softened, add to pot.

4. Add red pepper flakes, cider, brandy, and vinegar to pot. Cover and cook over low heat for 1 hour. (This recipe can be prepared the day before and refrigerated, improving the flavor.)

5. An hour before serving, add apricots, prunes, olives, whole onions, and capers. Cover and simmer for 45 minutes. First bring to a boil if you have taken the stew from the refrigerator.

*Available at specialty food markets; see list of suppliers (page 319).

**Available at most liquor stores.

---

servings: 10 to 12

6 hot Spanish chorizo sausages,* sliced

2 large chickens, each cut into 10 pieces

Salt and pepper to taste

4 tablespoons (½ stick) butter, or ¼ cup olive oil

3 medium onions, chopped or sliced

2 to 3 cloves garlic, thinly sliced

8 ounces fresh mushrooms, sliced

1 large green bell pepper, cut into bite-size pieces

¼ teaspoon hot red pepper flakes

1 cup apple cider

1 cup apple brandy (Calvados)**

2 tablespoons vinegar, preferably cider vinegar

4 ounces (about 1 dozen) each dried apricots and prunes

12 pimiento-stuffed green olives

2 dozen small white onions

2 tablespoons capers

Chicken Pot Pie

servings: 6

½ cup finely chopped onion

¼ cup vegetable shortening

onion biscuits

1½ cups sifted all-purpose flour

2¼ teaspoons baking powder

½ teaspoon salt

⅓ cup vegetable shortening

½ cup milk

filling

¼ cup all-purpose flour

¼ teaspoon pepper

½ teaspoon salt

2 cups chicken broth

2 cups cooked chicken, skin removed and cut into bite-size pieces

½ cup cooked peas

½ cup cooked diced carrots

¼ cup green bell pepper, sliced

¼ cup cooked pearl onions

This old-fashioned American single-dish meal, with its fragrant combination of chicken and vegetables topped with flaky biscuits, is the very definition of "comfort food."

1. Brown onion in shortening in a medium skillet over moderately high heat. Reserve.

2. For the biscuits, sift flour, baking powder, and salt into a bowl. Cut in shortening with pastry blender, with two knives, or with food processor fitted with a steel blade until mixture resembles coarse meal.

3. Add half of browned onions and the milk. Mix only until flour is dampened and dough forms a ball.

4. Remove ball from bowl to a floured work surface. Using the heel of a hand push the dough down and out once or twice to knead. Re-form ball and roll to ¼-inch thickness. Cut rounds with a 2-inch cutter.

5. Preheat oven to 450°F. For the filling, in a large skillet, reheat remaining browned onions. Blend in flour, pepper, and salt to form a paste. Cook over low heat, stirring, for 5 minutes.

6. Whisk in chicken broth, stirring constantly. Cook until thick and smooth.

7. Add chicken, peas, carrots, bell pepper, and pearl onions and cook for 10 minutes.

8. Pour mixture into a 6 x 10-inch baking dish. Place biscuits on top of hot filling. Bake in oven for 12 to 15 minutes.

Chicken, Artichoke, and Mushroom Casserole

The aroma of this casserole evokes a party atmosphere. It's ideal for entertaining, because it can be prepared in advance, refrigerated, and reheated just before serving.

1. Preheat oven to 350°F. Place seasoned flour in a plastic bag. Place chicken pieces in the bag and shake to coat.

2. Sauté chicken pieces in butter and oil until golden. Add additional butter or oil if needed.

3. Place chicken in a 2-quart ovenproof casserole. Add broth, wine, scallions, herbs, salt, and pepper.

4. Bake, covered, for 15 minutes. Stir in artichokes. Re-cover and bake an additional 15 minutes. Stir in mushrooms and bake uncovered another 15 minutes. Serve with rice.

servings: 4

- 1 cup all-purpose flour, seasoned to taste with salt and pepper
- 2 whole chicken breasts, boned, skinned, and cut into bite-size pieces
- 2 tablespoons butter
- 1 tablespoon vegetable oil
- 1½ cups chicken broth
- ½ cup dry white wine
- 2 tablespoons chopped scallions
- ½ teaspoon each: dried dill, thyme and oregano
- 1 tablespoon chopped parsley
- Salt and pepper to taste
- 1 package frozen artichoke hearts, thawed
- ½ pound small, fresh mushrooms

Roast Turkey

servings: 12

turkey

1 turkey (18 pounds)

16 tablespoons (2 sticks) unsalted butter

1 bunch fresh sage leaves

9 cups stuffing (see stuffing recipes, pages 202 and 232)

4 ribs celery, rinsed

4 carrots, peeled and sliced

1 quart chicken broth, turkey stock, or dry white wine

1 12 x 24-inch piece cheese cloth, or clean cotton cloth

gravy

¼ cup all-purpose flour

1 cup water

This native American fowl is the time-honored entrée at Thanksgiving.

1. Preheat oven to 450°F. Remove bag of neck, heart, and giblets from inside turkey. Rinse turkey inside and out with cold water. Pat dry with paper towels. Remove turkey fat from inside cavity and neck area. Gently separate breast skin by running fingers between the skin and meat, taking care not to tear the skin.

2. Flatten 4 pats of butter (1 tablespoon each) and stuff between skin and meat along with 4 large sage leaves.

3. Fill cavity and neck end of turkey with stuffing. Close each end of turkey by gently pulling skin and tying legs together and tucking neck flap under bird.

4. Place turkey, breast-side up, on a bed of the remaining sage leaves, the celery, and the carrots in a large roasting pan.

5. In a saucepan, melt the remaining 12 tablespoons butter. Brush butter over turkey. Dip cloth in butter and drape over breast.

6. Roast turkey for 20 minutes. Lower temperature to 325°F.

7. Baste turkey with melted butter every 20 minutes. Use broth, stock, or wine until enough pan juice has collected for basting.

8. Continue to roast turkey for about 4 hours or until instant-read thermometer inserted into thickest part of thigh registers 160°F. Remove cloth for last 45 minutes of cooking to brown evenly.

9. For gravy, remove turkey from oven and place on carving board to rest for about 20 minutes before carving. Remove sage and vegetables from pan and discard. Skim fat from surface of pan drippings. In a small bowl, blend flour with water until smooth. Add flour mixture to pan and place over moderate heat, stirring constantly to loosen bits stuck to pan. Continue cooking until pan drippings begin to thicken.

Lemongrass Chicken

Gā Xào Sa

Lemongrass, also called citronella root, is an aromatic tropical grass that is a notable element of Vietnamese cuisine. Serve this dish with rice and glazed carrots.

1. To prepare Vietnamese dipping sauce, *nuoc cham*, combine chili, garlic, and sugar in a mortar and pound to a fine paste. Add lime or lemon juice, vinegar, fish sauce, and the water. Stir to blend. Set aside.

2. Preheat oven to 425°F. In a mortar, pound lemongrass, garlic, shallots, chili peppers, and sugar to a paste. Add salt, butter or oil, and fish sauce. Stir to blend.

3. Carefully loosen skin on the breast and legs of the chicken by pushing fingers between the skin and meat to form a pocket. Rub half of the lemongrass paste under the skin and the rest over the skin and in the cavity. Let stand for 30 minutes.

5. Place chicken on a rack in a roasting pan, breast-side up, and roast in oven for 15 minutes. Reduce oven to 375°F and roast for 1¼ hours, basting chicken occasionally with pan juices. Chicken is done when a leg moves freely in its joint and the juices run clear when the thigh is pierced with a fork. Remove chicken from oven and let stand for 10 minutes.

6. Carve chicken into 10 pieces. Serve with Vietnamese dipping sauce.

Available at Asian food markets; see list of suppliers (page 319).

---

servings: 4

Vietnamese dipping sauce *(nuoc cham)**

- **1 small green chili pepper, seeded and minced**
- **2 small garlic cloves, crushed**
- **1 tablespoon sugar**
- **3 tablespoons fresh lime or lemon juice**
- **¼ cup rice vinegar**
- **¼ cup Vietnamese fish sauce *(nuoc mam)****
- **¼ cup water**

chicken

- **3 stalks fresh lemongrass,* outer leaves and tough upper part discarded, cut into thin slices and chopped**
- **6 garlic cloves, sliced**
- **4 shallots, sliced**
- **2 red chili peppers, seeded and chopped**
- **1 tablespoon sugar**
- **½ teaspoon salt, or more to taste**
- **2 tablespoons butter or vegetable oil**
- **1 tablespoon Vietnamese fish sauce *(nuoc mam)****
- **1 roasting chicken (4 pounds), rinsed and patted dry**

Belgian Endives au Gratin

Witloof met Hesp

servings: 4

8 endives, ends removed and brown leaves discarded

8 slices boiled ham

8 tablespoons (1 stick) butter

½ cup all-purpose flour

1¼ cups milk

6 ounces Emmenthal or Gruyère cheese, grated

Salt and pepper to taste

Paprika, for garnish

The delicate endive is Belgium's best-known food. Its history is fascinating: Legend has it that a farmer fled to escape the turmoil of the 1830 revolution, and upon his return, was amazed to discover that the chicory roots he had covered with earth in his cellar had grown tasty, elongated white shoots. Thus the endive was born. This labor-intensive crop must be planted twice—first to root the chicory, and then to force production of the white shoots in darkness.

1. Place endives in a medium saucepan containing about 4 cups boiling water and cook for 20 to 25 minutes. Drain well.

2. Wrap each endive stalk with a slice of boiled ham. Set aside.

3. Preheat broiler. In a medium saucepan over moderate heat, melt butter and add flour. Cook for 3 minutes, stirring. Slowly add milk, stirring constantly to break up lumps. Bring mixture to a boil, stirring constantly. Add cheese, salt and pepper.

4. Arrange wrapped endives in a 6 x 10-inch ovenproof dish and cover with sauce. Sprinkle with paprika and broil about 2 minutes. Serve with mashed potatoes.

CROATIA

Pork Tenderloin, Stubica-Style

Pisanica Stubica

As early as the 16th century, this dish was a specialty served in the stately homes of Croatian aristocracy. Even today, fine restaurants around Zagreb feature this rich and creamy dish on their menus. Serve with flat noodles, rice, or mashed potatoes and steamed vegetables.

1. Stuff half of the pitted prunes with a piece of butter each.

2. Channel a hole through the length of each pork tenderloin with a long thin knife. Stuff each with about 3 buttered prunes. Alternatively, make a slit running the length of the tenderloins, taking care not to cut through to the other side, putting 3 prunes in each slit and tying ends closed with cotton string. Sprinkle with salt and pepper.

3. Heat oil in a large heavy-bottomed pot over high heat until very hot, and brown the tenderloins on all sides. Cook in batches.

4. Cut the remaining prunes into thin strips and add to pot with the vegetable stock and wine. Add all tenderloins, cover, reduce heat and simmer about 20 minutes, or until meat is tender.

5. Add the sour cream and cream, stir, and return to a boil briefly.

6. Turn off heat, add vodka and stir.

7. Remove tenderloins and cut strings, if using, with scissors.

8. Slice meat on the diagonal and arrange on a warmed platter. Pour prunes and sauce over meat and sprinkle with parsley.

servings: 8 to 10

18 ounces (25 to 30) prunes, rinsed and pitted

7 tablespoons butter, cut into 15 pieces

5 pork tenderloins (about 4½ pounds total), rinsed and patted dry

Salt and pepper to taste

4 tablespoons vegetable oil

2 vegetable bouillon cubes, dissolved in 1 cup water, or 1 cup vegetable stock

1¼ cups white wine

1 cup sour cream

2 cups (1 pint) heavy cream

¼ cup 100-proof good-quality vodka

½ cup finely chopped fresh parsley, for garnish

Dublin Coddle

servings: 3 to 4

- **4 tablespoons (½ stick) butter**
- **5 medium onions, chopped**
- **1 pound Irish bacon,* cut into ½-inch-thick slices**
- **½ pound Irish sausages***
- **8 medium potatoes, peeled and cubed**
- **1 teaspoon salt**
- **½ teaspoon pepper**
- **1 teaspoon minced parsley**

To "coddle" means to simmer just below boiling point, or to pamper. An Irish grandfather insisted that this dish be prepared every March 17, St. Patrick's Day. And, on this special day, his family coddled him accordingly.

1. Melt butter over moderate heat in a large skillet, and sauté onions, stirring often. Place bacon and sausages over onions. Add potatoes, salt, and pepper. Add enough water to cover meat and bring to a boil. Reduce heat, cover, and simmer for 30 minutes.

2. With a slotted spoon, transfer bacon, sausages, and potatoes to a serving dish. Continue to simmer the onions and water, uncovered, until thickened. Spoon onion sauce over bacon, sausages, and potatoes, and garnish with parsley. Serve with Irish soda bread.

*Available at specialty meat markets; see list of sources.

JAPAN

Pork with Ginger Sauce

Butaniku no Shogayaki

Ginger juice makes this a deliciously full-flavored dish. For best results, use very high quality, tender pork, such as pork tenderloin. Serve with steamed rice and stir-fried vegetables.

1. Using a garlic press, squeeze ginger pieces over a very small bowl to capture drops of juice. (Alternatively, purée ginger pieces in a blender or food processor, place purée in a fine-mesh strainer, press with spoon to release juice into a small bowl.) Yield should be about 1 teaspoon ginger juice.

2. In a medium bowl, mix ginger juice, 1 tablespoon of the soy sauce, and the *sake* or wine. Add pork to sauce and let stand for 10 to 15 minutes.

3. To make ginger sauce, mix grated ginger, sugar, and remaining 1 teaspoon soy sauce. Set aside.

4. Heat oil and sauté pork slices in a large skillet over moderate heat, until cooked through, about 5 minutes. Cook in batches, if necessary.

5. Arrange cooked pork slices in a shallow dish or small serving platter and top with ginger sauce.

*Available at most liquor stores.

servings: 2 to 3

5-inch piece fresh gingerroot, peeled and cut into pieces

1 tablespoon plus 1 teaspoon soy sauce

1 tablespoon Japanese rice wine *(sake)** or white wine

1 pound boneless pork, sliced thin

1 tablespoon grated gingerroot

2 teaspoons sugar

2 tablespoons oil

Philippine Pork Stew

Dinuguan

servings: 4 to 6

- **1 pound pork shoulder, cut into ½-inch cubes**
- **⅔ cup vinegar**
- **1 large onion, thinly sliced**
- **½ teaspoon pepper**
- **1 teaspoon salt**
- **6 cloves garlic, thinly sliced**
- **2 tablespoons lard**
- **2 cups water**
- **½ teaspoon crushed peppercorns**
- **½ cup pork blood***
- **2 teaspoons sugar**
- **2 tablespoons Philippine fish sauce (patis)****
- **2 large jalapeño peppers**

A robust and delicious Philippine dish for which there are as many variations as there are cooks. A recipe that has been passed down through many generations of a UNIS family, its origins are reflected in its ingredients. Serve over steamed rice or steamed white rice cakes, known as puto.

1. In a medium bowl, combine pork, vinegar, onion, pepper, and salt. Set aside for 20 minutes.

2. Sauté garlic in lard for 20 seconds in a large skillet, stirring, over high heat. Add marinated pork, vinegar mixture, and the water. Bring to a boil. Cover, lower the heat, and simmer until pork is tender, about 30 minutes. Do not stir until vinegar has evaporated.

3. Add pork blood. Stir well. Add sugar, fish sauce, and hot peppers. Simmer for 10 minutes.

*Available at specialty food markets; see list of suppliers (page 319).

**Available at Asian food markets; see list of suppliers.

UNITED KINGDOM

Toad-in-the-Hole

This traditional British standby is a children's favorite. It combines savory sausages baked in a puffy Yorkshire pudding. Peas are the vegetable of choice with this dish.

1. Preheat oven to 425°F. Place butter and sausages in a 12-inch roasting pan. Bake for 10 minutes.

2. While sausages are baking, sift flour and salt into a medium bowl and beat in egg. Gradually add half the milk, beating to form a smooth batter. Pour in remaining milk and beat until very smooth.

3. Reduce oven to 400°F. Pour batter into roasting pan with sausages and bake 20 minutes. Reduce oven to 350°F and bake until batter rises and turns golden.

---

servings: 4 to 6

2 tablespoons unsalted butter

1 pound small pork link sausages

1 cup all-purpose flour

   Pinch of salt

1 egg

1 cup milk

Ground Pork in Tomato Sauce

Thit Heo Bam Cā Chua

servings: 4

Vietnamese dipping sauce *(nuoc cham)**

- **2 small garlic cloves, crushed**
- **1 small fresh green chili pepper, seeded and minced**
- **1 tablespoon sugar**
- **3 tablespoons fresh lime or lemon juice**
- **¼ cup rice vinegar**
- **¼ cup Vietnamese fish sauce *(nuoc mam)****
- **¼ cup water**

pork

- **1 small head soft-leaf lettuce, such as Boston, finely shredded**
- **4 scallions, finely shredded**
- **½ cup shredded mint leaves**
- **1 cup whole coriander leaves (about 1 medium bunch)**
- **2 tablespoons vegetable oil**
- **6 garlic cloves, chopped**
- **1 large onion, cut into slivers**
- **1 pound ground pork**
- **1 tablespoon sugar**
- **3 tablespoons Vietnamese fish sauce *(nuoc mam)****
- **3 large tomatoes, cored and diced**
- **1 cup chicken broth**
- **2 tablespoons tomato paste**
- **Freshly ground pepper**
- **6 cups cooked rice**

Served with rice, this attractive dish is to Vietnamese cuisine what spaghetti with meat sauce is to Italian.

1. To make dipping sauce, in a mortar, pound garlic cloves, chili pepper, and sugar to a fine paste. Add lime or lemon juice, vinegar, fish sauce, and the water. Stir to blend. Set aside.

2. In a large bowl, combine lettuce, scallions, mint, and coriander. Cover and refrigerate.

3. Heat oil in a wok or large pan over high heat. Add garlic and onion and cook, stirring, until fragrant, about 4 minutes. Add ground pork and cook for 8 minutes, stirring constantly to break up lumps. Add sugar and 1 tablespoon of the fish sauce and cook for 2 minutes. Add tomatoes, reduce heat to moderate, and cook for 5 minutes.

4. Add broth, tomato paste, and remaining 2 tablespoons fish sauce. Simmer, uncovered, stirring occasionally, for 15 minutes.

5. To serve, arrange lettuce mixture around a large serving platter, with rice in the center and meat sauce on top. Sprinkle with black pepper and drizzle with dipping sauce.

*Available at Asian food markets; see list of suppliers (page 319).

ITALY

Grilled Veal Chops

Braciole di Vitello ai Ferri

The pungent flavors of the olives, capers, and balsamic vinegar are a perfect complement to the veal. Serve with pasta and salad or seasonal vegetables.

1. In a medium bowl, combine tomato, onion, olives, capers, basil, red pepper flakes, 1 tablespoon of olive oil, vinegar, salt, and pepper.

2. Preheat broiler. Brush chops with remaining tablespoon of olive oil, sprinkle with garlic slices, and broil for 5 to 7 minutes, turn and continue broiling for 5 to 7 minutes.

3. Divide the arugula between 2 plates. Arrange veal chops on top, and cover with the tomato mixture.

servings: 2

1 medium tomato, diced

1 tablespoon diced red onion

7 Kalamata or other imported olives, pitted and sliced

1 tablespoon capers

1 tablespoon chopped fresh basil

⅛ teaspoon red pepper flakes

2 tablespoons olive oil

1½ tablespoons balsamic vinegar

Salt and pepper to taste

2 large veal loin chops, ½ to ¾ inch thick

1 clove garlic, sliced

½ bunch arugula or watercress, rinsed and thick stems removed

ITALY

Veal Chops with Raspberry Vinegar

Braciole di Vitello con Aceto di Lampone

---

servings: 4

4 loin veal chops, about ½ pound each

Salt and pepper to taste

2 tablespoons butter

4 cloves garlic, peeled

1 large bay leaf

4 sprigs fresh thyme, or 1 teaspoon dried

3 tablespoons raspberry vinegar

½ cup chicken broth

2 tablespoons coarsely chopped fresh chervil or parsley

The aromatic combination of garlic, thyme, chervil, and raspberry vinegar make for a delicately flavored veal dish. Serve with pasta or rice, and salad or vegetables.

1. Season chops on both sides with salt and pepper.

2. Heat butter in a large heavy-bottomed skillet and brown chops on both sides over moderate heat, about 5 minutes on each side.

3. Add garlic, bay leaf, and thyme. Cook, stirring about 3 minutes. Pour vinegar around chops, add chicken broth, cover, reduce heat and simmer for 15 minutes, or until chops are tender.

4. Remove garlic from skillet and mash into a paste. Return to skillet and blend with sauce. Cover and simmer for 5 minutes. Remove thyme and bay leaf and discard.

5. Place chops on warmed serving platter and sprinkle with chervil or parsley.

Zurich Veal with Potato Pancake

Züri Geschnätslets mit Rösti

This version of the classic Swiss-German dish features rösti, *an elegant grated and browned potato pancake. In Bern, it is served with boiled potatoes, without bacon or onions. Both versions include kidneys, a favorite of Swiss cooks. Serve with a salad.*

1. In a large skillet, melt 2 tablespoons of the butter over moderately high heat and brown the kidneys, if using. Remove kidneys from pan and keep warm. Sauté the veal in the same skillet until lightly browned, about 1 to 2 minutes per side. Remove veal and keep warm. Pour beef broth into skillet. Add mushrooms and cook 2 to 3 minutes. Pour the mixture into a bowl and set aside.

2. Melt the remaining 2 tablespoons butter in a skillet and sauté onion about 3 minutes. Add wine and return the veal, kidneys, mushrooms, and beef broth to the skillet. Stir and add cream. Simmer 2 to 3 minutes. Season with salt and pepper.

3. For the potatoes, melt the butter in a large skillet over moderately high heat. Add bacon and onion, and brown, stirring often. Add potatoes, salt, and pepper. Flatten potatoes with a spoon or metal spatula evenly in pan to form a pancake. Cover and cook until golden, about 10 minutes. Reduce heat. To turn pancake over, place a plate over skillet, and with one hand on the plate, quickly lift skillet with the other hand and invert over the plate. Slip pancake back into the skillet and cook another 10 minutes.

4. Pour veal mixture onto a serving platter and serve with the *rösti* potatoes. Garnish both with parsley.

servings: 5

veal

4 tablespoons (½ stick) butter

½ pound veal kidneys, soaked overnight in salt and water, thinly sliced (optional)

1½ pounds veal, sliced about ¼ inch thick

½ pound white mushrooms, thinly sliced

½ cup beef broth

1 small onion, minced

¾ cup dry white wine

½ cup heavy cream

Salt and pepper to taste

Chopped parsley, for garnish

potatoes

3½ tablespoons butter

2 to 4 slices bacon, sliced into thin strips

1 small onion, minced

1 pound potatoes, coarsely grated

Salt and pepper to taste

¼ cup chopped parsley, for garnish

UNITED STATES

Roast Loin of Veal with Mustard Seeds

servings: 8

- 1 loin of veal, boned and tied (about 3 to 4 pounds)
- ¼ cup olive oil
- ¼ cup black mustard seeds* (reserve 1 tablespoon for garnish)
- 1 teaspoon coarse (kosher) salt
- 1 teaspoon freshly ground black pepper
- ¼ cup fresh chopped rosemary, plus ¼ cup sprigs for garnish
- 3 heads roasted garlic, for garnish
- 1 cup demi-glace**
- 2 to 3 small heads radicchio, for garnish

Elegantly presented with a garnish of roasted garlic, radicchio blossoms, and rosemary sprigs, this is an impressive dish for a special occasion or buffet dinner. Serve with roasted potatoes and squash roasted with ginger.

1. Preheat oven to 400°F. Rub veal with olive oil.

2. Preheat a cast-iron skillet or heavy-bottomed pot large enough to hold the loin. Brown loin on all sides, about 15 minutes. Remove veal from skillet.

3. In a small bowl, mix mustard seeds, salt, pepper, and rosemary. Press onto veal, and place veal in a roasting pan.

4. Roast veal in oven for 35 to 45 minutes or until interior temperature reaches 130°F on a meat thermometer.

5. After placing veal in oven, sprinkle garlic heads with remaining tablespoon oil. Add to roasting pan with veal and roast until garlic is golden brown, about 30 minutes. To cut radicchio into blossom, grasp a head of radicchio with the stem end flat on the work surface. With a sharp knife make 2 deep intersecting **x**'s across the top, but do not cut through to the base. Gently spread the center so it resembles a flower in bloom. Set aside.

6. Remove meat from oven and let rest for 20 minutes before slicing into ½-inch slices. Slice on a slight angle.

7. Arrange veal slices overlapping one another on a platter. Cover with hot demi-glace and sprinkle with remaining 1 tablespoon mustard seeds. Garnish with roasted garlic heads, rosemary sprigs, and radicchio cut into blossoms.

*Available at Indian food markets and some supermarkets; see list of suppliers (page 319).
**Available at specialty food markets; see list of suppliers.

Ground Veal Medallions in Mustard Sauce

Medallions of ground veal in a light, cream-free sauce are simple to prepare, yet equally suited for guests or a family dinner. Serve with steamed rice, noodles, or boiled new potatoes tossed with butter, parsley, and lemon juice.

1. Place veal in a bowl and add egg, bread crumbs, parsley, and garlic. Mix well.

2. Form 1½- to 2-inch balls then flatten to form medallions. In a large skillet over moderate heat, melt 1 tablespoon of the butter and brown medallions well on both sides, about 5 minutes per side. Remove medallions from pan.

3. Melt remaining 4 tablespoons butter in skillet and add flour. Whisk to create a light paste and avoid lumps. Add chicken broth slowly, whisking constantly. Whisk in mustard and wine. Cook over low heat for 1 minute. Add medallions to sauce and simmer, covered, for 5 minutes. Season with salt and pepper.

servings: 4

1 pound ground veal

1 egg, lightly beaten

⅔ cup Italian bread crumbs

2 tablespoons minced Italian parsley

1 tablespoon minced garlic

5 tablespoons butter

1½ tablespoons all-purpose flour

1 cup chicken broth

2 teaspoons Dijon mustard

Splash of white wine

Salt and pepper to taste

Curried Goat

servings: 10

5 pounds goat stew meat (such as shoulder), cut into ½- to 1-inch pieces

1 teaspoon salt

1 tablespoon freshly ground black pepper

6 tablespoons curry powder, preferably Madras*

6 medium onions, sliced

5 cloves garlic, crushed and slightly cut

4 hot peppers, chopped

2 medium tomatoes, cored and chopped (optional)

¾ to 1 cup olive oil (4 tablespoons butter can be substituted for 4 tablespoons oil)

6 cups water

6 scallions, chopped, for garnish

Flavored with hot, fragrant Scotch bonnet peppers, habaneros, or the less fiery Jamaican hots, this is a dish for celebrations and family get-togethers in Jamaica. The Jamaican proverb regarding the goat is instructive: "Goat in a too much grass him tawl, you tek him put a kitchen corner him climb por stone." Which, loosely translated means, "One is never satisfied with what one has."

1. In a large bowl, season goat meat with salt, pepper, curry powder, onions, garlic, hot peppers, and tomatoes. Mix well and marinate for at least 30 minutes.

2. Remove onions from meat and set aside. In a large pot over moderately high heat, fry meat in olive oil until lightly browned on all sides, stirring often.

3. Add enough water to cover meat and bring to a boil. Reduce heat, cover, and simmer for 1 hour, stirring occasionally. Return onions to the pot and simmer 1 hour longer, or until meat is tender.

4. To let sauce thicken, remove lid during the last 30 minutes.

5. Garnish goat with scallions. Serve with white or basmati rice, roti bread, Caesar salad, and cold beer. Alternatively, serve with green bananas, boiled with skins on for 40 minutes.

*Available at Indian food markets; see list of suppliers (page 319).

Flemish Rabbit

Konÿm op zyn Vlaams

Rabbit is popular and commonly available in many countries of Europe, especially in France and Belgium. Pleasing accompaniments are boiled potatoes or yams.

1. In a large heavy pot, sauté bacon and onion in butter over moderate heat. When onion is translucent, add rabbit pieces and sauté about 5 minutes on each side. Add thyme, pepper, bay leaves, salt, flour, and water. Stir, scraping any browned bits from the bottom of the pot.

2. Cover, reduce heat, and simmer rabbit for 1 hour. Add the prunes, continue cooking for 20 minutes. Add a little water if rabbit seems dry during cooking.

3. Transfer rabbit to serving platter. Add wine or vinegar to pot, boil a few minutes to reduce sauce. Pour sauce over rabbit.

---

servings: 4

2 ounces bacon, about 4 thin slices

1 medium onion, chopped

5 tablespoons butter

1 rabbit (3½ to 4 pounds), cut by the butcher into 5 or 6 pieces

1 teaspoon dried thyme

Pepper to taste

2 bay leaves

Pinch of salt

1 tablespoon all-purpose flour

3 cups water

¼ pound dried prunes, pitted

3 tablespoons red wine, or 2 tablespoons tarragon vinegar

FRANCE

Rabbit with Mushrooms

Lapin aux Champignons

servings: 4

2 tablespoons butter

1 rabbit (3½ to 4 pounds), cut into
  6 pieces by the butcher

6 large white mushrooms, sliced, or
  10 to 12 cremini mushrooms, sliced

1 teaspoon dried thyme

1 clove garlic, chopped

  Salt and black pepper to taste

1 can (6 ounces) red peeled tomatoes

½ cup white wine

2 tablespoons heavy cream

1 tablespoon chopped parsley

The white-fleshed rabbit is as tender, versatile, and lean as chicken. Rabbits have been raised for the table in France for more than 300 years. This old family recipe cooks it to perfection. Serve with mashed potatoes or pasta.

1. Melt butter in a heavy-bottomed skillet over moderately high heat. Brown rabbit pieces, turning to brown evenly, about 5 minutes on each side.

2. Add mushrooms, thyme, garlic, salt, pepper, tomatoes, and wine. Bring to a boil, lower heat, cover and simmer for 20 minutes, or until the rabbit is tender when pierced with a fork.

3. Transfer rabbit to a serving platter. Keep warm.

4. Reduce sauce by boiling for 10 minutes over high heat. Lower heat and stir in cream. Do not allow cream to boil. Pour sauce over meat and garnish with parsley.

Fried Skate

Gebakken Rog

Skate, a large flat fish not common in the United States, is popular in homes and restaurants in Belgium and France. In Belgium, fish is a traditional Friday-night dinner for many people. Serve with roasted baby potatoes.

1. In a medium bowl, season flour with salt and pepper. Dip skate pieces in flour, coating thoroughly on both sides.

2. In a medium skillet, heat butter or oil over high heat. Sauté skate on both sides until brown, about 5 minutes total. Reduce heat and simmer for 10 minutes. Serve hot with lemon slices.

servings: 2

1 cup all-purpose flour

1 teaspoon salt

2 teaspoons pepper to taste

2 pieces skate fish, about ½ pound each, rinsed

4 tablespoons (½ stick) butter or vegetable oil (or a combination)

Lemon slices, for garnish

FRANCE

Monkfish with Herbs and Cognac

Lotte à l'Américaine

servings: 2

⅓ cup all-purpose flour

½ teaspoon each salt and pepper, or to taste

2 pieces monkfish, 7 ounces each

4 tablespoons olive oil

¼ cup plus 2 tablespoons Cognac or brandy

1 cup white wine

2 tablespoons tomato paste

4½ teaspoons minced fresh thyme

Dash of ground nutmeg

2 cloves

½ cup fish stock

1 medium onion, finely chopped

1 clove garlic, finely chopped

Zest of 1 lemon

White, firm monkfish blends beautifully with this Cognac-spiked sauce. This elegant and aromatic dish was passed down from the great-great-grandmother of a UNIS student. Serve with rice and a salad.

1. Mix flour with salt and pepper in a shallow dish. Dip monkfish pieces into the mixture, coating thoroughly.

2. Heat the oil over moderately high heat in a large heavy-bottomed skillet. Sauté fish quickly, about 2 minutes on each side. Pour ¼ cup of the Cognac or brandy over fish and carefully touch a lighted match to the liquid. Shake the skillet as the flames dance, then die out. Transfer fish to a plate and set aside.

3. Pour liquid from skillet into a large pot. Add wine, remaining 2 tablespoons Cognac or brandy, the tomato paste, thyme, nutmeg, cloves, fish stock, onion, garlic, and lemon zest. Season with salt and pepper to taste. Simmer sauce, covered, for 30 minutes.

4. Place monkfish in pot and simmer 10 to 15 minutes.

FRANCE

Red Snapper with Orange and Lemon Sauce

Rouget à l'Orange et au Citron

Asian accompaniments would be as harmonious as European ones with this simple and healthful dish enlivened by a tangy citrus sauce.

1. Preheat oven to 450°F. Cut 2 or 3 slits (1-inch each) on each side of each fish and insert bay leaves. Also, place 1 bay leaf in each fish cavity.

2. Rub each fish with 1½ tablespoons of the olive oil and season with salt and pepper.

3. Place fish on a rack set in a roasting pan containing about ½ inch hot water. Bake, uncovered, for 30 minutes.

4. While fish are cooking, in a small skillet, sauté orange and lemon cubes over moderate heat with remaining 3 tablespoons olive oil for 15 minutes. Stir frequently. Add salt and pepper to taste.

5. Arrange fish on serving platter. Pour citrus mixture over fish. Garnish with parsley sprigs.

servings: 4

2 whole small red snapper (or other firm white fish), 1 pound each, cleaned

12 bay leaves

6 tablespoons olive oil

Salt and pepper to taste

3 oranges, peeled, seeded, and cubed

2 lemons, peeled, seeded, and cubed

Parsley sprigs, for garnish

GREECE

Shrimp Santorini

Garides ala Santorini

servings: 4

2 cups minced onion (about 1 large onion)

3 tablespoons olive oil

2 cloves garlic, minced

¼ teaspoon red pepper flakes

2 cups crushed tomatoes, or about 10 finely chopped peeled plum tomatoes

½ cup tomato sauce

¼ cup minced fresh parsley

1 tablespoon minced fresh dill

1 pound medium shrimp, rinsed, peeled, and deveined

1 cup crumbled feta cheese

3 tablespoons ouzo* (optional)

This summery dish, first enjoyed in a restaurant on the beautiful Greek island of Santorini, includes feta cheese, a mainstay of Greek cooking. Feta may be eaten by itself, sprinkled on, or cooked into dozens of dishes. Feta is usually made from sheep's milk, so its flavor varies depending on the grasses and plants the sheep have eaten. Serve with a rice pilaf, crisp bread, and a well-chilled Greek wine.

1. Preheat oven to 350°F. In a medium skillet, sauté onion over moderate heat in oil until translucent, about 10 minutes.

2. Add garlic, pepper flakes, tomatoes, and tomato sauce. Reduce heat and simmer for 20 minutes.

3. Add parsley and dill and stir. Pour mixture into shallow 8-cup dish or casserole.

4. Stir in shrimp and sprinkle with feta cheese. Splash on ouzo.

5. Bake in oven for 15 to 20 minutes. Shrimp will turn pink.

An anise-flavored Greek spirit, available at most liquor stores.

Goa Shrimp Curry

Sungatache Hovman

This recipe originates in Goa, a balmy, palm-fringed former Portuguese colony on the western coast of India. In Goa, coconuts are an important cash crop and wealth is sometimes measured by the extent of one's coconut groves. Goan curries are usually made with seafood and coconut milk. A Goan mother notes, "The aroma will tell you when the flavors have mixed and the spices are no longer 'raw.' This is what makes a good curry." A firm-fleshed white fish may be substituted for the shrimp. Serve this fragrant curry with rice and mango chutney.

1. In a large skillet, sauté onion in oil over moderately high heat until soft, about 3 minutes. Stir often. Add ginger, garlic, curry powder, and tomato. Cook 1 minute, stirring.

2. Add coconut milk and chili peppers. Bring to a boil. Reduce heat and simmer, covered, for 15 minutes. Add shrimp, salt, and pepper. Cook for 6 to 7 minutes. Add cream if a richer flavor is desired.

3. Sprinkle with lemon or lime juice just before serving.

servings: 4

1 small onion, sliced

1 tablespoon corn oil

1-inch piece fresh gingerroot, minced

4 cloves garlic, peeled and chopped

1 heaping tablespoon curry powder

1 small tomato, chopped

1 can (8 ounces) unsweetened coconut milk

3 hot green chili peppers, or ½ teaspoon chili powder

1 pound medium shrimp, rinsed, peeled, and deveined

Salt and pepper to taste

1 tablespoon heavy cream (optional)

Juice of ½ lemon or lime

INDIA

Crab Curry

Kurli Masala

servings: 2

- 2 teaspoons chili powder
- ½ teaspoon pepper
- ½ teaspoon ground coriander
- 1½ teaspoon ground cumin
- ½ teaspoon whole mustard seeds
- 3 to 4 cloves garlic
- 1 teaspoon tamarind paste, or 1 to 2 sweet-and-sour tamarind balls*
- 2 medium onions, finely chopped plus ¼ onion, finely chopped
- 2¼ cups water
- 3 tablespoons vegetable oil
- 1 teaspoon tomato paste
- Salt to taste
- 6 medium hard-shell crabs, thoroughly cleaned and shelled (or 1 pound lump crabmeat, cleaned)

This delicious hot curry comes from a UNIS parent who grew up in Mangalore, on the Southwest coast of India. The secret lies in the preparation of the sauce. Sauté onions and spices over a low heat, until the onions float above the oil and the spices release their full fragrance. Serve with rice.

1. In a blender or food processor fitted with a steel blade, purée chili powder, pepper, coriander, cumin, mustard seeds, garlic, tamarind paste, 2 chopped onions, and a little of the water (up to ¼ cup) to make a paste.

2. Heat oil in a large heavy-bottomed pot. Add the remaining ¼ chopped onion and stir-fry until golden. Add tomato paste and continue stirring for about 1 minute. Reduce heat to low and add spice paste Stir-fry for 10 to 15 minutes until paste blends well with oil and gives off a fragrant aroma.

3. Pour remaining 2 cups of water into blender or food processor, blend to collect any remaining paste, and add to pot. Stir, add salt to taste, and raise heat to high until spice mixture comes to a boil. Immediately reduce heat to low, cover and simmer on low heat for 5 minutes.

4. Add crabs, cover, and cook for 15 minutes, adding some water if necessary.

*Available at Indian food markets; see list of suppliers (page 319).

Shrimp with Zucchini

Thinga aur Ghia

Although not found in India, zucchini is a good stand-in for the indigenous Indian squash that are often prepared with shrimp in coastal areas. Delicious served with basmati rice and red lentil dal.

1. Place zucchini in a colander and sprinkle with ¼ teaspoon of the salt. Toss to mix and set aside to drain for 30 minutes. Pat dry with paper towels.

2. Heat oil in a wide skillet over moderately high heat. Add garlic and sauté until medium brown.

3. Add shrimp and stir until opaque. Remove shrimp and set aside.

4. Add zucchini to skillet and sauté over moderately high heat about 3 minutes. Add tomatoes, the water, ginger, cayenne pepper, coriander, green chili pepper, turmeric, cumin, lemon juice, and remaining 1 teaspoon salt. Stir to mix.

5. Return shrimp to skillet. Cover, reduce heat, and simmer for 3 minutes.

6. Uncover, raise heat to moderate, and boil away extra liquid, if any, until sauce is reduced and thickened.

servings: 4

- 1 medium zucchini, trimmed, cut into 4 slices lengthwise, then into thirds crosswise
- 1¼ teaspoons salt
- 5 tablespoons vegetable oil
- 6 cloves garlic, finely chopped
- 1 pound shrimp, rinsed, shelled, deveined, and patted dry
- 3 small tomatoes, finely chopped
- ½ cup water
- 1 teaspoon minced gingerroot
- ¼ teaspoon cayenne pepper
- 1 cup finely chopped fresh coriander
- 1 fresh hot green chili pepper, seeded and finely chopped
- ½ teaspoon ground turmeric
- 1½ teaspoons ground cumin
- 1 tablespoon lemon juice

St. Peter's Fish with Mango Purée

Dag Amnon Hagalil im Machit Mango

---

servings: 4

Juice of 1 lemon

2 tablespoons Worcestershire sauce

Salt and freshly ground pepper to taste

2 fresh filets St. Peter's fish (also called John Dory), about 1¼ pounds each

¼ cup all-purpose flour

1 ripe mango, peeled, with fruit cut away from pit

2 teaspoons vegetable oil for frying

¼ cup butter

½ cup dry white wine

Originally from Lake Kinneret, the Sea of Galilee, St. Peter's Fish is Israel's most popular. It is now widely "farmed" and available in fish markets in the United States.

1. In a flat dish large enough for both filets, mix lemon juice, Worcestershire sauce, salt, and pepper. Add fish and coat well. Allow fish to marinate at least 30 minutes. Pour off marinade into a bowl and reserve.

2. Hold filets over the dish to drain. Place flour in a shallow dish. Dip filets in flour to coat lightly.

3. In a blender, purée half the mango. Thinly slice remainder.

4. Heat oil in a large skillet over moderately high heat. Cook fish for 1 minute on each side to color slightly. Remove fish, discard oil.

5. Add butter, wine, and reserved marinade to skillet. Add mango slices.

6. Return fish to skillet and cook until flesh flakes easily, about 5 to 7 minutes. Total cooking time of fish should not exceed 10 minutes per inch of thickness.

7. Place fish on hot platter, stir puréed mango into pan juices to warm, and pour over fish.

Jamaican Salt Fish Fritters

Salt fish, as salt cod is known, is a much-loved Jamaican specialty. Because the fish retains some saltiness despite its long soaking, these fritters are best accompanied by lots of water or icy beer. Serve with a fruit salsa and extra hot sauce on the side.

1. Shred cod in a medium bowl, using two forks, or pulse in food processor fitted with a steel blade.

2. Mix together salt cod, flour, scallions, garlic, cloves, thyme, pepper sauce, and egg. Form mixture into 3-inch patties.

3. Cook in a deep fryer containing oil preheated to 350°F. Alternatively, in a large skillet, heat about ¼ cup oil over moderately high heat, and sauté patties.

4. Fry in small batches for 4 to 8 minutes, until golden brown. Add oil as necessary and continue until all batter is used.

---

servings: 5

1 pound salt cod, soaked for 24 hours in cold water, changing water every 8 hours

¾ pound self-rising flour, or 1½ cups all-purpose flour mixed with 1½ teaspoons baking powder

4 scallions, trimmed and sliced

2 cloves garlic, minced

Pinch of ground cloves

2 tablespoons chopped fresh thyme, or ¾ teaspoon dried thyme

1 tablespoon Caribbean pepper sauce, such as Pick-a-Pepper or Jamaican Choice

1 egg, beaten

1 quart vegetable oil (approximately), for frying

Rolled Sushi

Maki-sushi

---

servings: 2

2 cups Japanese rice*

3 cups water

½ cup seasoned rice vinegar,* or
⅓ cup rice vinegar mixed with
3 tablespoons sugar and 1½
teaspoons salt

5 sheets roasted seaweed
(*sushinori*)*

½ pound raw tuna, sliced razor thin on
the diagonal

1 cucumber, peeled, seeded, and
thinly sliced lengthwise

1 avocado, peeled, pitted, and thinly
sliced

Japanese green mustard powder
(*wasabi*),* mixed with a little water
to make a thick paste

Pickled ginger slices*

Soy sauce

special equipment

1 bamboo rolling mat (*makisu*)* for
rolling sushi

Along with sukiyaki and tempura, sushi is one of the best-known Japanese dishes. Japanese mothers often make these rolls to mark special occasions, such as cherry-blossom viewing, school sports days, and festivals.

1. Place rice and water in a medium pot. Bring water to boil over high heat. Cover, reduce heat and simmer for 20 minutes. Remove from heat and let stand 10 to 15 minutes.

2. Turn cooked rice into large, non-aluminum bowl, separating kernels with a fork. While rice is still hot, add seasoned rice vinegar and toss gently to combine.

3. Unroll bamboo mat, glossy-side down. Place 1 sheet of the seaweed on bamboo mat.

4. Moisten hands with water. Place 1½ cups rice on seaweed. Press rice to side edges and bottom, covering three-quarters of the sheet. Place about 3 tuna strips, from left to right, across the center of the rice. Place cucumber strips right above tuna and avocado slices right above cucumber. Hold line of ingredients across rice firmly in place with fingertips. Using thumb, push near edge of bamboo mat up and over filling, pressing firmly to enclose filling. Lift edge of mat while rolling to avoid enclosing it in sushi roll. Firmly press bamboo mat around roll to shape.

5. Unroll mat and place sushi roll, seam-side down, on cutting surface. Cut crosswise into 8 equal slices. Repeat with remaining ingredients to make 5 rolls. Serve with *wasabi*, pickled ginger slices, and soy sauce. Sushi is best eaten soon after it is made.

Variations: Sushi rolls can be made with salmon caviar, raw salmon, steamed asparagus, blanched carrots, and boiled sliced shrimp.

*Available at Japanese food markets; see list of suppliers (page 319).

JAPAN

Salmon and Caviar with Rice

Ikura Donburi

Because salmon filet and eggs are prepared together in this recipe, in Japan this dish is charmingly known as "Mother and Child." Serve with miso soup.

1. Place rice and water in a large pot and bring to a boil over high heat. Cover, reduce heat and simmer for 20 minutes. Remove from heat and let stand for 10 minutes.

2. While rice is cooking, preheat broiler. In a small bowl, mix soy sauce, *sake*, and *mirin*. Place the salmon caviar in mixture and marinate for 10 to 15 minutes.

3. Place salmon filet in a small baking dish and pour lemon juice over filet. Broil filet for 10 to 12 minutes, until brown on top. Remove from broiler and flake salmon with a fork.

4. Place boiled rice on a platter and cover with flaked salmon. Spoon caviar mixture over salmon and sprinkle with seaweed. Serve with *wasabi*.

*Available at Japanese food markets and many supermarkets; see list of suppliers (page 319).

**Available at most liquor stores.

servings: 5

3 cups Japanese rice*

6 cups water

2 tablespoons soy sauce

2 tablespoons Japanese rice wine (sake)**

1 tablespoon sweet cooking wine (mirin)*

¼ pound salmon caviar

½-pound salmon filet

Juice of ½ large lemon

1 sheet dried seaweed (nori),* crushed

Japanese green mustard powder (wasabi),* mixed with a little water to make a thick paste

Malaysian Curried Shrimp

Curry Udang

servings: 8

1 pound medium shrimp, rinsed, peeled, and deveined

2 tablespoons hot curry powder

¾ teaspoon sugar

4 tablespoons vegetable oil

1 large onion, minced

10 curry leaves,* rinsed

7 ounces unsweetened coconut cream*

Salt to taste

Red chili peppers, for garnish, seeded and cut in thin strips

Coriander sprigs, for garnish

This old family recipe reflects Maylasians' fondness for spicy curries. Serve with rice.

1. In a medium bowl, toss shrimp with curry powder and sugar.

2. Heat oil in a large skillet over moderately high heat. Sauté onion and curry leaves until onion is soft, about 4 minutes. Stir often.

3. Add shrimp and stir-fry for about 3 minutes. Slowly add coconut cream and stir until shrimp turn pink. Add salt. Place on a serving plate and garnish with red chili pepper strips and coriander sprigs.

Available at Asian food markets; see list of suppliers (page 319).

Malaysian Shrimp in Spicy Gravy

Sambel Udang

The combination of shrimp paste and chilies is common in Malaysian cooking. The family of its contributor likes this dish so much, they insist on having it once a week. Serve with steamed white rice.

1. Using a mortar and pestle, a blender, or a food processor, purée shallots, garlic, turmeric, shrimp paste, and chili peppers into a smooth paste.

2. Heat oil in a wok over high heat and sauté paste, stirring until fragrant, about 2 minutes. Add lemongrass and sliced onion. Stir-fry for 4 minutes. Add tamarind juice, salt, and sugar and stir.

3. Add shrimp and stir-fry for 3 minutes, or until shrimp turn pink.

Available at Asian food markets; see list of suppliers (page 319).

servings: 4

- 6 shallots, peeled and finely chopped
- 4 cloves garlic, finely chopped
- ½-inch piece fresh or frozen turmeric,* peeled and minced
- 2 tablespoons shrimp paste*
- 2 tablespoons chopped red chili peppers, seeds removed, or to taste
- 3 tablespoons vegetable oil
- 2 stalks lemongrass,* tough outer leaves removed, upper 8-inches thinly sliced
- 1 medium onion, thinly sliced
- ½ cup tamarind juice*
- 1 tablespoon salt, or to taste
- 2 tablespoons sugar
- 1½ pounds medium shrimp, shelled and deveined, tails left intact

PHILIPPINES

Birthday Noodles

Pancit Bihon

servings: 4 to 6

- 3 quarts plus ½ cup water
- 12 ounces Korean sweet potato noodles*
- 3 tablespoons vegetable oil
- 1 tablespoon Asian sesame oil
- 4 cloves garlic, crushed
- 2 pounds medium shrimp, peeled and deveined
- 3 medium carrots, cut diagonally into ⅛-inch slices
- 1 pound string beans or snow peas, cut diagonally into 1½ x ⅛-inch pieces
- 3 stalks celery, cut diagonally into 1½ x ⅛-inch pieces
- 1 pound savoy green cabbage or Chinese cabbage, finely shredded
- 2 tablespoons vegetable or chicken broth
- Salt and pepper to taste
- 5 scallions, thinly sliced
- 1 cup minced fresh parsley

Popular throughout Asia, this dish has variations that use different kinds of noodles: egg, rice, and even sweet potato. Chicken or pork may be substituted for shrimp. Long noodles mean long life, the universal birthday wish.

1. In a large pot, boil 3 quarts of the water over moderately high heat. Add noodles and cook for 6 to 7 minutes. Drain in a colander and rinse twice in cold water. If desired, noodles may be cut into shorter lengths.

2. Heat vegetable oil and sesame oil in a nonstick skillet over moderate heat. Sauté garlic until light brown, stirring. Add shrimp and sauté for about 3 minutes, stirring. Remove shrimp and set aside.

3. Over high heat, stir-fry carrots for 1 minute. Add string beans, celery, cabbage, and ½ cup of the water and cover. Cook for 2 minutes.

4. Add noodles and shrimp to skillet and mix well. Add vegetable or chicken broth. Season with salt and pepper. Continue cooking for 1 minute. Remove from heat. Mix in scallions and parsley and serve.

Available at Asian food markets; see list of suppliers (page 319).

Grilled Swordfish with Soy Sauce

This is a recipe that even the most confirmed non-fish eaters will love. Serve with Asian noodles or rice.

1. Heat broiler to highest point. In a small bowl, mix mustard and mustard seeds together. Set aside.

2. For sauce, combine garlic, ginger, soy sauce, olive oil, and the water in a small saucepan and bring to a boil over high heat. Lower heat, and simmer for 15 minutes. Set aside.

3. While sauce is simmering, season fish with salt and pepper. Brush half the mustard mixture on one side of fish pieces. Place fish mustard-side up, in shallow broiler pan and broil 4 to 5 minutes. Turn fish pieces over and brush with remaining mustard mixture. Broil fish another 4 to 5 minutes, or until cooked through when pierced with the point of a sharp knife. Transfer fish to a heated platter.

4. Add coriander or parsley to sauce. Pour into a small bowl and serve alongside the fish.

servings: 5 to 6

1 tablespoon Dijon mustard

1 tablespoon mustard seeds

1 tablespoon crushed garlic

4 tablespoons finely chopped fresh gingerroot

3 tablespoons light soy sauce

4 tablespoons olive oil

¾ cup water

6 pieces fresh swordfish or tuna (about 3 pounds), cut 1 inch thick

Salt to taste

1 teaspoon pepper

2 tablespoons finely chopped coriander or parsley

Salmon with Cranberries and Lime

servings: 4

4 thick salmon filets (5 to 7 ounces each), skinned

Juice of 2 limes

½ cup water

¼ cup sun-dried cranberries, rinsed

Zest of 1 lime

1 tablespoon sugar

½ cup dry white wine

1 small shallot, chopped

1 cup fish stock* or clam juice

3½ tablespoons butter, cubed

Salt to taste

This delicately flavored, festively colored dish is great for a winter buffet, when citrus and cranberries are in season. If fresh cranberries are not available, golden raisins may be substituted. Serve with roasted baby potatoes and a vegetable purée.

1. Place salmon filets in a non-aluminum bowl. Add lime juice and marinate for ½ hour, turning to coat completely.

2. Preheat oven to 350°F.

3. Bring the water, cranberries, and lime zest to a boil in a small saucepan. Add sugar, stir, and turn off heat. Let mixture stand until cool. Drain cranberries and zest, reserving cranberry liquid.

4. Combine wine, shallot, fish stock or clam juice, 3 teaspoons of the cranberry liquid, and 2½ teaspoons of lime juice from salmon marinade in a medium saucepan over moderate heat. Boil until reduced to one-quarter volume, about 20 minutes. Remove from heat.

5. Place salmon filets in large baking dish and bake salmon for 20 to 25 minutes. Test for doneness by gently separating a section using a knife point and checking that interior is pale pink and moist.

6. Place filets on serving platter. Quickly reheat the cranberry-lime liquid and add cranberries and lime zest. Swirl in butter and salt. If sauce seems too thick, add more cranberry liquid or lime juice. Pour over salmon filets.

Available, fresh and frozen, at specialty food markets; see list of suppliers (page 319).

Honey Mustard Salmon

This easy-to-make party pleaser can be cooked in the oven or grilled out-doors in summer. The hot, sweet marinade can be fine-tuned to taste, using a dash of sesame oil or cayenne pepper or both. Do not substitute Dijon mustard, which is too strong in flavor.

1. In a blender, combine sugar, mustard, honey, olive oil, and tarragon to make a marinade.

2. Place salmon in a large plastic bag. Pour in marinade, coating salmon and its cavity. Seal bag and refrigerate for at least 6 hours or overnight. Toss bag once or twice to distribute marinade.

3. About 2 hours before baking, remove salmon from refrigerator and bring to room temperature.

4. Preheat oven to 400°F. Place a fresh sprig of tarragon inside the fish cavity. Tie the fish with string, criss-crossing string under and over the fish. Place fish belly-side down on a lightly oiled baking sheet and top with remaining marinade.

5. Bake fish for 35 to 40 minutes, or until it reaches an internal heat of 135°F on an instant-read thermometer. Another test for doneness is to insert a paring knife into the thickest part of the fish to check if it is cooked through. If it is, remove immediately.

6. Remove string and lightly cover fish with aluminum foil until ready to serve.

Note: The salmon can also be cooked hours ahead and served at room temperature.

*This hot and sweet mustard is available at specialty food markets; see list of suppliers (page 319).

servings: 16

- ½ cup dark brown sugar
- ½ cup Mendocino Mustard* or honey mustard
- ¼ cup wildflower or other floral honey
- 1½ cups olive oil
- 1 tablespoon chopped fresh tarragon, or 1 teaspoon dried
- 1 whole salmon (8 pounds), butterflied (backbone cut out), with head and tail intact
- 1 sprig of fresh tarragon

UNITED STATES

Tomato Fettucine with Oysters and Radicchio

servings: 2

1 teaspoon salt

4 to 6 slices bacon or pancetta

6 medium shallots, chopped

2 cloves garlic, chopped

½ head radicchio, separated, rinsed, dried, and cut into julienne strips

1 pound fresh tomato fettucine, or ½ pound dried fettucine

1 dozen Wellfleet oysters (more if they are small)

12 fresh basil leaves, rinsed, dried, and cut into julienne strips

Freshly ground pepper

Perhaps oysters are an aphrodisiac, perhaps not. But they distinguish this colorful pasta dish, which would make a great Valentine's Day entrée. Serve with a salad.

1. Bring to a boil at least 16 cups water with 1 teaspoon salt in a large pot.

2. Sauté bacon or pancetta in a 10-inch skillet, over moderate heat, until crisp. Drain on paper towels. Add shallots, sauté for 3 to 5 minutes, until soft. Add garlic and cook 3 additional minutes. Add radicchio and sauté until wilted, about 2 minutes. Transfer radicchio mixture to a medium bowl, and set aside.

3. Place pasta in boiling water and cook until *al dente* (firm to the bite), 3 minutes for fresh pasta and about 10 minutes for dried pasta. Drain in colander.

4. Add oysters and their juices to the skillet. Cook over low heat for about 3 minutes. Remove oysters to a warm plate.

5. Toss pasta and basil strips with radicchio mixture. Divide and mound in the center of two warmed dinner plates. Place oysters decoratively on pasta and crumble bacon on top. Sprinkle with freshly ground pepper.

UNITED STATES

Mesquite Tandoori Shark Fajitas

The contributor of this unique recipe, a UNIS alumnus, has roots in Sri Lanka, grew up in Long Island, New York, where he went shark fishing, and subsequently lived in San Antonio, Texas. The flavors of all his homes are brought together in a single dish. Salmon or tuna may be substituted for shark.

1. Place shark strips in a medium bowl, pour beer over fish and refrigerate for 2 hours. Remove shark from beer and coat with tandoori paste. Set aside. Meanwhile, soak mesquite chips in water to cover, about 20 minutes.

2. Heat barbecue grill. Remove mesquite chips from water and drain. When grill is hot, add mesquite chips. Place onions, bell peppers, and tomatoes on grill and cook for 10 minutes, turning often, until nicely browned and soft. Remove and set aside.

3. Grill shark for 3 to 5 minutes, turning often.

4. At the same time, warm tortillas on the side of the grill.

5. To serve, divide shark and vegetables evenly among warmed tortillas and roll up. Alternatively, serve the shark and vegetables on a warm platter, with the warm tortillas in a basket wrapped in a napkin, so your guests can roll their own. Serve with sour cream, *pico de gallo* and *Guacamole* (page 21), for topping on fajitas.

*Available at Indian food markets; see list of suppliers (page 319).

**Available at Latin American and specialty food markets; see list of suppliers.

servings: 8

1½ to 2 pounds mako shark, cut into ¾-inch wide strips (pieces from near the backbone, not the belly)

1 to 2 bottles light beer

1 jar tandoori paste*

2 cups mesquite chips, for grill

2 large onions, cut into ¾-inch slices

2 green or yellow bell peppers, cored, seeded and cut into ¾-inch strips

8 small tomatoes, cut in half

15 to 20 fresh tortillas

8 ounces sour cream

8 ounces *pico de gallo* salsa**

1 cup *Guacamole*

Cioppino

Spicy Seafood Stew

servings: 6

- 1 medium green bell pepper, chopped
- 1 large onion, chopped
- ¼ cup olive oil
- 3 cans (14 ounces each) Italian-style tomatoes, including juice
- 2 tablespoons tomato paste
- 2 cups dry red wine
- 2 tablespoons chopped fresh basil, or 1½ teaspoons dried, crumbled
- 2 tablespoons chopped fresh oregano, or 1½ teaspoons dried, crumbled
- 2 tablespoons chopped fresh thyme, or 1½ teaspoons dried, crumbled
- ½ bay leaf
- 2 teaspoons dried hot red pepper flakes, or to taste
- 1 parsley sprig, plus 6 tablespoons minced fresh parsley, for garnish
- 24 hard-shelled clams, scrubbed
- Salt to taste
- ¾ pound (about 18) shrimp, shelled with tails intact, deveined and butterflied (split almost in two and spread out like butterfly wings before cooking)
- 1½ pounds halibut or cod filet, cut into 1½-inch pieces
- ¾ pound sea scallops, halved if large

Despite its Italian name, which means "chopped a little," this fish and seafood stew hails from San Francisco, home to a large Italian-American population.

1. Cook the bell pepper and onion in oil in a large pot over moderately low heat, stirring until soft, about 4 minutes.

2. Add tomatoes with juice, tomato paste, wine, basil, oregano, thyme, bay leaf, pepper flakes, and parsley sprig. Bring liquid to a boil, stirring. Lower heat and simmer mixture, covered, stirring occasionally, for 1½ hours. (Stew can be prepared 2 to 3 days ahead to this point.) Bring mixture to a boil before proceeding to the next step.

3. Discard bay leaf and parsley sprig. Bring mixture to a boil, stir in clams, and cover. Using tongs, transfer clams to a bowl as they open. After 10 minutes, discard any unopened clams.

4. Season broth with salt. Add shrimp, halibut, and scallops. Stir gently. Simmer, covered, for 5 to 7 minutes, or until fish flakes.

5. Return clams to pot. Sprinkle with minced parsley, and serve with Garlic Parmesan Toasts for *Cioppino* (facing page).

Garlic Parmesan Toasts for *Cioppino*

Pour broth from Cioppino *over toast in each serving bowl to enhance both taste and texture.*

1. Preheat oven to 375°F. With the flat side of a knife, mash garlic with salt to make a paste.

2. Melt butter with garlic paste in a small saucepan, over moderate heat, stirring.

3. Brush garlic butter on 1 side of each bread slice. Bake half of slices in a large baking pan in the middle of the oven for 10 minutes.

4. Remove pan from oven and sprinkle toasts with half of the Parmesan cheese. Preheat broiler. Broil toasts in broiler, about 6 inches from the heat, for 30 seconds to 1 minute, or until the outer edges are golden and the Parmesan cheese begins to melt.

5. Bake and broil the remaining bread slices in the same manner. Serve with *Cioppino* (opposite page).

servings: 24 toasts

- **1 large clove garlic, minced**
- **¼ teaspoon salt**
- **6 tablespoons (¾ stick) unsalted butter**
- **24 slices Italian bread, ¼-inch thick, cut diagonally**
- **1 cup freshly grated Parmesan cheese**

Shrimp with Grits

servings: 4

4 cups water

1 cup regular grits

½ teaspoon salt

4 tablespoons butter

1 cup grated sharp Cheddar cheese

½ cup grated Parmesan cheese

Pinch each of white pepper, cayenne pepper, and ground nutmeg

6 slices bacon, diced

1 to 2 tablespoons peanut oil

1 pound fresh medium shrimp, rinsed, peeled, deveined, and patted dry

2 cups sliced mushrooms

1 cup sliced scallions

1 large clove garlic, crushed through a press or minced

4 teaspoons lemon juice (about ½ lemon)

Hot sauce (such as Tabasco), to taste

2 tablespoons chopped fresh parsley

Salt and pepper to taste

Nowadays, cooking with grits is particularly associated with the American South. Grits are made by grinding hominy—hulled, dried corn—somewhat coarsely, hence the "gritty" texture.

1. In a medium saucepan, boil the water and stir in grits. Reduce heat, and cook for 20 minutes, covered. Stir frequently. When grits become thick and tender, stir in salt, butter, Cheddar cheese, Parmesan cheese, white pepper, cayenne, and nutmeg. Adjust seasonings to taste.

2. While grits are cooking, cook bacon in a large skillet until just crisp. Drain and set aside.

3. Add enough oil to the bacon fat to coat the bottom of the skillet. Place skillet on medium heat until hot and add shrimp. Stir, adding mushrooms when shrimp start to color. Add scallions and garlic. Sauté for about 3 minutes. Season with lemon juice, hot sauce, parsley, salt, and pepper.

4. Divide cheese grits among four warmed plates. Top with shrimp and bacon and serve immediately.

Baked Ziti

Ziti al Forno

This dish incorporates some of the most classic ingredients in Italian cooking—pasta, tomatoes, onions, olive oil, and cheese. The combination of three cheeses—tangy Parmesan, mild ricotta, and mozzarella—makes a deliciously rich sauce. Serve warm with salad.

1. For the tomato sauce, heat oil in a large skillet over moderate heat. Add onion and garlic and sauté for 10 minutes. Add undrained tomatoes, tomato paste, the water, parsley, 1 tablespoon of the salt, the sugar, oregano, basil, and pepper. Mix well, mashing tomatoes with a fork. Bring sauce to a boil. Reduce heat and simmer, covered, for 1 hour, stirring occasionally.

2. Preheat oven to 350°F. Bring at least 16 cups of water to boil in a large pot. Add the remaining 1 teaspoon salt and the ziti. Cook until *al dente* (firm to the bite). Drain in a colander.

3. For the cheese sauce, combine ricotta, mozzarella, Parmesan, eggs, parsley, salt, and pepper. Stir until blended.

4. Lightly oil a 5-quart baking dish or casserole. Spoon some tomato sauce onto the bottom of the dish, and cover with a layer of ziti. Add a layer of cheese sauce. Repeat process 2 or 3 times, finishing with a layer of cheese sauce. Bake uncovered 45 minutes.

Note: This dish can be made ahead of time and refrigerated before baking. However, baking time should be increased 15 to 30 minutes. The recipe can be easily halved or doubled.

servings: 8 to 10

tomato sauce

- ¼ cup olive oil, plus more for baking dish
- 1 cup finely chopped onion
- 1 clove garlic, crushed
- 1 can (35 ounces) Italian tomatoes, or 1 can (19 ounces) tomato purée
- 1 can (6 ounces) tomato paste
- 1½ cups water
- 2 tablespoons chopped parsley
- 1 tablespoon plus 1 teaspoon salt
- 1 tablespoon sugar
- 1 teaspoon dried oregano
- ½ teaspoon dried basil
- ½ teaspoon pepper
- 1 pound ziti

cheese sauce

- 2 containers (15 ounces each) ricotta cheese
- 8 ounces mozzarella cheese, grated
- ⅓ cup grated Parmesan cheese
- 2 eggs
- 1 tablespoon chopped parsley
- 1 teaspoon salt
- ¼ teaspoon pepper

Red Pepper and Olive Pasta

Pasta con Olive e Pepe Rosso

---

servings: 6

1 pound penne pasta

2 to 3 tablespoons olive oil

4 scallions, trimmed and chopped

2 cloves garlic, minced

2 large roasted red peppers

⅔ cup pitted and chopped black Moroccan olives

⅔ cup pitted and chopped Italian green olives

½ to 1 teaspoon cayenne pepper

½ cup pine nuts, toasted

½ cup chopped sun-dried tomatoes in olive oil

The olive has been an important part of Mediterranean cuisine since time immemorial. Combined with roasted peppers and a generous amount of cayenne pepper, olives make for a colorful and mouth-watering vegetarian pasta.

1. In a large pot of boiling salted water, cook pasta until *al dente* (firm to the bite). Drain.

2. While pasta is cooking, heat oil in a large skillet and sauté scallions and garlic until soft, about 3 minutes, stirring. Add peppers, olives, and cayenne pepper. Stir and simmer over low heat for about 5 minutes.

3. In a serving bowl, toss pasta with sauce. Add pine nuts and sun-dried tomatoes. Toss again. Serve with a salad.

ITALY

Pasta with Seafood and Champagne

Pasta con Frutti di Mare e Champagna

In an Italian home, pasta is often served as a primo, *or first course, followed by a* secondo, *a second course of meat or fish. In preparing this aromatic dish, white wine can be substituted for Champagne.*

1. Sauté shallots and garlic in olive oil in a large skillet over moderate heat, until wilted and golden, about 4 minutes. Stir often. Do not let brown.

2. Add shrimp and scallops and cook over moderate heat until shrimp turn pink, about 3 to 5 minutes. Transfer seafood to a platter, and cover to keep warm.

3. Add Champagne or wine to skillet and boil rapidly over high heat until reduced by half. Add tomatoes, cover, and simmer over low heat for about 20 minutes.

4. In a large pot, bring to a rolling boil 16 cups water. Add the salt and pasta. Cook pasta until *al dente* (firm to the bite). For fresh pasta, cook 3 to 5 minutes; for dried, about 10 minutes. Drain pasta in a colander.

5. After Champagne and tomatoes have simmered, add cream, cooked seafood, and basil. Heat through for 2 to 3 minutes.

6. In a serving bowl, toss pasta with sauce. Serve with a green salad.

servings: 4

4 tablespoons minced shallots

2 cloves garlic, minced

3 tablespoons olive oil

¼ pound small shrimp, peeled and deveined

¼ pound small bay scallops

1 cup Champagne or sparkling white wine

6 tomatoes, chopped and seeded

1 teaspoon salt

1 pound pasta (fresh fettucine or any dried Italian pasta)

¼ cup heavy cream

½ cup fresh basil leaves, rinsed and coarsely chopped

Linguine with Garlicky Spinach and Clam Sauce

Linguini con Spinaci all'Aglio e Salsa de Vongole

servings: 4

5 cloves garlic, minced

1 teaspoon fresh thyme, or ½ teaspoon dried thyme

1 cup dry white wine

24 fresh clams, scrubbed, soaked in cold water with 2 tablespoons of cornmeal, drained, and rinsed

4 tablespoons extra-virgin olive oil

1 large bunch scallions, trimmed, finely chopped

2 medium Vidalia onions, finely chopped

Juice of 4 large lemons

Salt and freshly ground pepper

1 tablespoon red pepper flakes

1 pound spinach, rinsed, stems trimmed, well-drained, and chopped into small pieces

1 bunch fresh Italian parsley, chopped, or ½ cup chopped fresh basil

1 pound linguine

1 teaspoon salt

Hot sauce, such as Tabasco

Grated Parmesan or Romano cheese, to taste

From a family with roots in the Bari region of Italy, this dish shines when served with a green salad, Italian bread, and a crisp, cold Italian white wine.

1. In a large pot, place half of the minced garlic, the thyme, wine, and clams. Bring to a boil, cover, and cook until clam shells open, 5 to 8 minutes. Remove clams and set aside, discarding any unopened clams. Remove lid and continue cooking until broth is reduced by half. Set broth aside.

2. In a large skillet, heat 3 tablespoons of the oil and sauté scallions, onions, and remaining garlic over moderate heat, stirring, for 1 to 2 minutes.

3. Add lemon juice, salt, pepper, and reserved clam broth. Stir. Cover pan and simmer for 10 to 12 minutes. Add red pepper flakes, spinach, and parsley. Cook until spinach wilts completely, about 2 minutes. Add reserved clams in their shells and keep sauce warm.

4. While sauce is cooking, bring at least 12 cups water to a boil in a large pot. Add 1 teaspoon salt and remaining 1 tablespoon olive oil. Cook pasta until *al dente* (firm to the bite). Drain in a colander. Add a splash of olive oil to pasta and toss.

5. Put pasta on a large, flat serving dish. Spoon sauce over pasta and add salt, pepper, and hot sauce to taste. Toss well to coat. Arrange clams over pasta. Serve with grated Parmesan or Romano cheese. Serve with green salad.

Note: This dish can also be made with 2 or 3 cans of medium or baby clams plus 1 can chopped clams and 1 bottle clam juice. Add clams and clam juice with the lemon juice, salt, and pepper in Step 3.

ITALY

Spaghetti Carbonara alla John Ballato

In the early 1970s, when SoHo was still an undiscovered area of Manhattan, there were many places to eat—but only one place to dine. That notable exception was John Ballato's restaurant on Houston Street, a place where artists such as Jasper Johns and Roy Lichtenstein enjoyed the Italian-born restauranteur's culinary masterpieces. The contributor of this recipe spent 5 years experimenting to re-create this signature dish.

1. Place a pot containing 16 cups water on high heat. Meanwhile, sauté shallot with butter and olive oil in a large skillet over moderate heat, about 5 minutes. Add prosciutto, reduce heat and stir often, until prosciutto is shriveled slightly and shallots are transparent. Add chicken broth and simmer, covered, for 20 minutes.

2. Place spaghetti in boiling water and cook until *al dente* (firm to the bite), about 5 minutes for fresh pasta and 10 minutes or more for dried. Drain in colander. Add pasta to skillet and toss. Remove from heat. Add egg yolk and Parmesan cheese, stirring quickly. The sauce will thicken and become creamy yellow as the yolk cooks. When sauce coats each spaghetti strand, garnish with a fork and waste no more time! Serve with a green salad.

servings: 2

1 large shallot, peeled and finely chopped

2 tablespoons unsalted butter

1 tablespoon olive oil

3 to 4 thin slices prosciutto, minced

1 cup chicken broth

½ pound spaghetti

1 egg yolk, lightly whisked

2 tablespoons Parmesan cheese, or to taste

Asparagus Radicchio Pasta

Pasta con Radicchio e Asparagi

---

servings: 4

1 Vidalia onion, peeled and finely chopped

5 cloves garlic, minced

2 tablespoons olive oil

1 pound asparagus, stems trimmed, cut into 1-inch pieces

1 small head radicchio, rinsed and finely chopped

1 pound pasta (rigatoni or spaghetti)

1 teaspoon salt

Parmesan cheese, in a chunk, such as Parmigiano-Reggiano or Grana Padana, shaved in curls with vegetable peeler, for garnish

Although Vidalia onions are not Italian in origin, they are well-suited to this recipe as a sweet counterpoint to the bitter radicchio and salty Parmesan cheese. Serve this dish with a salad.

1. Heat a large pot containing at least 16 cups water over high heat. Meanwhile, in a large skillet, over moderately high heat, cook onion and garlic in olive oil, stirring, until onion is translucent.

2. Add asparagus and sauté for 5 minutes. Add radicchio and cook 5 minutes more. Stir frequently.

3. When water in pot boils, add pasta and salt. Cook until *al dente* (firm to the bite). Drain in colander.

4. In a large bowl, toss cooked vegetables with pasta. Garnish with Parmesan cheese curls.

ITALY

Linguine with Brie, Basil, and Tomatoes

Linguine con Formaggio Brie, Basilico e Pomodori

In Italy, this dish would likely be made with Pagliarino, a delicious soft-ripened cow's-milk cheese, or Taleggio, a rich buttery cheese from Lombardy. Because neither is widely available outside Italy, Brie makes an excellent stand-in. Serve with a loaf of crisp bread and a salad.

1. Combine tomatoes, basil, and garlic in a bowl and add 1 cup of the olive oil. Let stand at room temperature for at least 2 hours, or prepare the day before and refrigerate.

2. In a very large pot, bring 6 quarts of water to a rolling boil. Add linguine and cook until *al dente* (firm to the bite), about 10 minutes. Drain in a colander.

3. In a serving in bowl, toss linguine with remaining ½ cup olive oil. Add tomato mixture and Brie. Toss again.

servings: 6 to 8

- 4 large tomatoes, cut into small pieces
- 1 cup fresh basil leaves, rinsed, drained, and chopped
- 3 large garlic cloves, minced
- 1½ cups extra-virgin olive oil
- 2 pounds linguine
- 1 pound Brie, cut into small pieces (place in freezer for 10 minutes for easier cutting)

Pasta with Smoked Salmon in Cream Sauce

Tagliolini alla Panna e Salmone Affumicato

A true New York story: this recipe was given to a Filipina married to an American of Italian descent by the real estate broker who sold them their apartment. It's a terrific and festive way to "stretch" smoked salmon.

servings: 2 to 3

2 tablespoons butter

6 shallots, peeled and minced

3 cloves garlic, minced, or more to taste

8 ounces mushrooms, shiitake or Portobello, cut into thin strips

1 cup dry white wine

½ red chili pepper, seeded and minced

1½ cups heavy cream or half-and-half

Salt to taste

⅓ teaspoon freshly ground black pepper

2 tomatoes, blanched for 30 seconds, peeled, seeded, chopped, and cut into short strips

1 pound egg tagliolini or other fine pasta

½ pound smoked salmon, at room temperature, finely slivered

½ bunch basil, rinsed, stems removed, leaves patted dry, and cut into thin strips (about ½ cup)

1. In a a large pot, bring 16 cups water to boil.

2. Meanwhile, in a large skillet, melt butter and sauté shallots, garlic, and mushrooms over high heat for 1 minute, stirring.

3. Add wine and cook until wine has evaporated. Add chili pepper and cream and reduce by half. Add salt and pepper and remove from heat. Mix in tomato strips.

4. When water boils, add 1 teaspoon salt and pasta. Cook until pasta is *al dente* (firm to the bite), about 7 minutes. Drain in a colander. In a large bowl, toss pasta with sauce.

5. Place pasta on 2 or 3 individual plates. Sprinkle slivered salmon and basil on top. Serve at once.

Lentils with Rice and Pasta

Koshary

Freshly ground cumin is the secret of this simple, protein-rich vegetarian dish, a mainstay of Egyptian cuisine. This recipe comes with a greeting: B'el hana wal-shefa! *With happiness and health!*

1. In a large serving bowl, combine cooked rice, macaroni, and lentils. Set aside.

2. In a medium skillet, heat 3 tablespoons of the oil and sauté the small chopped onion until translucent over moderately high heat.

3. Add tomato sauce, cumin, vinegar, salt, pepper, and hot pepper flakes. Stir and cook for 5 to 7 minutes. Set aside.

4. In a separate large frying pan, heat remaining ⅓ cup oil. Over high heat, sauté remaining 5 onions until crisp and golden brown, stirring often, for about 10 minutes.

5. Before serving, sprinkle crisp onions over rice, macaroni and lentil mixture. Serve the sauce in a separate bowl to pour over entire dish.

*Rinse 1 cup dried lentils in a colander, picking out any stones. Cover lentils with water in a medium saucepan, bring to a boil and simmer for about 20 minutes, or until soft but not mushy. Add additional water, if necessary.

---

servings: 10 to 15

- 2 cups cooked rice
- 2 cups cooked macaroni
- 2 cups cooked lentils*
- 3 tablespoons plus ⅓ cup vegetable oil
- 1 small onion, chopped, plus 5 medium onions, chopped
- 2 cups tomato sauce
- 1½ teaspoons ground cumin
- 3 tablespoons white vinegar
- Salt and pepper to taste
- ½ teaspoon hot red pepper flakes or to taste

Tomatoes Stuffed with Rice and Pine Nuts

Domates Yemistes me Rizi

servings: 5

10 ripe tomatoes

3 large onions, finely chopped

2 tablespoons olive oil

1¼ cup long-grain rice

1 cup finely chopped fresh parsley

1 tablespoon finely chopped fresh mint

4 ounces pine nuts

¾ cup currants

Salt and pepper to taste

½ cup bread crumbs

This dish makes a light meal when served with a classic Greek salad (chopped tomato, cucumber, feta cheese, and black olives) or a simple chopped lettuce salad, accompanied by bread and feta cheese. Typically served at room temperature, it can also be eaten hot or cold.

1. Carefully slice tops of tomatoes so that the tops may be lifted but remain attached. Scoop pulp from inside of each tomato and chop. Set pulp aside.

2. Preheat oven to 350°F. Salt insides of tomato shells and place in a large, oiled baking dish.

3. Sauté onions in 1 tablespoon of the oil in a large skillet, over moderate heat, until onion begins to brown, about 6 to 8 minutes, stirring often.

4. Add rice and stir for about 3 minutes. Add tomato pulp, parsley, mint, pine nuts, currants, salt, and pepper. Cook over low heat, stirring, until the rice starts to thicken, about 10 minutes.

5. Fill tomatoes with mixture, close tops and rub a few drops of oil around openings. Sprinkle bread crumbs on top. Bake 1 hour.

Squash Stuffed with Indian Sprouted Beans

Bharele Tori

Although stuffed squash is not traditionally Indian, it is well suited for this dish, in which its smooth texture provides a pleasant contrast to the crunchy bean sprouts.

1. Preheat oven to 375°F. Place squash, cut-side down, in baking pan filled with 1½ cups (about 1 inch) water. Cover and cook for 20 to 30 minutes, or until squash is almost cooked. Remove squash and let cool.

2. Warm oil and mustard seeds in a medium saucepan, over moderate heat. As seeds begin to pop, add garlic and sprouted beans. Stir. Add ginger and remaining 2 tablespoons water. Cover and cook over moderately low heat for 15 minutes, stirring occasionally.

3. Add salt and cook for another 5 to 10 minutes, until sprouted beans are soft. Stir in lemon juice. Set aside.

4. Preheat oven to 400°F. Fill squash with sprouted bean mixture. Add more salt, if needed. Place squash on baking sheet or large baking dish, cover with aluminum foil, and bake for 20 minutes. Serve with bread.

*Available at Indian food markets; see list of suppliers (page 319).

**Available at many supermarkets, farmers' markets, and health food stores.

servings: 2

1¼ pound acorn or butternut squash, cut lengthwise, seeds removed

1½ cups water plus 2 tablespoons water

1 teaspoon salt

2 tablespoons vegetable oil

½ teaspoon mustard seeds*

2 cloves garlic, chopped

2 cups mixed sprouted beans**

1-inch piece gingerroot, minced

Salt to taste

2 tablespoons fresh lemon juice

Vegetable Cutlet with Mashed Potatoes and Mixed Vegetables

Alu Sabji Tikki

servings: 4 to 6

1 pound russet potatoes, peeled

1½ cups mixed raw vegetables, such as grated carrots, finely chopped cauliflower, peas, chopped green beans, and corn kernels

2-inch piece gingerroot, peeled and finely chopped

3 cloves garlic, minced

2 teaspoons curry powder, or to taste

2 teaspoons salt

Juice of ½ large lemon

Crushed hot pepper to taste

½ cup prepared bread crumbs

4 tablespoons vegetable oil

Mashed potatoes, rather than grains, such as bulgur wheat, make this vegetarian standard very smooth. Served with homemade tomato soup and coriander chutney, these cutlets make a great Sunday night supper. They're also excellent as miniature appetizers.

1. Bring to a boil 4 cups of salted water in a large pot. Add potatoes. Boil until tender, 20 to 30 minutes. Drain well and mash until smooth.

2. In a medium saucepan over moderate heat, boil vegetables with very little water until *al dente* (firm to the bite), about 3 to 5 minutes. Mash vegetables together lightly.

3. Once vegetables have cooled, mix with mashed potatoes. Stir in ginger, garlic, curry powder, salt, lemon juice, and hot pepper. Form round, oval or pear-shaped patties, 1 to 1½ inches thick. Roll in bread crumbs.

4. Heat vegetable oil over moderately high heat in a nonstick frying pan. When oil is hot, reduce heat to moderate and sauté vegetable cutlets. Turn to brown both sides, about 5 minutes per side.

INDIA

Bell Peppers with Carrots

Gajar Bharela Maracha

This unusual Indian stuffing for vegetables was the creation of a UNIS grandmother. Health-conscious before her time, she was a a tireless experimenter.

1. In a medium bowl, mix peanuts, carrots, sesame seeds, ginger, sugar, salt, asafetida, and turmeric.

2. Sprinkle a little salt into peppers and turn upside down for about 30 minutes.

3. Add 1 teaspoon of the oil to carrot mixture. Turn peppers right side up and stuff them with mixture and cover with tops.

4. Warm remaining oil in a small saucepan and arrange peppers upright. Cook, uncovered, over moderate heat for 10 to 12 minutes. Cover, reduce heat and cook for about 25 minutes. (If using a nonstick pot, use less oil.)

Available at Indian food markets; see list of suppliers (page 319).

servings: 3

¾ cup coarsely ground unsalted roasted peanuts

2 cups grated carrots

1 tablespoon sesame seeds

1 teaspoon grated gingerroot

1 teaspoon sugar

Salt to taste

Pinch of asafetida (optional)*

½ teaspoon turmeric powder

3 small green bell peppers, tops sliced off and reserved, stems trimmed, seeds and ribs removed

4 to 5 tablespoons oil

Egg Curry

Ande Masaledar

---

servings: 4

---

8 hard-boiled eggs, peeled and quartered

½ teaspoon ground turmeric

1 teaspoon red hot chili powder, or less to taste

¾ teaspoon Indian curry powder* (mild to hot, according to taste)

½ teaspoon salt

¾ teaspoon vegetable oil

1 teaspoon whole black mustard seeds*

8 to 10 curry leaves*

1-inch piece gingerroot, minced

2 large cloves garlic, peeled and finely chopped

2 large onions, peeled and finely chopped

1 teaspoon ground cumin

1 teaspoon ground coriander

3 plum tomatoes, finely chopped

4 to 5 tablespoons heavy cream or more to taste

2 tablespoons chopped fresh coriander

An original recipe, this aromatic Indian entrée is a "wet" curry—that is, sauced. The addition of cream enhances the texture of the sauce. Serve with generous amounts of Indian bread for scooping up the delicious, silky sauce, and basmati rice. This recipe is easily multiplied to serve at a large gathering.

1. Place eggs in a shallow bowl. In a small bowl, mix turmeric, chili powder, curry powder, and the salt. Sprinkle spice mixture over eggs and rub egg pieces gently with spices. Set aside for 15 to 20 minutes.

2. Heat vegetable oil in a large saucepan over moderate heat. When hot, add mustard seeds. When the seeds pop, about 30 seconds, add curry leaves, ginger, and garlic. Sauté, stirring, for 30 seconds. Add onions and cook for 6 to 7 minutes, or until soft, stirring often. Add cumin and coriander. Stir for 30 seconds. Add chopped tomatoes and salt to taste. Sauté tomatoes for 5 to 6 minutes, or until mixture is soft. Add cream.

3. Gently fold in spiced eggs. Add 1 tablespoon of the fresh coriander and stir. Cover and cook over low heat for 10 to 12 minutes. For a creamier sauce, add additional cream.

4. Sprinkle with remaining coriander and serve hot.

Available at Indian food markets; see list of suppliers (page 319).

ITALY

Eggplant Parmesan

Melanzane alla Parmigiana

If there is a "typical" vegetable of southern Italy, it must be the eggplant. Eggplant Parmesan has traveled far beyond Italian shores and has gained many devotees. It may be made a day in advance, refrigerated, and reheated when guests arrive. It's perfect served with a crisp, green salad and crusty bread.

1. Sauté onion in 3 tablespoons of the oil until golden, in a small saucepan over moderately high heat, stirring often. Add tomatoes and salt. Cover and simmer for 40 minutes.

2. Sprinkle each eggplant slice lightly with salt. In a small bowl, beat egg, add the water and mix well. Quickly dip each slice of eggplant in egg mixture and then into flour to lightly coat.

3. Pour the oil to a ¼-inch depth in a large skillet. Place over high heat. When very hot, cook eggplant, a few slices at a time, until lightly browned on each side. Add additional oil to pan, as needed, and sauté remaining eggplant slices. (Be sure the oil is hot before adding more eggplant slices to skillet.)

4. Preheat oven to 400°F. In a lightly oiled 9 x 11 x 2-inch baking dish, evenly cover bottom with one-third of tomato sauce. Layer half the fried eggplant slices over sauce. Spread all the mozzarella slices on top of eggplant. Sprinkle on half the Parmesan cheese. Cover with another one-third of the tomato sauce. Layer remaining eggplant slices, sprinkle on remaining Parmesan cheese and cover top with remaining tomato sauce.

5. Bake for 15 to 20 minutes, or until top bubbles.

servings: 4

- 1 small onion, peeled and finely chopped
- 1½ cups plus 3 tablespoons virgin olive oil
- 2 cups crushed tomatoes
  Salt to taste
- 2 medium eggplants, sliced lengthwise into ¼-inch slices, ends discarded
- 1 egg
- ⅓ cup cool water
- 1½ cups all-purpose flour
- ¾ pound aged mozzarella *(scamorza)*, cut into ¼-inch slices
- 1 cup freshly grated Parmesan cheese

Tomatoes Stuffed with Rice

Pomodori Ripieni di Riso

servings: 6

6 large, ripe, round tomatoes

½ cup extra-virgin oil

Pinch of sugar

Salt and pepper to taste

2 cloves garlic, peeled and minced

¼ cup minced fresh basil leaves

¼ cup freshly grated Parmesan cheese

¾ cup Arborio rice

A simple, summertime favorite in the Italian countryside, this dish is much appreciated by citified palates as well. It is versatile and easy.

1. Preheat oven to 350°F. Slice off tomato tops and set aside. With a spoon, remove tomato pulp, leaving a hollow shell. Chop pulp and set aside. Rub insides of tomato shells with oil and sugar.

2. Lightly oil bottom of a 9 x 12-inch baking dish. Arrange tomato shells in dish, side by side.

3. In a medium bowl, combine tomato pulp, salt, pepper, garlic, basil, and Parmesan cheese.

4. In a large skillet, sauté rice in remaining oil, reserving 1 tablespoon, over moderately high heat for 3 minutes. Add tomato-pulp mixture and cook another 3 minutes.

5. Fill tomatoes with rice mixture and cover with tomato tops. Sprinkle stuffed tomatoes with reserved 1 tablespoon oil and salt.

6. Bake in oven for 1 hour, or until tomatoes appear wrinkled and brownish on top. Rice should be fully cooked. Serve warm or at room temperature.

Note: Chunks of raw potatoes can be placed between the tomatoes and cooked along with the stuffed tomatoes.

Japanese Dolls

Hinazushi

female   male

On March 3, Girl's Day, Japanese families set up special dolls called hina ningyo *to inspire their daughters to be good-natured.*

1. Place rice and water in a medium saucepan and bring to a boil over high heat. Cover. Lower heat, simmer for 20 minutes. Remove from heat and let stand, covered for 10 minutes.

2. In a separate saucepan, mix vinegar, sugar, and salt and boil, stirring to dissolve sugar. Combine thoroughly with cooked rice while it is still hot. Let cool.

3. To prepare egg crêpes, mix together eggs, cornstarch, and *sake*. Heat a little oil in a small skillet. Spoon 2 tablespoons of the batter evenly in skillet. Repeat to make 8 crêpes, adding oil as necessary. Each crêpe should be about 6 inches in diameter.

4. Remove mushrooms from water and pour off and reserve clear liquid *(shiru)*, discarding sandy dregs. Slice mushrooms into thin strips. In a small saucepan, mix half of *shiru* with 1 tablespoon each soy sauce and *mirin*. Bring to a boil. Place mushrooms in mixture and bring to boil again.

5. In a separate pan, boil shredded carrot in remaining *shiru* with 1 teaspoon soy sauce and a pinch of sugar.

6. Add string beans, mushrooms, carrot, and white sesame seeds to cooked rice. On four plates, form rice mixture into two 3-inch-high cones as "bodies" for the dolls.

7. Fold egg crêpes in half and drape them around the rice bodies to form "kimonos." Place 1 quail egg on top of each body for a head. Use the *nori*, black sesame seeds, and red coloring to form the hair, eyes, and mouth. Four of the dolls should be female and four male.

*Available at Japanese food markets; see list of suppliers (page 319).

**Available at most liquor stores.

---

servings: 4

rice

2 cups Japanese rice,* soaked in water for 1 hour and drained

2 cups water

⅓ cup rice wine vinegar*

2 tablespoons sugar, plus a pinch for filling

1 teaspoon salt

crêpes

4 eggs, lightly beaten

½ teaspoon cornstarch

1 teaspoon Japanese rice wine *(sake)***

Vegetable oil, for cooking crêpes

dolls

4 dried Japanese mushrooms,* soaked in tepid water with a pinch of sugar

4 teaspoons soy sauce

1 tablespoon sweet Japanese cooking wine *(mirin)**

½ carrot, shredded

¼ pound string beans or snow peas, briefly boiled with a pinch of salt, cut lengthwise into thin strips

2 tablespoons white sesame seeds

8 quail eggs,* boiled for 7 minutes and shelled

1 sheet seaweed *(nori)**

Black sesame seeds *(kurogoma)**

Red food coloring, for decorating

Tofu "Steak" with Watercress and Miso Sauce

Tofu Dengaku

servings: 4

- 2 firm, fresh tofu cakes* (*momen tofu*)
- 30 sprigs watercress, thick stems removed
- Pinch of salt
- 4 tablespoons white miso (*shiro-miso*)**
- 4 tablespoons Japanese sweet cooking wine (*mirin*)** or dry sherry
- 4 tablespoons red miso (*aka-miso*)**
- 2 tablespoons sugar
- 2 tablespoons Japanese rice wine (*sake*)***
- 1 tablespoon Asian sesame oil
- 4 tablespoons vegetable oil

The versatile soybean is an indispensable part of Japanese cuisine. Introduced to Japan in the 6th century, it was called the "meat vegetable," an apt name since it has been a primary source of protein in the Japanese diet ever since. The following recipe uses tofu and soybean curd as the "steak" of this dish, and miso, a paste made from cooked, fermented soy beans. There are various types of miso, including the two used here, delicate and fine-textured white miso and robust red miso.

1. In a medium saucepan over medium heat, boil tofu in water to cover for 1 to 2 minutes. Squeeze out excess water by placing tofu between 2 plates or cutting boards for 10 to 20 minutes. Cut each tofu cake in half crosswise, then in half again lengthwise.

2. Cook watercress in salted boiling water for 1 to 2 minutes. Cool in cold water. Coarsely chop watercress.

3. Mix watercress, white miso, *mirin*, and salt in a small bowl.

4. In a separate bowl, combine red miso, sugar, *sake*, sesame oil, and 2 tablespoons of the vegetable oil.

5. Heat remaining 2 tablespoon vegetable oil in a skillet over moderately high heat. Sauté tofu quickly on both sides until browned.

6. Place 2 pieces of tofu on each plate. Pour white and red miso mixtures over tofu and garnish with watercress.

*Available at Japanese food markets and most supermarkets; see list of suppliers (page 319).

**Available at Japanese food markets; see list of suppliers.

***Available at most liquor stores.

MEXICO

Three-Bean Vegetarian Chili

Chile Vegetariano con Tres Frijoles

Zesty spices and a healthy trio of beans give this original chili a flavor that even meat-lovers will enjoy. This chili gains flavor if cooked a day ahead. Serve with rice, chopped scallions, grated Cheddar cheese, and sour cream.

1. In a large bowl, soak beans overnight in water to cover by 2 inches. Drain. In a large pot, cover beans with fresh water and cook until tender, approximately 1½ hours. Drain. Set aside.

2. Heat oil in a large pot, add onions and cook over moderately high heat until translucent, stirring often. Add bell peppers and cook until they begin to soften. For a spicier chili, add diced jalapeño peppers. Add the chili powder, cumin, and coriander, stirring often. Sauté until fragrant, 4 to 5 minutes.

3. Add all remaining ingredients, including the cooked, drained beans. Cover, reduce heat, and simmer for 15 minutes.

servings: 6 to 8

¾ cup dried black beans

¾ cup dried kidney beans

¾ cup dried pinto beans

4 tablespoons olive oil

2 large onions, chopped

2 green bell peppers, chopped

1 to 2 seeded, stemmed, and diced jalapeño peppers (optional)

4 teaspoons chili powder

2 teaspoons ground cumin

1 teaspoon ground coriander

1 medium zucchini, quartered and sliced

1 pound (2 cups) frozen corn kernels

1 can (28 ounces) chopped tomatoes

1 can (12 ounces) tomato paste

1 teaspoon dried oregano

½ teaspoon dried thyme

Cayenne pepper to taste

SWITZERLAND

Cheese Fondue
Fondue de Fromage

servings: 4

2 cloves garlic, pressed or crushed

1¼ cups very dry white wine

1½ pounds Gruyère cheese, grated

5 ounces Vacherin or Emmenthal cheese, grated

3 teaspoons cornstarch

2 tablespoons kirsch (cherry brandy)

Pepper to taste

Dash of nutmeg

2 Swiss or French bread loaves, 1 or 2 days old, cut into small cubes (slightly less than ½ pound per person)

A wonderful winter dinner with friends, cheese fondue, a specialty uniquely associated with Switzerland, is at its best when made with Swiss cheeses and wines. A light white wine is a perfect accompaniment. Many Swiss like the crust-like bottom remnant the best. They fry an egg on it or cover it with kirsch, light it with a match, and roll it up like an omelette. Some engaging customs have developed around the fondue pot: If a chunk of bread is lost in the fondue pot, the loser must forfeit a bottle of wine or give a kiss. Greedy eaters who dip two chunks at a time must finish the fondue!

1. Rub clay *caquelon** or fondue pot with garlic. In the middle of the table, place pot on a stand with alcohol heat or fondue pot on a portable stove. Pour in wine and bring to a boil.

2. Add cheeses and melt, stirring constantly with a wooden spoon. Mix cornstarch with kirsch. When cheese is creamy and barely simmering, add cornstarch mixture and blend well. Stir until mixture bubbles. Add pepper and nutmeg.

3. To serve, spear bread cubes for dipping with long-handled forks, coat well, and eat. The fondue must simmer at all times.

Note: If fondue is too thick, add more white wine while stirring. If it's too thin, add cornstarch mixed with white wine. Use approximately ½ cup wine per ½ pound cheese.

Available at speciality cookware stores; see list of suppliers (page 319).

TURKEY

Eggplant Soufflé

Fritada de Berenjena

Eggplant dishes are a standby in the cuisine of Sephardic Jews from Greece and Turkey. Fritada *is the word for fried dishes in Ladino (a language combining Spanish and Hebrew, spoken by Jews from Spain, Greece, and Portugal), a name that dates from the days before people of the region had home ovens. Today, however, the term refers to baked dishes that are served cold in summer.*

servings: 4

1 large eggplant, about 2 pounds
½ pound farmers' cheese
½ cup grated Parmesan cheese
3 eggs, beaten
½ teaspoon salt
2 tablespoons corn oil

1. Preheat broiler. Puncture eggplant skin all over with a fork. Broil whole eggplant on a baking sheet, turning often, for 30 to 40 minutes. If eggplant skin blackens before flesh is tender, remove eggplant from the broiler and finish cooking, covered with foil, in the oven at 350°F until fork-tender. When the skin is charred, let cool slightly, then peel and remove as many seeds as possible. Chop eggplant flesh and place in a large bowl.

2. Add farmers' cheese and Parmesan cheese and mix well. Add eggs and salt and mix again.

3. Preheat oven to 375°F. Grease a 9-inch ovenproof pie dish with oil and pour in eggplant mixture. Bake for 30 minutes.

Note: At step 2, the soufflé can be flavored with 1 to 2 teaspoons dried basil, oregano, or thyme and 1 or 2 cloves minced garlic.

accompaniments

BRAZIL

Manioc with Vegetables and Fruit

Farofa

Farofa is a distinctly Brazilian dish made from manioc flour, farinha de mandioca. *Manioc is a versatile root vegetable that produces everything from tapioca flour to the starchy mashes called* pirao. *Lightly toasted manioc flour is sometimes served as a side dish to sprinkle over dishes such as Black Bean Stew,* Feijoada, *(page 91). This colorful dish, one of many variations of* farofa, *is usually served on holidays and special occasions.*

1. Heat the oil over moderately low heat in a large pan and add the butter. Sauté garlic for 1 minute, stirring. Add onion and sauté until golden, about 5 minutes, stirring often.

2. Stir in eggs and cook for 2 to 3 minutes, stirring often. Remove from pan and chop eggs into ½-inch dice. Return to pan and add scallion.

3. Slowly pour manioc flour into the center of pan, stirring gently to incorporate all ingredients. Add more butter or manioc flour if necessary; the consistency should be moist but not greasy.

4. Add bell peppers and cook for 2 minutes. Add dried fruits, mixing gently.

5. Stir in the parsley, salt, pepper, and Tabasco. Break up any lumps of manioc and cook another 3 minutes. Serve with Black Bean Stew or grilled meat.

*Available at Brazilian food markets; see list of suppliers (page 319).

servings: 12

1 tablespoon vegetable oil

4 tablespoons (½ stick) butter or margarine

3 garlic cloves, finely chopped

½ cup finely chopped onion

3 large eggs, lightly beaten

½ cup thinly sliced scallion

3 cups manioc flour* (or more, as needed)

½ cup diced yellow bell pepper

½ cup diced red bell pepper

½ cup raisins

½ cup dried apricots, quartered

½ cup pitted prunes, quartered

½ cup chopped fresh parsley

1 teaspoon salt

½ teaspoon freshly ground black pepper

Dash of Tabasco

CHINA

Cold Sesame Noodles

Liáng Miàn

servings: 6 to 8

6 tablespoons soy sauce

6 tablespoons sesame seed paste or tahini paste*

¼ cup sugar

3 tablespoons white vinegar

3 tablespoons dry white wine or Chinese tea

1 pound thin spaghetti or vermicelli noodles

2 to 3 tablespoons Asian sesame oil

⅓ cup sesame seeds

1½ teaspoons minced garlic

¼ cup shredded carrots, for garnish

¾ cup thinly sliced scallions, for garnish

Noodles have been eaten in China for at least 3,000 years. Although rice became the staple food of the central and southern regions during the Sung dynasty more than 1,000 years ago, noodle dishes such as this continue to be typical in northern China, where the cool climate favors the cultivation of wheat. Popular with children, these noodles can be served alone for lunch or with grilled shrimp or meat for dinner.

1. Combine soy sauce, sesame seed paste, sugar, vinegar, and wine. (Sauce will keep indefinitely, refrigerated in an airtight jar.)

2. In a large pot of boiling water, cook noodles until *al dente* (firm to the bite). Drain well. Transfer to a large bowl and toss with the sesame oil. Cover and refrigerate for at least 3 hours.

3. Toast sesame seeds over moderate heat in a small, dry skillet, stirring constantly, until light brown.

4. Just before serving, mix toasted sesame seeds and garlic into sauce. Pour over noodles and mix well. Garnish with shredded carrots and scallions.

Available at Asian, Indian, and Middle Eastern food markets; see list of suppliers (page 319).

Glazed Carrots with Ginger

Carottes Glacées au Gingembre

The key ingredient in this French-Vietnamese side dish is nuoc mam, *or* fish sauce. *A staple in Vietnamese cooking, it is a thin brown liquid made from fermenting salted fresh anchovies. Its concentrated taste loses pungency while cooking and in this dish is further softened by the addition of sugar, butter, ginger, garlic, and coriander. For a complete meal, serve with Lemongrass Chicken (page 135) and rice.*

servings: 6 to 8

- 2 pounds carrots, peeled, trimmed, and cut diagonally into ½-inch-thick discs
- Salt to taste
- 4 tablespoons (½ stick) butter
- 1 tablespoon chopped garlic
- 1 cup chicken broth or water
- 1 tablespoon Vietnamese fish sauce (*nuoc mam*)*
- 1 tablespoon sugar
- 1½ teaspoons minced fresh gingerroot
- 2 tablespoons chopped fresh coriander
- Freshly ground black pepper

1. Drop carrots in a large pot of boiling salted water and cook for 6 minutes or until *al dente* (firm to the bite). Drain. Rinse under cold water to stop cooking.

2. Melt butter over moderate heat, in a large frying pan. Add garlic and fry a few seconds, stirring. Do not let garlic brown.

3. Add carrots, broth, fish sauce, sugar, and ginger, and bring mixture to a boil.

4. Reduce heat, simmer 6 to 7 minutes, stirring occasionally. Carrots should be tender but not mushy, and the sauce should be lightly thickened and reduced to about ¼ cup.

5. Sprinkle with coriander and black pepper to taste. Serve immediately.

Available at Asian food markets; see list of suppliers (page 319).

accompaniments 199

Cauliflower Soufflé

Blumenkohl Auflauf

---

servings: 4

....

1 medium cauliflower (about 1¼ pounds), rinsed, trimmed, and broken into florets (discard stems and core)

4 tablespoons (½ stick) butter

¼ cup all-purpose flour

1¼ to 1½ cups milk

2 eggs, beaten

Salt and pepper to taste

1 cup grated Swiss or Gruyère cheese

1 tablespoon dry bread crumbs

When properly prepared this dish has a rounded, golden puffed top, the source of its name. Broccoli or a combination of cauliflower and broccoli give an equally appealing result.

1. Boil or steam cauliflower until tender, about 5 minutes.

2. Preheat oven to 350°F. Melt butter in a skillet and add flour. Lower flame to moderately low, stir to blend mixture, and cook for 5 minutes, stirring often. Add milk, stirring constantly, until mixture is smooth and thick. Remove from heat and whisk in eggs, salt, pepper, and cheese.

3. Place cauliflower in a lightly greased 6 x 3-inch round soufflé dish or casserole, just large enough to hold it (if dish is too big, the soufflé will not puff properly). Pour sauce over cauliflower. Sprinkle with bread crumbs. Bake about 45 to 60 minutes, or until top is puffed and golden brown.

GERMANY

Bread Dumplings

Brot Klösse

Bread dumplings are a popular dish in southern Bavaria. They are often served, one dumpling per person, with roast pork and sauerkraut. They are also delicious in chicken soup. Sadly, the art of making good bread dumplings is disappearing, but they can still be found in the countryside and at village restaurants.

1. Place bread slices in a large bowl. Pour boiling milk over bread, mix well and let stand for 1 hour.

2. Melt butter over moderate heat in a saucepan and sauté onion until translucent, stirring often, about 4 minutes. Remove pan from heat, and mix in parsley and lemon rind. Add to bread mixture and season with salt. Add eggs and mix well.

3. Wet hands and shape mixture into 3-inch balls for dumplings.

4. Boil water in a 6- to 8-quart pot, add salt and one dumpling to test. If dumpling stays together, add remaining dumplings. If trial dumpling falls apart, add some flour to dumpling dough. When dumplings float to the top of the water, reduce heat, partially cover pot, and simmer for 20 to 25 minutes. Dumplings should be light and fluffy. Remove dumplings with a slotted spoon and carefully place in serving bowl.

Note: The dumplings can be made with fewer eggs, and without parsley or lemon, according to taste. They can be made into 1½-inch balls if a smaller dumpling is preferred. Finely chopped chives may be used instead of parsley.

servings: 6 to 8

1 pound stale white rolls (about 10), or stale white bread (do not use seeded or whole-grain bread), thinly sliced

2 cups boiling milk

2 tablespoons butter

1 large onion, peeled and finely chopped

3 tablespoons finely chopped fresh parsley

Rind of 1 lemon, finely chopped

2 teaspoons salt, or to taste, plus more for boiling dumplings

3 eggs

GREECE

Turkey Stuffing, Greek-Style

Yemisi ya Galopoula

servings: 8

- 8 tablespoons (1 stick) butter
- 2 cups onion, finely chopped
- 2 tablespoons olive oil
- 2 pounds chopped ground beef (round or sirloin)
- 1 cup seedless white raisins
- ¾ pound cooked chestnuts, coarsely chopped*
- ½ cup pine nuts
- 1 teaspoon cloves
- 1 teaspoon cinnamon
- ½ cup chopped fresh parsley
- 1 cup cooked rice
- 1 can (8 ounces) tomato sauce
- 1 cup dry red wine
- ½ cup chicken broth
- 1 turkey (18 pounds)

The rich combination of raisins, chestnuts, and sweet spices make this poultry filling well suited for festive occasions with family and friends. This recipe makes enough stuffing for an 18-pound bird.

1. Melt butter and sauté onion in a large skillet over moderately high heat, until translucent, stirring often.

2. Add olive oil and ground meat. Sauté meat, stirring often, until browned.

3. Add raisins, chestnuts, pine nuts, cloves, cinnamon, and parsley. Stir in rice, tomato sauce, wine, and broth. Reduce heat and simmer until liquid evaporates, about 30 minutes.

4. Fill bird cavity with stuffing. Follow tying instructions in Roast Turkey recipe (page 134). Stuffing should not be placed inside bird until just before roasting. Wrap any remaining stuffing in aluminum foil, or place in a covered casserole dish and bake for 30 minutes.

5. When bird is roasted, immediately transfer stuffing from cavity to a serving bowl, adding any cooked in foil or casserole. Stuffing should be slightly moist. Add additional chicken broth, if necessary.

Available in jars at specialty food markets; see list of suppliers (page 319).

GREECE

Cucumber and Yogurt Salad

Tzatziki

A typical accompaniment to Greek family meals, this salad can be served with pita bread and olives as an appetizer, or with grilled chicken, fish, or lamb.

1. Place yogurt in a cheesecloth-lined sieve over a bowl. Drain overnight in the refrigerator and discard liquid.

2. Drain the cucumbers as follows: Place grated cucumbers in a fine sieve or colander lined with cheesecloth. Sprinkle with salt and let stand for 45 minutes to 1 hour. Squeeze gently to remove excess water.

3. In a medium bowl, combine cucumbers, garlic, vinegar, olive oil, ½ teaspoon of the salt, and pepper.

4. Add drained yogurt and blend. Serve with pita bread.

---

servings: 2 cups

2 cups plain yogurt

2 large cucumbers, peeled, seeded, and coarsely grated

½ teaspoon salt, plus more for sprinkling

1 tablespoon minced garlic

1 tablespoon white vinegar

2 tablespoons olive oil

Pepper to taste

Cassava Puffs

servings: 3 dozen

1½ cups peeled and coarsely chopped cassava*

1 egg, lightly beaten

1¾ tablespoons butter or margarine

¼ teaspoon cayenne pepper

1 teaspoon salt, or to taste

1⅔ teaspoons baking powder

½ cup all-purpose flour

Vegetable oil for frying

When the Spanish explorers arrived in the Americas, cassava (also called yucca and manioc) was the "staff of life," venerated by Amerindians of the Caribbean, who prepared it as bread and in many other ways. Cassava puffs also make a good snack or appetizer.

1. Cover cassava with water and boil until tender, about 20 minutes. Drain well. While still hot, mash until smooth.

2. In a medium bowl, combine cassava, egg, butter or margarine, cayenne pepper, salt, and baking powder. Mix thoroughly.

3. Form mixture into small balls and roll in the flour to coat.

4. In a large skillet, pour oil to ¼-inch depth. Heat the oil over moderately high heat and fry balls until golden brown, about 5 minutes, turning as they cook to brown evenly. Drain on paper towels. Serve with by Coriander Chutney (facing page) or Mango Chutney (page 206).

Note: Other Latin American vegetables such as *eddoes, tannias,* and hard yams can also be used.

Available at Latin American food markets; see list of suppliers (page 319).

Coriander Chutney

Hara Dhania Chutney

India is a source of some of the world's tastiest condiments. This piquant chutney is an outstanding accompaniment to a variety of fish, meat, and vegetable dishes.

1. Blend coriander, chili peppers, lemon juice, ginger, sugar, salt, and water to a fine paste in a blender or food processor. Serve as a spread for vegetable sandwiches or with vegetable cutlets. The chutney can be refrigerated for 1 week or frozen in an airtight container for up to 3 months.

Variation: Add 2 tablespoons grated coconut and 2 tablespoons chopped mint leaves.

---

servings: 1½ to 2 cups

1 large bunch fresh coriander, rinsed, stems removed, and chopped (about 1½ cups)

2 green chili peppers (or to taste), chopped

1 teaspoon fresh lemon juice

1-inch piece gingerroot, peeled and minced

½ teaspoon sugar

½ teaspoon salt

Water to thin paste, if needed

Mango Chutney

Aam Chutney

servings: 2 cups

2 large mangoes, still firm to the touch, peeled, cut away from pit, and cubed

8 tablespoons sugar

2-inch piece fresh gingerroot, peeled and minced

10 cloves garlic, mashed

½ cup cider vinegar

1 teaspoon salt

2 teaspoons chili powder

¼ cup raisins

Chutneys are sweet-and-sour condiments, often consisting of tropical fruits like mango cooked in vinegar, sugar, and spices to a jam-like consistency. The contributor learned this recipe from her mother in Goa and refined it when she was part of the international community in Somalia.

1. In a medium bowl, mix mango cubes with sugar and set aside for 1 hour.

2. Purée ginger, garlic, and vinegar in a blender or food processor, or pulverize with a mortar and pestle.

3. Add salt, chili powder, and mangoes to ginger mixture.

4. Cook over low heat in a large skillet, until mango pieces are tender, about 5 minutes. Add raisins and cook another 2 to 3 minutes.

5. Let cool and serve with Indian curries or leg of lamb. Chutney will keep for 1 week in the refrigerator or up to 3 months in the freezer, in an airtight container.

INDIA

Peas and Potatoes with Cumin and Yogurt

Dahi Aloo Mutter

This vegetable dish from the Gujarat region of western India will please the most tender palate. Its spiciness is tempered by the cooling addition of yogurt. Serve with rice or Indian breads.

1. Boil potatoes until tender. Let cool and peel.

2. Heat shortening in a large skillet, over moderately high heat and cook cumin seeds until they begin to pop, about 30 seconds. Add curry powder, stirring for about 20 seconds, then add ginger, boiled potatoes, and peas. Mix well.

3. Blend the yogurt and salt with a spoon. Add to the vegetables. Lower heat and simmer, covered, for 10 minutes.

4. Add more curry powder, if desired, and sprinkle with coriander.

servings: 4

- **1 pound small potatoes**
- **1 tablespoon solid vegetable shortening or vegetable oil**
- **2 teaspoons whole cumin seeds**
- **1½ teaspoons curry powder, preferably Indian**
- **1-inch piece gingerroot, peeled and minced**
- **1½ cups peas, fresh or frozen**
- **1 container (16 ounces) plain yogurt**
- **Salt to taste**
- **½ cup chopped fresh coriander**

INDIA

Red Lentil Curry

Masoor Dal

---

servings: 4

2 cups Indian red lentils *(masoor dal),** discolored grains discarded, rinsed and drained

6 cups water

¼ teaspoon ground turmeric

Salt to taste

1 tablespoon butter

½ teaspoon whole black mustard seeds*

½ teaspoon whole cumin seeds

1 dried hot red chili pepper

½-inch piece gingerroot, peeled and minced

3 or 4 whole black peppercorns

Pinch of asafetida* (optional)

1 large onion, peeled and thinly sliced

2 plum tomatoes, coarsely chopped

2 tablespoons finely chopped fresh coriander

Lentils, known as dal *across India, are an important source of protein in the Indian diet. Besides their nourishing properties, they are well adapted to a wide array of spices, as this fragrant dish flavored with the bitter, pungent resin asafetida confirms.*

1. Place lentils in a heavy pot with the water and turmeric. Partially cover and cook over moderately high heat until lentils are soft, about 15 minutes. Add salt.

2. Melt butter in a small skillet over medium heat. When hot, add mustard seeds, cumin seeds, hot chili pepper, ginger, peppercorns, and asafetida. When mustard seeds begin to pop, about 30 seconds, add onion and sauté for 4 to 5 minutes, stirring frequently. Add tomatoes and cook for 4 minutes. Add onion mixture to pot of cooked lentils. Stir well and simmer over moderately low heat for 3 to 4 minutes. Add more water if lentils are very sticky. The lentils should have the consistency of gravy.

3. Remove pot from heat and add coriander. Serve hot with basmati* or regular rice or Indian bread.

*Available at Indian and Middle Eastern food markets; see list of suppliers (page 319).

INDIA

Sour Chickpeas

Khatte Chole

Served warm or at room temperature, these chickpeas, with a sour-and-spicy combination of lemon juice and spices, are ideal for picnics and hot weather buffets because they keep well for hours without refrigeration.

1. Put 2 tablespoons of the chopped onions, ½ teaspoon of the salt, the chili pepper, ginger, and lemon juice in a small bowl. Mix well and set aside.

2. Heat oil in a pot over moderately high heat. When oil is hot, add remaining onions.

3. Stir for 8 to 10 minutes, or until onions turn reddish brown. Add tomatoes and continue to stir-fry for another 5 to 6 minutes, mashing tomato pieces with a fork.

4. Add coriander, cumin, and turmeric and cook, stirring, about 30 seconds.

5. Add drained chickpeas, the water, the remaining 2 teaspoons salt, the *garam masala*, and cayenne pepper. Stir.

6. Simmer, covered, for 20 minutes, stirring occasionally.

7. Add lemon juice mixture and stir. Serve hot, warm, or at room temperature. Garnish with chopped coriander.

Note: Powdered pomegranate seeds (*anardana* powder), available at Indian food markets, can be added to make the sauce darker and more sour. Sprinkle on top of sauce before serving.

*Garam masala, a blend of ground coriander, cumin, ginger, black pepper, cinnamon, pimiento, cardamom, bay leaves, and nutmeg, is available at Indian food markets; see list of suppliers (page 319).

servings: 6

3 medium onions, peeled and finely chopped

2½ teaspoons salt

1 hot green chili pepper, finely chopped

1 tablespoon finely chopped fresh gingerroot

4 tablespoons fresh lemon juice

6 tablespoons vegetable oil

2 medium tomatoes, finely chopped

1 tablespoon ground coriander

1 tablespoon ground cumin

½ teaspoon ground turmeric

1 can (31 ounces) chickpeas, rinsed and drained, or 1½ cups dried chickpeas, cooked according to package directions

1¾ cups water

1 teaspoon *garam masala**

½ teaspoon cayenne pepper

Chopped fresh coriander, for garnish

INDIA

Curried Roast Cauliflower

Dum Phool Gobi

servings: 4 to 6

2 onions, peeled and finely chopped

1 teaspoon ground turmeric

1 teaspoon hot paprika or chili powder

1-inch piece gingerroot, peeled

3 to 4 cloves garlic

1½ teaspoons Indian curry powder, such as Madras, or *garam masala***

2 tablespoons water, if necessary

1 medium cauliflower (about 1¼ pounds), rinsed, lower stems and leaves removed, cut into florets

2 tablespoons vegetable oil

2-inch piece cinnamon stick

4 whole cloves

4 cardamom pods* (optional)

1½ pounds tomatoes, chopped

1 cup raw peas

1 teaspoon salt, or to taste

½ cup plain yogurt or light sour cream

2 tablespoons chopped fresh coriander, for garnish

The ordinary cauliflower is transformed in this delicious combination of herbs, spices, and tomatoes. Baked slowly in a smooth sauce, it's an ideal side dish with roasted chicken or fish, or as part of a vegetarian meal.

1. Make a spice paste by puréeing onions, turmeric, paprika or chili powder, gingerroot, garlic, curry powder, or *garam masala* and the water in a food processor or blender.

2. Cook cauliflower in boiling water for 5 minutes and drain.

3. Preheat oven to 375°F. In a large pot, heat the oil over moderate heat. Add cinnamon, cloves, cardamom, and remaining onion and sauté until golden brown, stirring often, about 5 minutes. Add spice paste, stir, and cook for 2 to 3 minutes. Add tomatoes, peas, and salt and cook another 3 to 4 minutes. Add yogurt or sour cream and mix well.

4. Place partially cooked cauliflower in an ovenproof serving dish. Carefully spread sauce on top and in between cauliflower florets. Cover with foil and bake for 25 to 30 minutes. Garnish with coriander.

*Available at Indian food markets; see list of suppliers (page 319).

**Garam masala, *a blend of ground coriander, cumin, ginger, black pepper, cinnamon, pimiento, cardamom, bay leaves, and nutmeg, is available at Indian food markets; see list of suppliers.*

Dona Elena's Never-Fail Festive Rice Pilaf

Ram Baan Majedar Pulav

In the monsoon of 1933, Senhor Teodosio had promised Dona Elena a wild fowl curry for dinner, but shot her rooster by mistake. While he was cooking the chicken curry, Dona Elena set about preparing her rice pilaf. Although Dona Elena and Senhor Teodosio washed down their meal with a glass each of tinto, *a Portuguese red wine, the meal goes equally well with Indian beer. In her recipe book, Dona Elena suggests garnishing the rice with raisins and sliced hard-boiled eggs. We bring you the recipe, updated for our times.*

servings: 4 to 6

- 2 cups basmati rice*
- 4 tablespoons extra-virgin olive oil
- 4 cardamom pods*
- 6 cloves
- 1 small onion, peeled and finely chopped
- ½ teaspoon ground turmeric
- 1 small tomato, chopped
- 1 teaspoon sugar
- 2 cups chicken broth, chilled and defatted
- Salt to taste
- 1¾ cups water
- ½ cup raisins, for garnish
- 2 hard-boiled eggs, thinly sliced, for garnish

1. Thoroughly rinse rice in water three times. Drain and set aside.

2. Place 2-quart saucepan over moderate heat. When hot, add oil, wait 10 seconds. Add cardamom pods and cloves. Stir briefly.

3. Add chopped onion and stir-fry until lightly golden. Add turmeric and tomato. Fry 2 minutes.

4. Raise heat to moderately high, add rice and sugar. Fry for 2 minutes, stirring constantly.

5. Add chicken broth. Stir twice. Add salt and the water. Stir and bring to a boil. Stir twice, turn heat to low, and cover.

6. Simmer 15 minutes. Liquid will be absorbed.

7. Uncover rice and fluff. Keep on low heat 1 more minute. Fluff again before serving. Garnish with raisins and eggs.

Note: Senhor Teodosio and the widow Dona Elena are fictional characters in Victor Rangel-Ribeiro's novel about the mythical Goan village of Tivolem. This recipe and Senhor Teodosio's Chicken Curry (page 116), however, are very real; guests have enjoyed both dishes on occasion, with no leftovers!

Available at Indian food markets; see list of suppliers (page 319).

Lemon Rice with Indian Yogurt

Limbu Chawal Ke-Sath Dahi Raita

A popular dish from South India, served at special occasions like weddings, which are often elaborate two-day affairs, and for the Tamil New Year in January.

servings: 4

lemon rice

2 tablespoons vegetable oil

1 teaspoon black mustard seeds*

7 or 8 curry leaves*

1 tablespoon dried white beans (urad dal)*

1 tablespoon yellow split peas (chana dal)*

1 teaspoon ground turmeric

1 green chili pepper, slit lengthwise

2 tablespoons shelled roasted peanuts

2 cups cooked rice, cooled and grains separated

1 tablespoon chopped fresh coriander

Juice of 1 lemon

Indian yogurt

4 tablespoons plain yogurt

1 teaspoon sour cream

½ teaspoon salt

1 teaspoon vegetable oil

½ teaspoon black mustard seeds*

1 green chili pepper, finely chopped

1 plum tomato, chopped

1 teaspoon chopped fresh coriander

1. For the rice, heat oil in a large frying pan until oil ripples, and add mustard seeds. When seeds pop, about 30 seconds, add curry leaves, white beans, and yellow split peas. Lower heat and sauté until beans and peas turn light brown and fragrant, about 30 to 60 seconds.

2. Add turmeric, chili pepper, and roasted peanuts. Mix well. Add rice, a little at a time, stirring constantly. When all the rice is incorporated, take pan off heat. Add coriander and lemon juice and mix.

3. For the yogurt, in a small bowl, mix yogurt and sour cream. Beat until smooth. Add salt.

4. In a small saucepan, heat the oil. When hot, add mustard seeds, chili pepper, and tomato. Sauté for 2 minutes. Let cool and add mixture to yogurt. Garnish with coriander.

5. Serve lemon rice at room temperature with Indian or plain yogurt.

Available at Indian food markets; see list of suppliers (page 319).

`INDIA`

Creamed Spinach with Indian Cheese

Palak Paneer

One of the most noted dishes of northern India, this is traditionally made with fresh chopped spinach. But, as this recipe demonstrates, frozen prepared creamed spinach is a fine substitute. The mild Indian cheese absorbs the flavors of the spinach and spices.

1. Heat oil in a 5-quart pan over moderate heat until hot but not smoking.

2. Add onion and garlic-ginger paste and sauté until onion is soft.

3. Add ground coriander, turmeric, cumin, paprika, cayenne, salt, and tomato. Cook until tomato is soft, about 5 minutes.

4. Add creamed spinach and cook for 8 minutes.

5. Add *paneer* cheese and *garam masala*, and cook an additional 5 minutes. Stir well before serving.

*Available at Indian food markets; see list of suppliers (page 319). Garam masala is a blend of ground coriander, cumin, ginger, black pepper, cinnamon, pimiento, cardamom, bay leaves, and nutmeg.

servings: 4

....

2 tablespoons vegetable oil

¾ cup finely chopped onion

1 teaspoon garlic-ginger paste*

½ tablespoon ground coriander

½ teaspoon turmeric

½ teaspoon ground cumin

¼ teaspoon paprika (optional)

¼ teaspoon cayenne pepper

½ teaspoon salt, or to taste

1 large tomato, chopped

1-pound package frozen creamed spinach, defrosted

1 package (12 ounces) *paneer* cheese* or 12 ounces firm tofu, cut into small cubes

½ teaspoon *garam masala**

ITALY

ITALY

Saffron Risotto

Risotto allo Zafferano

---

servings: 4

....

1¾ cups chicken broth

½ teaspoon saffron threads

2½ tablespoons olive oil

½ cup chopped onion

¾ cup Arborio rice, rinsed

¾ cup dry white wine

Salt and pepper to taste

2 tablespoons butter

1 teaspoon heavy cream (optional)

2 tablespoons grated Parmesan cheese

Risotto, made with famed Arborio rice slowly simmered in wine or broth, is Milan's most celebrated contribution to the cuisine of Italy.

1. Mix chicken broth with saffron threads and heat to warm in a medium saucepan.

2. Heat olive oil in a separate medium saucepan over moderate heat, and stirring, sauté the onion for 5 minutes, or until soft. Add rice, stirring frequently with a wooden spoon, to completely coat all grains, about 3 minutes. Continue stirring and add wine. Lower heat to simmer, and allow rice to absorb wine. Add ¾ cup of the warm chicken broth. Once absorbed, slowly add remaining broth, stirring often. Add salt and pepper to taste.

3. When all the broth is fully absorbed and rice is *al dente* (firm to the bite) about 18 minutes, quickly stir in butter, cream, and Parmesan cheese. Serve with *osso buco* or lamb shanks, or with a green salad as a luncheon meal.

KOREA

Korean Noodles with Vegetables

Chap-chae

This is one of Korea's best-known noodle dishes. It is made with dried rather than fresh mushrooms, because they have a more concentrated flavor.

1. Soak dried shiitake mushrooms in warm water to cover for about 15 minutes, squeeze out water, then cut into julienne strips. Season with 1 teaspoon of the soy sauce, 1 teaspoon of the sugar, the scallions, sesame seeds, black pepper, 1 teaspoon of the sesame oil, and the garlic.

2. Heat 1 tablespoon of the vegetable oil in a wok or skillet. Sauté onion, carrot, bell peppers, and spinach, stirring. Add salt to taste and mushrooms. Cook, stirring, until onion is translucent and peppers are softened. Set aside.

3. Beat egg. In a separate skillet, heat remaining vegetable oil and pour in the egg. Cook in a very thin layer until set. Cut into ¼-inch strips and set aside.

4. In a medium pot, boil water. Add noodles to boiling water, turn off heat, and set aside for about 10 minutes. Drain, rinse well with cold water and drain again. Place in a bowl and season with the remaining 2 tablespoons sesame oil, the remaining 1½ tablespoons soy sauce, and the remaining 1 tablespoon sugar.

6. In a wok or skillet, stir-fry noodles and vegetables together. Add salt or soy sauce to taste and garnish with egg strips. Serve warm or cold.

*Available at Asian food markets; see list of suppliers (page 319).

---

servings: 6

- **10 medium sized dried shiitake (*pyogo*) mushrooms***
- **1 teaspoon plus 1½ tablespoons soy sauce**
- **1 teaspoon plus 1 tablespoon sugar**
- **1 tablespoon chopped scallions**
- **1 teaspoon sesame seeds**
- **¼ teaspoon black pepper**
- **1 teaspoon plus 2 tablespoons Asian sesame oil**
- **½ teaspoon finely chopped garlic**
- **1½ tablespoons vegetable oil**
- **1 cup onion, peeled and cut into thin strips**
- **½ cup carrot, cut into 2-inch matchsticks**
- **½ cup thin strips red and green bell pepper**
- **1 cup cooked spinach, chopped**
- **Salt to taste**
- **1 egg**
- **5 ounces cellophane noodles (*Dang Myun*)***

accompaniments

Spicy Mixed Vegetables with Pineapple and Peanuts

Achar

servings: 6 to 8

6 large shallots (about 1 pound), peeled

8 fresh red chili peppers, seeds and stems removed

1 to 2 tablespoons chili powder

1 tablespoon shrimp paste*

1 to 2 tablespoons ground tumeric

¼ cup water

1 small cabbage (about 1½ pounds), quartered and cut into 1-inch strips

Salt to taste

1 white radish (daikon),* peeled, quartered, and cut diagonally into 1-inch strips

2 large carrots, peeled, quartered lengthwise, and cut diagonally into 1-inch strips

2 large cucumbers, quartered and cut diagonally into 1-inch strips

½ pound Chinese long beans or string beans, cut into 1-inch lengths

½ cup vegetable oil

1 cup rice wine vinegar

3 tablespoons sugar

¼ cup sesame seeds

½ fresh pineapple, peeled, cored, and cut into bite-size chunks

½ cup ground roasted peanuts

Popular in Malaysia and Singapore, this colorful vegetable dish can be served with rice, curries, meat, or chicken.

1. Purée shallots, fresh chilies, chili powder, shrimp paste, and turmeric with the ¼ cup water in a blender or food processor. Set aside.

2. In a large pot, blanch cabbage leaves in boiling water for 1 to 2 minutes. Let cool under running water.

3. Sprinkle salt on cut white radish, carrots, cucumbers, and long beans or string beans. Let sit for 30 minutes. Squeeze liquid from vegetables using a clean cloth or paper towels.

4. In a wok or large skillet, stir-fry shallot mixture in oil for about 2 minutes, until fragrant. Add vinegar, sugar, and salt, and simmer for 2 minutes. Remove from heat.

5. Toast sesame seeds over moderate heat in a small dry skillet, stirring constantly, until light brown.

6. Add all vegetables and the pineapple to shallot mixture. Mix in sesame seeds and peanuts. Serve chilled or slightly warm, with rice.

Available at Asian food markets and health food stores; see list of suppliers (page 319).

RUSSIA

Garlic Rosemary Potato Pancakes

Latkes

The addition of garlic and rosemary puts a contemporary twist on the traditional potato pancake. Although enjoyed year-round, latkes are a tradition of Chanukah, the Jewish Festival of Lights. These potato pancakes are also delicious with smoked salmon and sour cream.

1. Coarsely shred potatoes, using food processor fitted with a grating disk. Transfer potatoes to a colander and press out as much liquid as possible.

2. Using a food processor fitted with a steel blade, roughly purée about one-third of the grated potato mixture with garlic and rosemary.

3. In a large bowl, combine both potato mixtures with egg, salt, pepper, baking powder, and matzo meal. Mix until thoroughly combined. Chill for at least 30 minutes.

4. Preheat oven to 200°F. In a 10- or 12-inch skillet, preferably cast iron, heat about ¼-inch oil over high heat until hot but not smoking. Drop ¼ cup batter into pan, and flatten with a spatula. Cook no more than 4 or 5 pancakes at a time.

5. Regulate heat carefully, reducing to moderate as the pancakes fry until golden and crisp, about 4 minutes each side. Transfer to paper towels to drain. Continue in the same manner until all batter is used. (If necessary, add more oil to the pan, but heat oil before frying a new batch.)

6. Keep pancakes warm in the oven on an ovenproof platter, lined with paper towels. They are best served immediately.

---

servings: 4 to 5

- 3 large all-purpose potatoes, peeled
- 2 tablespoons chopped garlic
- 1 tablespoon chopped fresh rosemary
- 1 large egg, beaten
- ¾ teaspoon salt, or to taste
- ¼ teaspoon freshly ground pepper, or to taste
- ½ teaspoon baking powder
- 1 tablespoon matzo meal or flour
- Vegetable oil for frying

Baked Green Bananas

servings: 4 to 6

- 3 to 4 pounds unripe (green) bananas, peeled*
- 1 bunch scallions, trimmed and chopped
- ½ pound Cheddar cheese, grated
- 1 can (12 ounces) evaporated milk
- 3 large eggs
- ¾ cup bread crumbs
- Salt, pepper, and tarragon or thyme, to taste

Green bananas are the national dish of the Caribbean island of Saint Lucia, often served on December 13, a national holiday commemorating the day in 1502 when Christopher Columbus first set foot on its shores. In Saint Lucia, this dish is often served with codfish.

1. Boil bananas in a pot of water until they are soft, about 30 minutes. Drain and let cool for 5 minutes. Mash with a fork while still hot.

2. Preheat oven to 350°F. Grease a 10 x 10-inch baking pan. Mix all remaining ingredients with mashed bananas, reserving some bread crumbs and cheese for the topping.

3. Pour banana mixture into pan. Sprinkle top with remaining bread crumbs and cheese.

4. Bake until top is golden brown and knife inserted in center comes out clean, 40 to 45 minutes.

Do not use plantains.

Singapore Rice Noodles

Passed down through many generations, this family recipe shows the influence of three cultures—Indian, Chinese, and Malay—that have infused the cooking of Singapore with its distinctive flavors.

1. Heat oil in a large frying pan or wok over high heat. Fry garlic until slightly brown, about 2 minutes, stirring constantly.

2. Add shrimp and bean sprouts. Stir-fry, tossing, for 2 minutes or until shrimp turn pink. Add rice vermicelli, chicken broth, scallions, and chili peppers. Stir-fry for 3 to 4 minutes, mixing well.

3. Mix in curry powder, soy sauce, white pepper, and salted black bean sauce, if using. Fry for 1 more minute over moderate heat. Garnish with egg.

*Available at Asian food markets; see list of suppliers (page 319).

---

servings: 4

- ½ cup vegetable oil
- 3 teaspoons minced garlic
- 1 pound small shrimp, peeled and deveined
- 1 cup fresh bean sprouts
- 1 pound rice vermicelli, softened in boiling water for 2 to 4 minutes, drained and rinsed under cold water for 30 seconds
- ¼ cup chicken broth
- 8 scallions, trimmed and chopped
- 3 to 4 dried red chili peppers, minced
- 1 tablespoon curry powder, preferably Indian
- 3 tablespoons light soy sauce
- ½ teaspoon white pepper
- 1 tablespoon salted black bean sauce* (optional)
- 1 egg, fried or scrambled

Sweet Potatoes with Sherry and Black Walnuts

servings: 10

3 large sweet potatoes, cooked, peeled, and mashed

½ cup dry sherry

1 teaspoon salt

½ cup brown sugar

2 eggs, lightly beaten

½ cup melted butter

½ cup chopped black walnuts*

Although this recipe can be made with ordinary walnuts, it is even tastier with black walnuts, which have a greater depth of flavor. Because black walnuts have exceptionally hard shells, it's best to buy them already shelled.

1. Preheat oven to 350°F. Butter a 6- to 8-cup ovenproof casserole. Beat mashed potatoes, sherry, salt, sugar, eggs, and butter with an electric mixer until fluffy. Fold in nuts.

2. Pour into casserole and bake 20 minutes.

Available at specialty food markets; see list of suppliers (page 319).

Hoppin' John

Hoppin' John is traditionally served in the American South on New Year's Day, when a shiny coin is buried in the dish before serving, bringing the finder good luck for the entire year. Serve with collard greens, corn bread, or biscuits.

1. Rinse peas. In a bowl, cover peas with cold water by at least 2 inches and soak overnight. For a quicker method, cover peas with boiling water and soak for 1 hour.

2. Drain peas and rinse again in cold water.

3. Place onion, pepper, salt, thyme, and ham hock or smoked turkey wings, if using, in a large pot of boiling water. Add peas to pot. Water should cover peas by 1 inch. Bring to a boil again, lower heat and simmer, covered, for 2 hours or until tender, stirring occasionally. Stir cooked rice into the peas during the last 20 minutes of cooking. Remove from heat, when most of the water is absorbed.

Available at specialty food markets; see list of suppliers (page 319) and in some supermarkets.

servings: 6

1 pound dried black-eyed peas

1 large onion, peeled and chopped

½ teaspoon black or cayenne pepper, or to taste

1 teaspoon salt, or to taste

1 teaspoon dried thyme, or to taste

1 ham hock or 4 smoked turkey wings* (optional)

½ cup cooked rice

Sesame Spring Spinach

---

servings: 3 to 4

....

4 cloves garlic, chopped

1 tablespoon sesame seeds

2 tablespoons olive oil

1 pound fresh spinach, well-rinsed
and patted dry

½ tablespoon Asian sesame oil

2 tablespoons soy sauce

The sautéed sesame seeds and pungent sesame oil give this dish an Asian touch.

1. In a wok or deep skillet, over moderately high heat, sauté garlic and sesame seeds in olive oil until garlic is soft and seeds are toasted, about 3 minutes. Stir constantly.

2. Add spinach and sauté until wilted, about 3 minutes, stirring often.

3. Add sesame oil and soy sauce and toss. Serve immediately.

Spring Vegetable Casserole

This healthy recipe originated in Trinidad, where it is often served at Easter. Vary, if desired, by adding or substituting other seasonal vegetables.

1. Preheat oven to 325°F. Melt butter in a small ovenproof casserole. Add carrots, turnip, onions, and celery. Add vermouth or wine and season with salt and pepper.

2. Butter a circle of waxed paper to fit the size of the casserole and place it on top of the vegetables. Cover with a lid or aluminum foil and cook for 1 hour or until vegetables are tender. Remove waxed paper and top with parsley.

servings: 4

2 tablespoons butter

6 medium carrots, cut into thin 2-inch matchsticks

1 turnip, peeled, cut into thin 2-inch matchsticks

2 small onions, peeled and thinly sliced

4 tender inner celery stalks, thinly sliced diagonally

⅓ cup dry white vermouth or white wine

Salt and freshly ground pepper to taste

¼ cup chopped fresh parsley, for garnish

Cauliflower Gribiche

servings: 4 to 6

- 1 medium cauliflower, about 1¼ pounds, lower stems and leaves removed
- 1 cup water
- ¼ cup sour gherkin pickles, coarsely chopped
- ⅓ cup diced red onion
- 2 ounces flat anchovy filets in oil, cut into ¼-inch pieces
- 1 tablespoon red wine vinegar
- 2 tablespoons virgin olive oil
- ½ teaspoon salt
- ½ teaspoon freshly ground black pepper
- 1 large hard-boiled egg, peeled and chopped into ¼-inch pieces

The word "gribiche" in the name of this recipe recalls a French sauce containing hard-boiled egg, vinegar, and capers. This version substitutes gherkins for capers, because of its creator's fond memories of the pickles made on the farm where her mother grew up.

1. Separate the cauliflower into 1-inch florets.

2. Place cauliflower in a large saucepan and add the water. Bring water to a rolling boil, cover and cook over high heat for 3 to 4 minutes, until water has evaporated. Remove cauliflower to a bowl.

3. Combine pickles, onion, anchovies, vinegar, olive oil, salt, and pepper and mix well. Add to cauliflower.

4. Transfer mixture to a serving platter, sprinkle chopped egg on top, and serve immediately. Serve with roasts, grilled meats, or chicken.

Fried Green Tomatoes

A classic from the American South reminiscent of family dinners on warm summer nights.

1. Mix eggs, milk, and water together in a medium bowl. Set aside.

2. In a separate medium bowl, mix Parmesan, oregano, salt, and pepper together. Set aside.

3. In a large bowl, mix flour, cornmeal, and sugar together. Set aside.

4. Slice green tomatoes about ⅓ to ¼ inch thick.

5. Dip each slice into the egg mixture, then the Parmesan mixture, then the flour mixture.

6. Place coated tomatoes on a rack and chill in the refrigerator for 15 to 20 minutes to set batter.

7. Heat olive oil and butter in a large heavy skillet. When hot, fry tomatoes in batches until golden brown on each side. Drain on paper towels and serve hot.

servings: 4

2 large eggs, beaten

½ cup milk

1 tablespoon water

⅔ cup grated Parmesan cheese

2 teaspoons dried oregano, crumbled

2 teaspoons salt

¼ teaspoon black pepper

1 cup all-purpose flour

1 cup coarse yellow cornmeal

1 tablespoon sugar

1½ pounds unripe (green) tomatoes

1½ tablespoons olive oil

2 tablespoons butter

Roasted Squash with Ginger and Charred Peppers

servings: 6 to 8

2 large butternut squash, halved and seeded

2 large red bell peppers

6 medium shallots, peeled and diced

3 tablespoons olive oil

2 cloves garlic, minced

½ cup coarsely chopped blanched, roasted almonds

¼ cup candied ginger, cut into ¼-inch pieces

1 tablespoon chopped fresh thyme, or ½ teaspoon dried thyme, crumbled

1 tablespoon chopped fresh rosemary, or ½ teaspoon dried rosemary, crushed

Salt and pepper to taste

A dish that can be made a day ahead and reheated in the oven just before serving. Any hard winter squash, such as dumpling or acorn squash can be prepared this way. Roasting squash intensifies its flavor.

1. Preheat oven to 375°F. Roast squash, cut-side down, on a greased baking sheet or in a roasting pan until tender, about 30 to 45 minutes. Cool, peel, and chop into 1-inch cubes.

2. Place bell peppers directly on burner flame, turning until skin is blistered and blackened. Let cool, uncovered. When cool, remove seeds, leaving skin on. Slice into julienne strips. Alternatively, in preheated broiler, broil bell peppers about 2 inches from heat, turning frequently, until skins are blistered and blackened, about 8 to 12 minutes.

3. Sauté shallots in olive oil in a large skillet or pot, over moderate heat until soft, about 4 minutes. Add garlic and continue to cook until soft, about 4 minutes. Mix in almonds. Add squash and ginger and toss. Just before serving, add thyme, rosemary, salt, and pepper, and toss again.

4. Arrange pepper strips decoratively over squash mixture in serving dish.

UNITED STATES

Roasted Asparagus

Roasting asparagus imparts a delicious, nutty flavor that is further enhanced by the Parmesan cheese and lemon zest.

1. Preheat oven to 350°F. Arrange asparagus spears in a single layer on a nonstick roasting pan or jelly roll pan.

2. Sprinkle with lemon zest, salt, pepper, and Parmesan cheese. Drizzle with oil.

3. Roast 10 minutes, or until tender.

Note: If using very thick asparagus, peel the tough skin at the bottom of the stalk before cooking.

servings: 2 to 4

1 pound thick asparagus spears, rinsed and trimmed

Zest of 1 lemon, grated or thinly sliced

Salt to taste

Freshly ground pepper to taste

½ cup grated Parmesan cheese

¼ cup olive oil

Roasted Baby Potatoes with Olives, Lemon, and Garlic

servings: 6 to 8

4 pounds baby potatoes, such as Yukon Gold, scrubbed

2 tablespoons olive oil

½ pound good quality black olives (about 1 cup), pitted

Zest of 1 lemon, removed with a vegetable peeler and cut into thin strips

2 tablespoons peeled and chopped garlic

2 tablespoons fresh thyme, or 1½ teaspoons dried thyme, crumbled

Juice of 1 lemon

Salt and pepper to taste

The brininess of the olive purée and the tartness of the lemon juice are perfect counterpoints to the sweetness of the tender baby potatoes.

1. Preheat oven to 400°F. Cover potatoes with water and boil until barely cooked, about 15 minutes. Drain.

2. Cut potatoes into bite-size pieces. Toss with the olive oil. Place potatoes on a baking sheet and roast for 20 minutes, or until tender when pierced with a fork.

3. Purée olives in a food processor or blender.

4. While potatoes are still hot, toss with olive purée, lemon zest, garlic, thyme, lemon juice, salt, and pepper.

Wild Rice and Mushrooms

This mixture of rice, mushrooms, and seasonings makes an elegant side dish as well as an excellent stuffing for a chicken, or, by tripling the recipe, for an 18-pound turkey.

1. Melt butter over moderate heat in a 1-quart pot. Sauté garlic, onion, and mushrooms, stirring until onion is softened. Add brown rice and wild rice and stir about 5 minutes. Add broth, parsley, thyme, pepper, bell peppers, and carrot.

2. Cover pot and bring contents to a boil. Reduce heat, and simmer 35 to 45 minutes. Let stand, covered, for 10 minutes. Place in a serving bowl and sprinkle almonds over top.

servings: 4

4 tablespoons (½ stick) butter

3 cloves garlic, peeled and minced

1 onion, peeled and chopped

6 to 8 white mushrooms, thinly sliced

⅓ cup brown rice

⅓ cup wild rice

2 cups chicken or vegetable broth

1 tablespoon chopped fresh parsley

⅓ teaspoon dried thyme

   Pepper to taste

½ cup diced red bell pepper

½ cup diced green bell pepper

1 large carrot, peeled and diced

½ cup slivered almonds

Curried Mushrooms with Onions

servings: 4

- 1 tablespoon olive oil or butter, or a mixture of both
- 1 medium Vidalia or other sweet onion, peeled and finely chopped
- 1 pound white mushrooms, cleaned and sliced
- 2 teaspoons Madras or other Indian curry powder, or to taste
- ½ cup chicken or vegetable broth (or 1 bouillon cube dissolved in ½ cup water)
- ¼ cup heavy cream
- Pinch of salt
- Pepper to taste

This recipe, an original not to be found in any other cookbook, is the creation of an inventive UNIS parent who was in the mood for Indian food, had some ingredients on hand, and used her know-how to combine them. Serve with any kind of meat or as an appetizer with melba toasts.

1. Heat oil in a medium-size heavy saucepan, add onions and sauté over moderate heat until translucent, about 3 minutes.

2. Add mushrooms and stir until the liquid released evaporates and mushrooms are lightly browned.

3. Sprinkle in curry powder. Add broth and cream; stir to combine.

4. Cover and cook over low heat until the sauce thickens, about 30 minutes. During the last 5 to 10 minutes of cooking, stir constantly to prevent scorching.

5. Add salt and pepper to taste.

UNITED STATES

Red Cabbage with Apples

Mark Twain, the great American writer and wit, may have disdained the cabbage as "a cauliflower without an education." But the addition of apples, garlic, onions, and spices makes for a well-educated and delicious side dish.

1. Preheat oven to 375°F. Sauté cabbage, onion, and garlic in butter until wilted, about 10 minutes. Cover and simmer for 5 minutes.

2. Combine cabbage mixture with apples in a medium-size oven-proof casserole. Season with nutmeg, allspice, cinnamon, thyme, caraway seed, salt, pepper, and orange rind.

3. Add brown sugar, wine, and vinegar. Mix well, cover with a lid or aluminum foil, and bake at 375°F until tender, about 20 minutes. Check once or twice, adding a little hot water if cabbage seems too dry.

servings: 4 to 6

- **2 pounds red cabbage, outer leaves and center ribs removed, shredded**
- **2 cloves garlic, minced**
- **4 tablespoons (½ stick) butter**
- **1 pound apples, peeled, cored, and quartered**
- **1 large onion, sliced**
- **¼ teaspoon each nutmeg, allspice, cinnamon, thyme, and caraway seeds**
- **Salt and pepper to taste**
- **1 teaspoon grated orange rind**
- **2 tablespoons brown sugar**
- **½ cup dry white wine**
- **2 tablespoons white wine vinegar**
- **3 tablespoons hot water or more, if needed**

UNITED STATES

Savory Turkey Stuffing

servings: stuffing for 18-pound bird

- 7 to 8 cups homemade bread crumbs from 2½-pound loaf of white bread
- 1 tablespoon vegetable oil or butter
- Turkey liver, gizzard, heart, or giblets (optional)
- 1 cup water
- 1 large onion, peeled and diced
- 4 stalks celery, diced
- 1 carrot, grated
- 1½ teaspoons ground sage
- 1½ teaspoons dried thyme
- 1 teaspoon poultry seasoning
- Salt and pepper to taste
- 1½ cups chicken or turkey broth

One of many versions of traditional stuffing for Thanksgiving turkey.

1. To make bread crumbs, shred bread into small bits or chop in food processor, fitted with a steel blade.

2. Heat ½ tablespoon oil or butter in a large frying pan over moderately high heat, and add liver, gizzard, heart, and giblets, if using. Sauté until browned. Add 1 cup water, reduce heat and simmer 30 minutes or until soft. Remove from pan, let cool slightly, and dice into small pieces. Reserve liquid and set aside.

3. In same pan, heat remaining ½ tablespoon oil or butter, sauté onion and celery until onion is translucent.

4. In a large mixing bowl, combine bread crumbs, turkey pieces, onion, celery, carrot, sage, thyme, poultry seasoning, salt, and pepper. Toss mixture and let cool for 10 minutes. Add broth or reserved liquid and mix.

5. Immediately before cooking turkey, stuff cavity of bird until completely filled, but do not pack too tightly. Alternatively, stuffing may be cooked outside bird in a large ovenproof dish, in a 350°F oven, covered, for 45 minutes, and uncovered for an additional 20 minutes. For added flavor, place uncooked turkey neck and wing tips on top of stuffing mixture in dish while cooking.

Note: 1 cup of raisins, nuts, raw cranberries, diced dried apricots, cooked chestnuts, or mushrooms may be added to stuffing mixture.

Apricot Chutney

Chutneys, typically a sweet-and-spicy combination of fruits and spices cooked with vinegar, are endlessly varied. This one is distinguished by its tart and tangy taste.

1. Combine apricots, water, onion, and ¼ cup of the brown sugar in a large saucepan. Simmer uncovered until liquid is absorbed, about 25 minutes, stirring occasionally. Mash lightly.

2. In a separate pan, combine vinegar, salt, grated ginger, crystallized ginger, curry powder, cinnamon stick, and the remaining ¾ cup brown sugar. Simmer for 5 minutes. Add raisins, remove from heat, and let stand 5 minutes. Remove cinnamon stick. Pour into apricot mixture. Cook, stirring, until mixture is hot and thick, about 5 to 8 minutes.

3. The chutney can be stored in an airtight container in the refrigerator for 1 week or frozen for up to 3 months.

servings: 4 cups

2 cups chopped dried apricots

2 cups water

1 medium onion, finely chopped

1 cup light brown sugar

1½ cups cider vinegar

½ teaspoon salt

1 tablespoon peeled grated gingerroot

3 pieces crystallized ginger, minced

1 teaspoon curry powder

1 cinnamon stick

2 cups golden raisins

Cranberry Chutney

servings: 2 cups

3 cups fresh or frozen whole cranberries, rinsed, stems and discolored berries discarded

2-inch piece fresh gingerroot, peeled and minced

3 red Thai chili peppers*

1 cup fresh lime juice (from 3 or 4 limes)

Grated rind of 1 lime

1 cup dark brown sugar

The cranberry, a relative of the European lingonberry, has been a feature of American cooking since colonial times. This chutney, which is equally delicious with Indian, Thai, or American food, would make a tasty alternative to ordinary cranberry relish on Thanksgiving.

1. Combine and chop 2 cups of the cranberries, the ginger, and chili peppers in a food processor fitted with a steel blade.

2. Place mixture in a medium saucepan with remaining 1 cup cranberries, the lime juice, lime rind, and brown sugar. Stirring constantly over moderate heat, bring to a boil.

3. Reduce heat to low and stir occasionally until chutney thickens, about 20 to 30 minutes.

4. Cool and serve with poultry or game. The chutney can be stored in an airtight container in the refrigerator for 1 week or frozen for up to 3 months.

*Available at Asian food markets; see list of suppliers (page 319).

Red Pepper Hollandaise

Hollandaise, a classic sauce of egg yolks and melted butter, receives a contemporary interpretation in this gorgeous rosy sauce made with puréed sweet red pepper.

1. Roast the red bell pepper directly on burner flame, turning with tongs, until skin is blistered and blackened. Let cool uncovered. When cool, rub skin off. Core, seed, chop, and purée the pepper in a blender or food processor. Alternatively, in preheated broiler, broil about 2 inches from heat turning frequently, until skin is blistered and blackened, about 8 to 12 minutes.

2. Beat egg yolks with lemon juice and mustard in the top of a double boiler or in a stainless steel bowl set over a pot of simmering water. Stir in red pepper purée and continue stirring until sauce begins to thicken, 10 to 15 minutes. Stir in butter, a piece at a time, whisking constantly, until all butter has melted and been incorporated and sauce is smooth and thick, about 10 to 15 minutes. Stir in hot sauce and season with salt.

3. If sauce curdles, pour back into the blender or food processor immediately and blend until smooth. Serve over eggs Benedict, fish, or steamed asparagus.

servings: 4

- **1 red bell pepper**
- **2 egg yolks**
- **2 tablespoons lemon juice**
- **¼ teaspoon Dijon mustard**
- **6 tablespoons (¾ stick) frozen unsalted butter, cut into pieces**
- **¼ teaspoon hot pepper sauce (such as Tabasco)**
- **Salt to taste**

Sun-Dried Tomato and Pistachio Pesto

servings: 2½ cups

- 1 cup sun-dried tomatoes packed in oil
- ½ cup unshelled, unsalted roasted pistachio nuts
- ½ cup Pecorino Romano, Parmesan, Asiago or other aged, hard Italian cheese, cut into cubes
- 1 small clove garlic
- ½ cup extra-virgin olive oil

The pistachio nut, long used in Mediterranean and Middle Eastern cooking, makes a new appearance in this one-minute gourmet sauce created by an inventive UNIS family.

1. In the bowl of a food processor, place tomatoes, nuts, cheese, and garlic.

2. With the motor running, slowly add olive oil and blend until somewhat smooth but with a bit of texture remaining. (If a purée is desired, add more olive oil and continue processing.)

3. Toss with favorite cooked pasta and vegetables or use as a sauce for baked chicken breast, fresh tuna, or swordfish. Pesto will keep for about 2 weeks in an airtight container in the refrigerator.

Stuffed Zucchini

Zapallitos Rellenos

In Uruguay, zucchini and other squash have been a native crop cultivated since ancient times. The many Italian immigrants who settled in Uruguay readily adapted this vegetable to preparations familiar from their homeland.

1. To make bread crumbs, shred bread into small bits or chop in food processor, fitted with a steel blade.

2. Preheat oven to 375°F. Place zucchini in a lightly oiled oven-proof dish and bake for 30 minutes, or until soft but not mushy. Set aside to cool.

3. Heat olive oil in a small saucepan, over moderately high heat, and sauté onions until golden.

4. In a bowl, quickly soak the ½ cup bread crumbs in milk. Drain off excess milk. Mix bread crumbs with cooked onions. Add egg and salt and mix until smooth.

5. Raise oven temperature to 400°F. Cut zucchini in half lengthwise and scoop out inside pulp. Coarsely chop pulp and add to bread mixture. Stir to combine.

6. Fill zucchini shells with mixture. Cover with the ¼ cup buttered bread crumbs and bake for 20 minutes, or until bread crumbs are golden brown.

servings: 4

½ cup bread crumbs (made from day-old French bread), plus ¼ cup bread crumbs mixed with 1½ tablespoons melted butter

2 medium zucchini

2 tablespoons olive oil

3 tablespoons minced onion

¼ cup warm milk

1 egg, beaten

1 teaspoon salt

desserts

AUSTRIA

Emperor's Nonsense

Kaiserschmarren

Legend has it that at an Austrian Emperor's dinner, a new cook made a mistake and thought he had burned the dessert ("What a nonsense!"). It had to be served to the Emperor anyway, who liked it very much. Since then, this dish has been called Emperor's Nonsense.

1. In a large bowl, whisk flour, salt, egg yolks, 1 tablespoon of the sugar, milk, and raisins into a thin batter.

2. Melt 2 tablespoons of the butter in a 10-inch skillet and pour in half the batter so that it fills the pan evenly. The batter should be ¼ to ½ inch thick.

3. Fry until golden brown on each side, about 5 minutes altogether. Cook remaining batter in the same manner.

4. Shred the 2 pancakes into little pieces with two forks. Sprinkle with remaining 1 teaspoon sugar. Serve with stewed cranberries or other fruit.

Note: The batter can be prepared ahead and quickly cooked after dinner for dessert. A bit of vanilla sugar (recipes on pages 245 and 271) and a few drops of Grand Marnier may be added.

servings: 6 to 8

1½ cups all-purpose flour
   Pinch of salt
3 egg yolks
1 tablespoon sugar, plus 1 teaspoon for topping
4 tablespoons (½ stick) butter
1 cup milk
½ cup raisins

AUSTRIA

Malakoff Torte

servings: 12

1 cup milk

3 tablespoons rum or Cognac

20 tablespoons (2½ sticks) unsalted butter, at room temperature

6 egg yolks

3 ounces sugar

1¼ cups ground almonds, plus 1 cup chopped almonds, for garnish

1 cup heavy cream

40 ladyfingers

½ cup confectioners' sugar, or 1 cup heavy cream, whipped, for decorating top of cake

"Malakoff" is the name given to various classic cakes that contain nuts. This confection is one of many luscious desserts from Vienna, the pastry capital of the world.

1. Wrap aluminum foil or plastic wrap around the outside of a 9½-inch springform pan to prevent seepage. Secure with a rubber band or string.

2. In a bowl, mix milk with 1 tablespoon of the rum or Cognac. Set aside.

3. In a large bowl, beat butter until very soft with an electric mixer. Blend in egg yolks, sugar, ground almonds, remaining 2 tablespoons rum or Cognac, and the heavy cream. Set mixture aside.

4. Dip ladyfingers, one at a time, into milk-rum mixture and cover bottom of springform pan with a layer of ladyfingers. Add a layer of almond mixture just thick enough to cover ladyfingers.

5. Alternate layers of ladyfingers and almond mixture, ending with ladyfingers (There should be 3 layers in all). Cover with aluminum foil or plastic wrap and weigh down with a wooden board or plate. Refrigerate for at least 24 hours.

6. Uncover, carefully run a thin, sharp knife around the inside of the pan, and release torte. Top with confectioners' sugar or whipped cream. Press chopped almonds around the sides or sprinkle over top.

AUSTRIA

Ischler Tarts

Ischler Törtchen

Ground almonds lend a slightly crunchy texture to these petite and delicious Austrian jam tarts.

1. With a pastry cutter, or in the bowl of a food processor fitted with a steel blade, or with two kitchen knives, cut butter into flour until mixture resembles fine bread crumbs.

2. Add almonds and lemon juice and pulse briefly, or knead by hand, until dough forms a ball.

3. Flatten dough ball, wrap in plastic, and let rest 30 minutes in refrigerator.

4. Remove dough from refrigerator and allow to come almost to room temperature. Roll out slightly chilled dough to ¼-inch thickness.

5. Preheat oven to 350°F. With a floured cookie cutter or drinking glass, cut dough into 3- to 3½-inch circles. Cut 3 small holes in half of the circles.

6. Place on baking sheet and bake until lightly brown, 10 to 15 minutes. Allow to cool.

7. Spread jam on plain circles, place perforated circles on top. Sprinkle with confectioners' sugar.

servings: 12 to 15

16 tablespoons (2 sticks) butter, at room temperature

1 cup all-purpose flour

½ cup finely ground blanched almonds

1 tablespoon fresh lemon juice

⅔ cup apricot or red currant jam

¼ to ½ cup confectioners' sugar, for sprinkling

desserts   **243**

CANADA

Canadian Spice Cake

servings: 10

8 tablespoons (1 stick) butter, softened

1 cup brown sugar

1 can (10¾ ounces) condensed tomato soup

1⅓ cups all-purpose flour, sifted

1 teaspoon cinnamon

½ teaspoon ground cloves

½ teaspoon baking soda

½ teaspoon ground nutmeg

½ teaspoon salt

½ cup each currants, raisins or dried cranberries, and walnuts or macadamia nuts

Although tomato soup may seem a surprising ingredient for this recipe, which dates from the 1940s, it gives a rich, velvety texture to the cake.

1. Preheat oven to 325°F. Grease an 8-inch square pan.

2. Blend butter with sugar. Gradually add the tomato soup.

3. Into a large bowl, sift the flour, cinnamon, cloves, baking soda, nutmeg, and salt.

4. Add the flour mixture to soup mixture and blend well. Stir in currants, raisins or cranberries, and nuts.

5. Pour into pan and bake 45 minutes. Let cool and cut into squares.

Croatian Fritters with Brandy

Fritule prshulate

A typical sweet from the Dalmatia region of Croatia. The brandy, or grappa, plus fresh orange and lemon zests makes these fritters light and flavorful.

1. For the starter, in a small bowl, dissolve sugar in the lukewarm water, flour and yeast. Allow yeast to dissolve and bubble, about 15 minutes.

2. For the fritters, combine cooled potatoes, eggs, vanilla sugar, rum, lemon zest, orange zest, *grappa* or brandy, nutmeg, and starter.

3. Mix flour, salt, and raisins together, and add to potato mixture (if necessary, a little warm milk or water may be added to thin). The batter should have the consistency of light bread dough.

4. Beat fritter mixture with a wooden spoon for 15 minutes (or in an electric mixer fitted with a dough hook for 10 minutes) until dough becomes smooth and glossy. Cover and put in a warm place for 1 hour to rise.

5. In a large heavy pot, heat oil to 350°F with a frying thermometer (try to maintain this temperature throughout frying). Dip a spoon into hot oil. Take spoonfuls of fritter mixture and drop them into the hot oil. Fry until golden, about 2 to 3 minutes on each side. Drain on paper towels. Serve hot, sprinkled with sugar.

servings: 25 fritters

starter

- 1½ tablespoons sugar
- 1 cup lukewarm water
- 2 tablespoons all-purpose flour
- 1 tablespoon fresh yeast, crumbled, or 1 package dried yeast

fritters

- 1 pound white potatoes, boiled, peeled, and riced or mashed
- 2 eggs, beaten
- Vanilla sugar (¼ teaspoon vanilla extract mixed with ¼ cup sugar)
- 2 tablespoons rum
- 2 teaspoons fresh lemon zest (rind of 1 lemon)
- 2 tablespoons fresh orange zest (rind of 1 medium orange)
- 1 teaspoon *grappa* or brandy (optional)
- ½ teaspoon grated nutmeg
- 1¾ cups all-purpose flour
- 1 teaspoon salt
- ⅓ cup raisins
- ¼ cup warm milk or water (optional)
- 4 cups vegetable oil, for frying
- Sugar, for sprinkling

DENMARK

Danish Ice Cream

Gloedeis

---

servings: 4

2 cups heavy cream

6 egg yolks

7 to 8 tablespoons sugar

Seeds of 1 split vanilla bean or
½ teaspoon vanilla extract

A simple ice cream can be made right in the freezer without using an ice-cream maker.

1. Place a 4-cup flat-bottomed glass dish in the freezer for at least 15 minutes.

2. In a mixing bowl, beat cream with an electric mixer until very stiff.

3. In a separate bowl, whisk egg yolks, sugar, and vanilla seeds or extract.

4. Fold cream into egg mixture and pour mixture into frozen dish. Freeze for at least 4 hours. Serve with fresh berries or other fruit.

Variation: For rainbow ice cream, divide the ingredients above into three portions. Mix 1 portion with 4 ounces melted, cooled chocolate. Mix a second portion with ½ cup chilled puréed strawberries. Pour the plain vanilla portion into a pre-frozen deep glass dish and freeze for 30 minutes to 1 hour. Pour chocolate portion over vanilla and freeze for an additional 30 minutes to 1 hour. Pour strawberry portion over the chocolate portion and freeze for 30 minutes to 1 hour.

FRANCE

Chocolate Mousse

Mousse au Chocolat

Children growing up in France are taught the basics of French cuisine at their mother's knees. Recalling the experience of learning to make chocolate mousse, a UNIS mother says, "I was only allowed to do two things: hold the bowl and lick the chocolate when my mother was finished. Now I make mousse with my own children and let them do the same two things."

1. Over very low heat, melt chocolate in the top part of a double boiler set over water. Slowly add Cognac or Grand Marnier, espresso, and orange juice, stirring thoroughly between additions. Let cool to room temperature.

2. Add egg yolks, one at a time, to cooled chocolate mixture. Beat thoroughly after adding each yolk.

3. Beat egg whites until stiff. Gently fold into chocolate mixture.

4. Whip cream with sugar and vanilla until stiff. Gently fold half the whipped cream into chocolate mixture, reserving the rest for garnish.

5. When mixture is evenly blended, pour into a decorative serving bowl or individual serving cups. Refrigerate, covered, for 3 to 4 hours. Serve with remaining whipped cream and slivers of candied orange peel.

servings: 6

8 ounces high-quality bittersweet dark chocolate, (preferably Lindt), broken into pieces

2 tablespoons Cognac or Grand Marnier

1 tablespoon strong espresso coffee

1 tablespoon orange juice

4 large eggs, separated

1 cup heavy cream

2 tablespoons sugar

½ teaspoon pure vanilla extract

Slivers of candied orange peel, for garnish (optional)

FRANCE

Almond Torte

Tarte aux Amandes

servings: 6 to 8

6 large egg whites

¾ cup plus 2 tablespoons sugar

1 cup finely ground almonds

¼ cup all-purpose flour

8 tablespoons (1 stick) melted butter

1 tablespoon confectioners' sugar

This is inspired by a version of frangipane, *the classic French confection made with ground almonds.*

1. Preheat oven to 375°F. Grease a 10-inch solid-bottom tart pan (or equivalent). In a large bowl, combine egg whites and sugar and whisk lightly.

2. Add almonds, flour, and butter and mix well. Pour into tart pan. Bake for 50 minutes.

3. Place confectioners' sugar in a mesh strainer and shake gently over top of torte. The torte tastes best when freshly baked.

FRANCE

Raspberry and Custard Pastry

Clafoutis aux Framboises

The easy-to-prepare clafoutis *originated in the Limousin region of France, where black cherries are traditionally used. The dish takes its name from the word* clafir, *meaning "to fill" in the provincial dialect. Peaches and other tender summer fruits can be added or substituted for the berries or cherries.*

1. Preheat oven to 375°F. Melt butter in a deep 9-inch pie or cake pan.

2. Mix flour, sugar, baking powder, and salt in a large bowl. Add milk and stir until smooth.

3. Pour batter into pan. Pour fruit, including any juices, into the middle of the batter. Do not stir. Bake 40 to 50 minutes, until firm. Serve warm or cold with whipped cream, if desired.

servings: 4 to 6

3 tablespoons unsalted butter

1 cup all-purpose flour

1 cup sugar

1½ teaspoons baking powder

½ teaspoon salt

¾ cup whole milk

2½ cups fresh raspberries, sweetened with ⅓ cup sugar, (or 12-ounce bag unsweetened frozen berries), or pitted black cherries

Whipped cream (optional)

Flourless Chocolate Cake

Gâteau au Chocolat

servings: 10 to 12

- 16 tablespoons (2 sticks) unsalted butter, plus more for greasing pan
- 2 tablespoons plus ¾ cup light brown sugar
- 9 ounces high-quality dark chocolate (such as Lindt or Valrhona), broken into pieces
- 1 tablespoon solid vegetable shortening or oil
- 1 teaspoon vanilla extract
- 8 large eggs, separated
- ¼ teaspoon salt
- Confectioners' sugar, for dusting

This rich cake would make a wonderful gift. Serve plain, with vanilla ice cream, or with a dollop of whipped cream.

1. Preheat oven to 300°F. Generously butter a 10-inch or 10-cup Bundt pan or springform pan. Sprinkle sides and bottom with 2 tablespoons of the sugar and shake out excess sugar. Melt chocolate in the top of a double boiler set over simmering water. Stir butter and shortening into chocolate. When fully incorporated, remove pan from heat. Mix in the remaining ¾ cup vanilla and the sugar.

2. Add egg yolks, one at a time, to chocolate mixture. Beat well with electric mixer after each addition. Let cool.

3. In a large non-aluminum bowl, beat egg whites with salt until soft peaks form.

4. Gently stir one quarter of the egg whites into the chocolate mixture to lighten it. Fold in remaining egg whites.

5. Pour batter into prepared pan. Bake, undisturbed, for 1 hour and 15 minutes.

6. Remove from oven and place cake pan on a rack for 10 minutes. While still warm, run a knife around inside edge of pan and unmold onto a large plate by holding plate over pan and quickly inverting. (If using a springform pan, loosen sides before inverting.)

7. When cool, dust with confectioners' sugar.

FRANCE

Three Kings Cake

Galette des Rois

From a recipe book kept for five generations by a family who ran a restaurant in Provence, this cake is customarily served on January 6, the feast of the Epiphany, commemorating the arrival of the Three Kings in Bethlehem to pay homage to the infant Jesus. French legend has it that they came loaded with gifts, including this cake. Traditionally a fava bean, fève, is placed in the filling of the cake before it is baked. The person who finds the fève becomes King or Queen for the day and gets all wishes granted, a great source of suspense and entertainment for all.

servings: 6

- 7 tablespoons butter, softened
- 1 cup finely ground almonds
- 1 cup sugar
- ½ cup rum
- 2 eggs, plus 1 egg, separated, for glazing
- ½ pound frozen puff pastry, thawed but still very cold
- Butter, for greasing
- 1 fava bean (optional)

1. Preheat oven to 425°F. Whip butter, almonds, sugar, and rum together in a large bowl using a whisk or electric hand mixer, or in a food processor fitted with a steel blade. After about 4 minutes, or when mixture is light and fluffy, add the 2 eggs, one at a time, whipping until sugar dissolves, about 1 minute.

2. Divide puff pastry in half. On a lightly floured work surface, roll each half into a 9-inch circle, about ⅛ inch thick. Place 1 circle on a buttered cookie sheet.

3. Spread filling evenly, leaving a 1-inch edge. Brush edges of pastry with beaten egg white. (Place fava bean in filling, if desired.) Place remaining pastry circle on top. Brush off any flour on upper pastry. Firmly press edges of pastry together to seal. With a sharp knife, trim edges and cut 5 or 6 evenly spaced decorative notches on the outside rim of the cake. Mix yolk into remaining beaten egg white, and lightly brush on pastry.

4. Bake for 15 minutes. Do not open oven door or pastry will not puff.

5. Brush top again with remaining egg mixture. Reduce heat to 350°F and bake for 45 minutes, or until the pastry is firm.

FRANCE

Minute Crêpes

Crêpes Minute

---

servings: 6 crêpes

4 tablespoons (½ stick) butter, plus more for frying

1⅓ cups warm milk

1 cup all-purpose flour

3 large eggs

½ teaspoon salt

2 tablespoons water

Most recipes for crêpes require a long wait while the batter "rests." These crêpes are absolutely delicious and take just minutes to make.

1. Add 4 tablespoons of the butter to warm milk.

2. In a medium bowl, mix flour, eggs, salt, and the water. Stir in milk mixture.

3. Heat a little butter in a nonstick frying pan. When moderately hot, ladle ½ cup batter into pan, tilting and spreading evenly to make a very thin layer. Cook until bottom is lightly brown and edge lifts easily from pan. Crêpe should slide easily in pan. Flip over with a spatula and cook the other side for 1 to 2 minutes. The crêpe should brown in spots. Continue making crêpes and stacking them atop each other until all batter is used.

Note: For dessert, fill crêpes with grated chocolate and thinly sliced bananas, or a few drops freshly squeezed lemon juice and sugar. For a savory lunch dish, fill crêpes with ham and melted Râclette or Gruyère cheese or mushrooms in a béchamel sauce.

FRANCE

Fruit-and-Pastry–Filled Cabbage Leaves

Tartouillats

This unusual French dessert is made with the unlikely combination of cabbage leaves filled with a pancake-like batter and brandy-spiked cherry custard. The use of cherries is typical of Burgundy, whereas in the Nivernais and Morvan regions chopped apples would be used.

1. Sift flour with salt into a bowl. Stir in sugar and make a well in the center. Add eggs and ½ cup of the milk. Whisk until mixture is smooth. Stir in remaining milk to form a batter. Cover the bowl and let batter stand for about 30 minutes.

2. Preheat oven to 400°F.

3. Bring a large pan of water to a boil. Blanch cabbage leaves until somewhat limp, about 5 minutes. Drain and blot dry. If stems of the leaves are large and tough, cut them out. Butter eight 6-ounce ramekins (ovenproof ceramic cups), and line them with the cabbage leaves.

4. Stir the fruit and marc or kirsch into batter. Spoon mixture into cabbage leaves. Trim edges of leaves with scissors to leave a neat, generous border not more than 1 inch above the ramekin edges.

5. Set ramekins on a baking sheet with a rim and bake in the center of the oven until the filling is firm and cabbage leaves are slightly brown, 25 to 35 minutes. The filling will puff up but shrink again as it cools.

6. Let *tartouillats* cool slightly before unmolding onto a serving dish or individual plates. They can be cooked several hours ahead. Serve warm or at room temperature.

Note: Three Bosc pears or apples, peeled, cored, and diced can be substituted for the cherries.

servings: 8

1 cup all-purpose flour

½ teaspoon salt

1¼ cup sugar

4 large eggs

1 cup milk

8 large rounded cabbage leaves, with no holes

2 cups black cherries (about 1 pound), pitted

2 tablespoons marc (brandy) or kirsch (cherry brandy)

GERMANY

Plum Torte

Pflaumentorte

---

servings: 10

1½ cups all-purpose flour

¾ teaspoon baking powder

¼ cup sugar

¾ pound (3 sticks) unsalted butter, softened

1 egg

3 pounds plums, pits removed, cut into ¼-inch pieces

Sugar and cinnamon, for sprinkling

Plums are the best-known topping for this torte, but apricots or cherries will work equally well. Serve with sweetened whipped cream, flavored with a couple drops of almond extract.

1. In a small bowl, combine flour, baking powder, and sugar.

2. Cut in butter using your fingertips until mixture resembles fine bread crumbs. Add the egg and continue to blend until dough is smooth. Refrigerate dough for 30 minutes.

3. Preheat oven to 425°F. Butter a 9-inch springform pan. Gently press dough against the bottom of the pan. Place plums on dough, leaving a narrow border of dough around the edge.

4. Place torte in the oven and immediately lower heat to 350°F. Bake for 35 to 45 minutes.

5. Sprinkle sugar and cinnamon on torte while it is still warm.

Cherry and Almond Bread Pastry

Kirschen-Michel

A special dessert in the German state of Hessen, where cherries are the first fresh fruit of the season.

1. Preheat oven to 350°F. Butter a 10-cup ovenproof dish. In a large bowl, soak bread slices in milk.

2. In a medium bowl, beat butter, sugar, and egg yolks until frothy. Stir in cinnamon, lemon peel, and soaked bread.

3. In a separate bowl, beat egg whites until foamy. Gently add cherries and bread mixture, stirring to combine. Pour batter into baking dish, sprinkle with almonds, and bake for 1 hour, or until puffed and golden.

servings: 4

- 4 thin slices day-old bread
- 2 cups milk
- 8 tablespoons (1 stick) butter, at room temperature
- ½ cup sugar
- 4 eggs, separated
- 1 teaspoon ground cinnamon
  Grated peel of ½ lemon
- 2 pounds cherries, pits removed
- ¼ cup chopped almonds

German Coffee Ring

Frankfurter Kranz

servings: 6

pastry batter

10 tablespoons (1¼ sticks) unsalted butter or margarine

¾ cup sugar

4 eggs

1½ cups all-purpose flour

⅔ cup cornstarch

3 teaspoons baking powder

filling and frosting

4 tablespoons (½ stick) butter, at room temperature

¾ cup sifted confectioners' sugar

2 cups prepared vanilla pudding, at room temperature

crunchy topping *(krokant)*

1 tablespoon butter

4 tablespoons sugar

½ cup chopped walnuts or almonds

A key feature of this wreath-shaped cake is the nut-brittle topping, called krokant. *The pudding-style frosting and filling are typically German. Originating in Frankfurt, this dessert is traditionally served on Saturdays and Sundays with an assortment of other cakes.*

1. Preheat oven to 350°F. Grease a 10-inch Bundt pan.

2. For pastry batter, in a large bowl, with an electric mixer, beat butter or margarine and sugar until fluffy. Add eggs, one at a time.

3. In a separate bowl, mix flour, cornstarch, and baking powder. Add flour mixture to egg mixture 1 tablespoon at a time, beating well after each addition. Pour batter into prepared pan and bake for 50 to 60 minutes, or until toothpick inserted in center comes out clean. Let cool on a wire rack.

4. For the filling and frosting, beat butter and sugar together in a medium bowl. Add pudding to mixture 1 tablespoon at a time, beating well after each addition. Refrigerate.

5. For the topping, in a small pan, heat butter and sugar. Add chopped nuts and cook over moderate heat, stirring constantly, until sugar mixture turns golden brown, about 5 minutes. Immediately pour nut mixture onto aluminum foil. Allow to cool. Bend up edges of foil and cover with another sheet. Using a rolling pin, break up topping into small pieces.

6. Cut cooled cake twice horizontally to form three separate layers. Place first layer on a serving platter. Spread one-third of filling on layer. Place middle cake layer on top and spread another third of filling on top. Add remaining layer. Spread remaining filling around sides and top of cake. Unwrap topping and gently apply evenly to top and sides of cake.

Greek Custard Pastry

Galaktoboureko

In Greece, thick sheep's or goat's milk is used to make this luscious flaky phyllo pastry filled with a rich custard.

1. In a large saucepan, scald 7 cups of the milk with the vanilla bean. Cool slightly. Remove vanilla bean and scrape seeds into milk.

2. In a large bowl, beat eggs until frothy, about 2 minutes. Gradually beat in sugar and cream of rice cereal. Add vanilla and remaining 1 cup milk.

3. Add egg mixture to warmed milk. Place saucepan over low heat until mixture thickens, about 10 to 15 minutes, stirring constantly. *Do not allow mixture to boil.* Pour into a bowl, cover with plastic wrap, and let cool.

4. Preheat oven to 400°F. Lightly butter a 9 x 11 x 2-inch baking dish. Lay a sheet of phyllo in dish and brush lightly with melted butter. Layer about 12 sheets, buttering every other sheet. Spread cooled custard evenly over phyllo. Layer remaining phyllo sheets on top in the same manner. Trim edges to 1 inch and fold in. (Keep phyllo sheets covered with a damp cloth until using.)

5. Bake 15 minutes. Lower heat to 350°F and bake another 45 minutes, or until top of pastry is golden brown and flaky.

6. While pastry is cooking, prepare syrup. In a medium saucepan, combine all ingredients except vanilla. Bring to a boil over low heat, stirring constantly, until syrup thickens, about 15 minutes. Remove the lemon, orange, and cinnamon stick. Let syrup cool, add vanilla, and stir to mix. Pour over warm pastry.

---

servings: 40 pieces

pastry

8 cups (2 quarts) milk

1 vanilla bean

6 large eggs

2 cups sugar

1 cup cream of rice cereal

¼ teaspoon pure vanilla extract

1 pound phyllo pastry

1 pound (4 sticks) unsalted butter, melted

syrup

3 cups water

3 cups sugar

½ medium orange

½ medium lemon

1 cinnamon stick

¼ teaspoon pure vanilla extract, or 1 vanilla bean, split lengthwise (for more intense flavor)

Sweet Potato and Coconut Pudding

Pudding aux Patates Douces et aux Noix de Coco

---

servings: 8

½ cup sugar

1½ cups boiled, peeled, and mashed sweet potatoes

1 cup freshly grated coconut, about ½ peeled fresh coconut

½ teaspoon ground cinnamon

¼ teaspoon ground or grated nutmeg

¼ teaspoon ground allspice

4 tablespoons (½ stick) butter, melted

¾ cup milk

½ cup water

2 eggs, lightly beaten

Sweet potatoes have been cultivated for food in the Americas for nearly 5,000 years. They grow abundantly in the West Indies, where they appear in many dishes, including this delicous tropical pudding.

1. Preheat oven to 400°F and butter a 6-cup ovenproof baking dish.

2. In a medium bowl, beat together sugar, sweet potatoes, coconut, cinnamon, nutmeg, and allspice until smooth. Add butter, milk, and the water, and beat thoroughly.

3. Add eggs to mixture, one at a time, beating after each addition until creamy and smooth.

4. Put mixture in prepared baking dish and bake about 30 minutes, or until golden brown.

HUNGARY

My Grandmother's Dobos Torte

Dobos Torta

A uniquely Hungarian torte layered with rich butter cream and crispy wafers. It is often served on holidays.

1. Preheat oven to 375°F. Grease outside bottoms of four 8-inch round cake pans with butter.

2. In a large bowl, beat egg yolks with sugar until light. Mix in cake flour, baking powder, and 1 teaspoon of the vanilla.

3. In another bowl, beat egg whites until stiff with an electric mixer. Gently fold into yolk mixture.

4. Spread about ⅓ cup of cake batter onto the bottom of each inverted cake pan, forming an even layer. Do not let batter spread to the edge (keep within ½ inch). Repeat on as many inverted pans as the oven can accommodate at one time.

5. Place inverted cake pans in the oven and bake for about 8 to 12 minutes. Layers are done when they spring back when touched. Closely watch layers, as they burn easily. Remove from oven and let cool for 10 minutes. Gently scrape each layer off bottom of pan with a thin-edged knife and place on a kitchen towel or a rack lined with paper towels, to cool further. Batter will yield 8 to 12 layers.

6. For mocha butter cream frosting, beat together the 16 tablespoons butter, the cocoa, confectioners' sugar, remaining 1 teaspoon vanilla, and coffee. Put a dab of frosting on the center of a serving plate to prevent layers from slipping. Place a cake layer on the plate and spread with a thin layer of frosting. Continue until all layers are used, making sure to reserve some frosting to cover top and sides of cake.

servings: 8

16 tablespoons (2 sticks) unsalted butter, plus more for greasing

6 eggs, separated

1 cup sugar

1 cup cake flour, sifted

¼ teaspoon baking powder

2 teaspoons pure vanilla extract

4 tablespoons cocoa

1 pound confectioners' sugar

2 tablespoons cold coffee

INDIA

Indian Semolina Pudding

Sheero

---

servings: 6 to 8

....

clarified butter *(ghee)*

---

2 pounds (8 sticks) unsalted butter

1 tablespoon water

(or ¾ cup ready made *ghee*)*

pudding

1½ cups semolina or farina (Cream of Wheat)

1 tablespoon powdered almonds

1 tablespoon pistachio nuts

2 to 3 tablespoons ground cardamom

Pinch of saffron

3½ to 4 cups milk, warmed

1¼ cups sugar

1 tablespoon red or golden raisins

Slivered almonds, for garnish

A traditional dessert from the Gujarat region of India. It uses ghee, *or clarified butter, which is an important element of Indian cuisine. This recipe is prepared to honor Lord Vishnu, the second member of the Hindu trinity of Brahma, Vishnu, and Shiva.*

1. To make *ghee*, in a heavy saucepan, melt butter over moderate heat, stirring constantly. When butter starts to brown and a light yellow liquid separates from whitish residue, carefully add water. Remove from heat. Strain *ghee* through a fine metal strainer set over a bowl. Yield will be approximately 4 cups. *Ghee* can be stored in a glass jar in the refrigerator for 3 months.

2. For pudding, in a large pot, heat ½ to ¾ cup *ghee* over moderately low heat. Add semolina or farina and stir until mixture is aromatic and turns light pink. Set aside.

3. In a large bowl, add almonds, pistachios, cardamom, and saffron to warmed milk. Stir mixture into semolina. Cook over moderate heat for 5 minutes, stirring to prevent lumps. Lower heat to a simmer. Once milk is absorbed, semolina should be soft. If not, gradually add more milk. Add sugar and stir for 4 to 5 minutes. (Some *ghee* will separate from the mixture when semolina is fully cooked.)

4. Add raisins. Spoon pudding into a serving dish and decorate with slivered almonds.

*Available at Indian food markets; see list of suppliers (page 319).

IRAQ

Baklava

Almond and Phyllo Pastry with Syrup

One of the grandest pastries of the Middle East, baklava is served at every occasion.

1. In a bowl, combine nuts, sugar, cinnamon, and allspice.

2. Butter all surfaces of a 13 x 9 x 2-inch baking dish.

3. On a large work surface, lay out phyllo sheets flat on a piece of plastic wrap and then cover with damp paper towels to prevent them from drying out.

4. Preheat oven to 350°F. Place 1 sheet of phyllo in prepared pan and brush top with melted butter. Continue this process until at least 10 sheets are layered. Gently spread nut mixture evenly on the top layer.

5. Place each remaining sheet of phyllo over the filling, brushing each layer with butter.

6. With the tip of a small knife, score 4 squares by 6 squares through the top couple of layers of phyllo (24 squares in all). Then score each square in half diagonally to make 48 triangles.

7. Bake for 35 to 40 minutes until top layer turns golden brown.

8. Prepare syrup by placing all syrup ingredients in a medium saucepan. Bring to a boil. Reduce heat and simmer for 10 minutes. Let cool completely.

9. When the pastry has cooled, slowly pour half the syrup evenly over top. After 20 minutes, slowly pour on remaining syrup.

10. Let pastry rest for several hours before cutting. Using a sharp knife, cut through all layers along the scored lines. Gently lift out triangles with a spatula and fork. Serve at room temperature.

Note: Baklava is best made a day before serving.

---

servings: 48 pieces

pastry

2 cups finely chopped fresh blanched almonds, walnuts, or pistachios, or a combination of the three

½ cup sugar

1 tablespoon ground cinnamon

1 teaspoon ground allspice

16 tablespoons (2 sticks) unsalted butter, melted over hot water in the top of a double boiler

1 pound phyllo dough

syrup

12 cups sugar

½ cup water

2 teaspoons lemon juice

1 teaspoon rose water, orange-flavored water, or pure vanilla extract

desserts 261

My Sainted Grandmother's Shortbread Hearts

servings: 24 cookies

16 tablespoons (2 sticks) unsalted butter, softened

½ cup brown sugar

⅛ teaspoon salt

1¾ cups all-purpose flour

1¼ cup potato starch*

The secret ingredient of these cookies is the potato starch, which makes them extremely light.

1. Beat butter, sugar, and salt with an electric mixer until fluffy, about 5 minutes.

2. Sift together flour and potato starch. Add to butter mixture, blending thoroughly.

3. Dust dough with flour. Between 2 sheets of plastic wrap or waxed paper, roll out dough to ¼-inch thickness. Slip onto cookie sheet and freeze for 30 minutes or overnight.

4. Remove cookie sheet from freezer and remove wrap or paper. Preheat oven to 300°F.

5. Cut dough into hearts or other shapes, using a 2-inch cookie cutter or by hand. Place on baking sheet and bake for 30 minutes, or until golden brown. Let cool on baking sheet for 5 minutes before removing.

*Available in many supermarkets.

Jackfruit Pudding

Nangka Puding

Jackfruit, nangka *in Malay, is the national fruit of Malaysia. Sweeter than a peach, a jackfruit is the size of a watermelon and has many seeds. In Malaysia, the seeds are boiled in salted water, like beans, and served with tea.*

1. Preheat oven to 350°F. Grease an 8-cup baking dish (approximately 11 x 7 inches). In a large bowl, mix sugar with coconut milk. Stir in eggs. Pour in milk, jackfruit with syrup, salt, and vanilla; mix again.

2. Pour mixture into baking dish. Bake until top becomes slightly brown, 20 to 25 minutes. Let pudding cool before serving.

*Available at Asian food markets; see list of suppliers (page 319).

servings: 8

½ cup sugar

1 can (13.5 ounces) unsweetened coconut milk

6 eggs, beaten

1 can (12 ounces) evaporated milk

1 can (10 ounces) jackfruit,* with syrup, chopped

½ teaspoon salt

1 teaspoon pure vanilla extract

Bananas Baked with Orange Juice

Plátanos al Horno con Naranja

servings: 4

4 bananas, peeled

8 to 10 tablespoons dark brown sugar

2 teaspoons ground cinnamon

2 tablespoons unsalted butter

⅓ to ½ cup orange juice

A dessert of Mayan origin from Mérida, in the Yucatán peninsula in Mexico, where it is served on festive occasions.

1. Preheat oven to 350°F. Arrange bananas in baking dish and sprinkle with sugar and cinnamon.

2. Pour on orange juice and dot with butter.

3. Bake for 30 minutes or until bananas are soft, the sugar has caramelized, and the orange juice has turned into a sauce. Serve with vanilla ice cream.

MIDDLE EAST

Almond Fingers

Assabih bil Looz

Rose water, used in this recipe, is a time-honored ingredient in Middle Eastern desserts.

1. Preheat oven to 350°F. Butter a 9 x 13 x 2-inch baking pan.

2. In a small bowl, mix sugar, almonds, cinnamon, and rose water.

3. Slice each phyllo sheet lengthwise into 3 rectangles. Keep covered with plastic wrap until used, as phyllo dries out quickly. Brush 1 rectangle with melted butter. Place about 1 tablespoon of the nut mixture in the center about 1 inch from the edge. Fold 1 inch of phyllo over filling, fold in sides, and roll into a cigar shape. Repeat process with all the phyllo rectangles. Place rolls in a row in baking pan.

3. Bake for 30 minutes, or until pastry is golden. Remove, let cool, and dust with confectioners' sugar.

servings: 4 to 5

4 tablespoons (½ stick) unsalted butter, melted

¼ cup sugar

¾ cup ground almonds

1 teaspoon ground cinnamon

1 teaspoon rose water

12 sheets phyllo pastry

   Confectioners' sugar, for dusting

MYANMAR

Burmese Semolina Pudding

Sanwinmakin

servings: 16 to 20

2⅔ cups semolina or farina (Cream of Wheat)

1¾ cups sugar

1½ teaspoons salt

8 cups unsweetened coconut milk

8 tablespoons (1 stick) butter or peanut oil

3 egg whites, stiffly beaten

1 cup raisins

¾ cup sesame seeds, or ¼ cup blanched almonds, thinly sliced

A member of the UNIS community recalls enjoying this dessert as a novice priest in Burma when he was a child. When he was asked to try it by an older monk, he liked the taste of the pudding very much and felt warmed by the good will of the Order of Monks of Lord Buddha.

1. In a large bowl, stir semolina or farina, sugar, and salt into coconut milk. Let stand 30 minutes.

2. Pour mixture into a large pot. Bring to a boil, stirring constantly. Add butter or peanut oil. Reduce heat to low, and cook, stirring steadily in one direction until thickened. Remove from heat and let cool. Fold in the egg whites and raisins.

3. Preheat oven to 325°F. Butter a 2-quart baking pan or casserole. Pour pudding into pan. Sprinkle top with sesame seeds or almonds. Bake for 45 minutes. Cool completely. Remove from pan and serve in slices.

Pavlova

Meringue Cake with Whipped Cream

This felicitous combination of meringue and cream was created to celebrate the visit of the famous Russian ballerina Anna Pavlova to Australia and New Zealand in the late 1920s. There has been a friendly rivalry ever since between Australians and New Zealanders over where the dessert originated.

1. Preheat oven to 300°F. Beat egg whites, sugar, vinegar, and vanilla together until very stiff, about 10 to 15 minutes.

2. Place mixture on a foil-lined cold baking sheet and shape into a mound.

3. Bake for 30 to 40 minutes. Let cool on a rack; the mound will sink.

4. Cover with whipped cream and garnish with sliced kiwis, strawberries, or passion fruit.

Note: These can be made as individual desserts by making 6 to 8 small mounds on the foil-lined baking sheet. If cooking in advance, store meringue in an airtight container in a dry place. Do not refrigerate or cover with whipped cream until ready to serve.

servings: 6 to 8

4 large egg whites

1 cup sugar

1 teaspoon white vinegar

1 teaspoon pure vanilla extract

1 cup heavy cream, whipped

Sliced kiwis, strawberries, or passion fruit for garnish

Norwegian Sour Cream Waffles

Norske Fløtevafler

---

servings: 6

5 eggs

¾ cup confectioners' sugar

1¾ cups all-purpose flour

1 teaspoon ground cardamom or ginger

1 cup sour cream

4 tablespoons (½ stick) unsalted butter, melted

2 tablespoons water

1 cup raspberry or lingonberry jam

1 cup heavy cream, whipped

A UNIS family became acquainted with these waffles when posted in Norway, where they are prepared on a special heart-shaped waffle iron. A few years later, while living in The Hague in Holland, they prepared them for a dinner party. When the time came for dessert, they discovered that their dog had devoured every single waffle. The family served the raspberry jam and whipped cream with cookies, and no one was the wiser. And the family still has the dog!

1. In a medium bowl, whisk eggs and sugar together until smooth. With a rubber spatula, fold in half of the flour, the cardamom, and sour cream. Fold in the remaining flour.

2. Gently stir in butter and the water and set batter aside for 10 minutes. Cook batter according to instructions for waffle iron.

3. Serve with jam and whipped cream.

Flan

This Filipino version is one of many variations of the centuries-old Spanish custard.

1. Preheat oven to 350°F. Melt sugar in a heavy saucepan over low heat, shaking the pan as the sugar melts. Cook until sugar turns to a golden-brown syrup, stirring constantly, about 10 minutes.

2. Pour immediately into a 9-inch round ovenproof pan. Tilt to spread evenly, as syrup hardens quickly. Make sure the bottom is completely covered. Set aside and let cool until syrup hardens.

3. Combine egg yolks, condensed milk, evaporated milk, vanilla, and lemon juice in a large mixing bowl. Pour into pan on top of caramel. Set pan in a larger baking pan. Fill outer pan with 1 inch hot water.

4. Place pans in oven and bake for 45 minutes, or until a knife inserted comes out clean. Remove from oven and let cool. Remove inner pan from water bath. Place serving platter over custard and invert pan, allowing caramel to coat top and sides. Serve warm or chilled.

servings: 8

- ½ cup sugar for caramel syrup
- 6 egg yolks
- 1 can (14 ounces) condensed milk
- 1 can (12 ounces) evaporated milk
- ½ teaspoon pure vanilla extract (optional)
- ½ teaspoon fresh lemon juice (optional)
- 2 cups sliced fresh fruit such as peaches, kiwi, or pineapple (optional)

Likusya's Torte

servings: 8 to 10

dough

- 2 teaspoons (1 packet) dry yeast, or ½ cake (¼ ounce) fresh yeast
- ½ cup slightly warm milk
- 12 tablespoons (1½ stick) unsalted butter or margarine, softened
- 2 cups all-purpose flour
  Pinch of salt
- 2 cups shelled walnuts
- 1 egg
- ½ cup sugar
- ½ teaspoon pure vanilla extract
- 2 tablespoons confectioners' sugar

A recipe handed down by a UNIS grandmother, who was born in Odessa in 1887. Her granddaughter remembers shelling walnuts for the torte from the time she was 3. The granddaughter left Russia in 1977, after her grandmother's 90th birthday, and kept up the tradition of serving this at family gatherings. She has since lived in Israel and the United States and has traveled widely but has never came across anything similar. The recipe can be doubled, but don't count on leftovers!

1. In a large bowl, stir yeast into milk and set aside until yeast has dissolved, about 10 minutes. In a separate bowl, combine 8 table-spoons of butter, the flour, and salt. When bubbles begin to form on top of yeast mixture, gradually add flour, kneading until soft, light, and no longer sticky. Form dough into a ball, flatten a little and refrigerate at least 1 hour or up to 2 days. Alternatively, chill dough in the freezer for 30 minutes. Preheat oven to 350°F.

2. Meanwhile, make walnut spread by blending walnuts, egg, sugar, vanilla, and the remaining 4 tablespoons butter in a blender or in a food processor fitted with a steel blade to make a paste.

3. After dough has chilled, divide into 3 pieces, with one slightly larger than the others. Roll larger piece to ¼-inch thickness and patch, if necessary. Place in a 10-inch round or square baking pan, pressing to form a ½-inch-high edge in the pan. Evenly spread with half of the nut mixture. Roll out second piece of dough and place on top of nut mixture. Spread with remaining nut mixture. Roll out remaining piece of dough and cover torte, pressing the dough to meet the dough at the edge.

4. Bake torte, in the middle of the oven, 40 to 50 minutes until golden. Remove from oven. Immediately cut into 2-inch squares and sprinkle with confectioners' sugar. When torte cools, transfer squares to a serving plate.

Chilled Lemongrass Soup

The citrusy flavor of lemongrass infuses this unusual dessert soup topped with delicate almond cookies called tuiles. *This original recipe was contributed by Gray Kunz, a UNIS parent and the executive chef at Lespinasse, considered by many to be the finest restaurant in New York City.*

1. For the soup, combine milk, vanilla bean, and sugar in a saucepan and bring to a boil. Add lemongrass. Remove mixture from heat, and allow to infuse and cool. Strain into a clean saucepan and place in an ice bath in the refrigerator.

2. For the *tuiles*, preheat oven to 375°F. In a medium bowl, combine almonds, cornstarch, sugar, and egg white. Mix until smooth and creamy. Stir in egg yolk and orange juice. Roll dough into 4 balls the size of walnuts. Place 2½ inches apart on a greased, parchment-lined baking sheet.

3. Bake until just brown around the edges, about 7 to 10 minutes. Remove from oven. Working quickly, while still hot, remove *tuiles* from baking sheet with a thin spatula and form them into small bowls. (This can be done by draping them over a teacup to create a bowl shape). *Tuiles* are pliable while hot; if they cool and become brittle before molding them, slip them back into the oven for a few seconds to allow them to soften. Set aside to cool and harden. Transfer to an airtight container.

4. To serve, ladle chilled soup into four bowls and float a *tuile* in the center of each.

Note: *Tuiles* may be made 2 days ahead and kept in an airtight container at room temperature. To make vanilla sugar, bury a whole or split vanilla bean in a container holding 1 pound of extra fine granulated sugar. Cover tightly. Sugar will be sufficiently scented with vanilla in about 1 week.

*Available at Asian food markets and some supermarkets; see list of suppliers (page 319).

---

servings: 4

soup

- 3 cups milk
- 1 vanilla bean, split
- 6 tablespoons sugar
- 3 stalks lemongrass,* tough outer leaves removed, bottom 3 inches finely chopped

tuiles

- ½ cup skinned and ground almonds
- ½ teaspoon cornstarch
- ¼ cup sugar
- 1½ teaspoons vanilla sugar
- 1 egg white
- 1 small egg yolk
- 1½ teaspoons orange juice

Impossible Pie

servings: 4

4 large eggs

4 tablespoons (½ stick) unsalted butter

1 cup sugar

½ cup self-rising flour

¼ teaspoon salt

2 cups milk

1 cup shredded unsweetened coconut

1 teaspoon pure vanilla extract

The name of this dish is ironic, for making it is easy. Or perhaps it's impossible to believe that its simple preparation results in a pie with a crust, filling, and topping!

1. Preheat oven to 350°F. Place all ingredients in a blender or work bowl of food processor, fitted with a steel blade. Blend just until thoroughly mixed. Pour into buttered 10-inch pie pan and bake for 1 hour.

2. When cooked, crust will be on the bottom, custard in the middle, and coconut on top.

UNITED KINGDOM

Christmas Cake

Much like a traditional dark fruitcake, this holiday cake will keep for weeks.

1. Soak raisins and mixed dried fruit in brandy overnight.

2. Preheat oven to 325°F. Grease a 10-inch Bundt pan or two 9 x 5-inch loaf pans and line with waxed paper. In a large bowl, beat brown sugar and butter until light and fluffy.

3. Gradually add flour to butter, alternating with eggs. Mix in cinnamon, allspice, nutmeg, baking soda, salt, vanilla extract, and almond extract.

4. Gradually mix in brandied fruit and nuts.

5. Bake in the center of the oven for 2 hours in a Bundt pan or for 1½ hours in the loaf pans, or until knife inserted in the center comes out clean. Remove from oven and let cool before removing waxed paper. Store in aluminum foil in an airtight container. Christmas Cake will keep for 1 to 2 months in the refrigerator.

servings: 12

- **4 cups raisins (1 pound)**
- **1 cup mixed dried fruit, including glacé cherries**
- **½ to 1 cup brandy, to taste**
- **1 cup brown sugar**
- **16 tablespoons (2 sticks) unsalted butter**
- **2½ cups all-purpose flour, sifted**
- **4 medium eggs, lightly beaten**
- **2 teaspoons each ground cinnamon and allspice**
- **1 teaspoon ground or grated nutmeg**
- **1 teaspoon baking soda**
- **Pinch of salt**
- **1 teaspoon each pure vanilla extract and almond extract**
- **1 cup chopped walnuts, almonds, or a combination of both**

Dr. Gottesman's Persimmon Pudding

servings: 8

3 **medium very ripe persimmons, cored, peeled, and seeded**

2 **eggs**

2 **cups milk, or 1¾ cups milk and ¼ cup brandy**

¼ **cup walnut oil or butter, melted**

¾ **cup sugar**

1½ **cups all-purpose flour**

1 **teaspoon baking powder**

1 **teaspoon baking soda**

½ **teaspoon salt**

2 **teaspoons ground cinnamon**

1 **teaspoon ground ginger**

½ **teaspoon ground nutmeg**

1 **cup raisins, or 1 cup walnuts, coarsely chopped, or ½ cup each (optional)**

Dollop of whipped cream (optional)

The beloved doctor of a member of the UNIS community made this pudding with ripe persimmons from his garden in the Santa Ynez Valley, north of Santa Barbara, California. Persimmons, the fruit of a tree of Japanese origin, now also flourish in California and are available during the fall and winter.

1. Press persimmons through a sieve placed over a bowl to yield 2 cups persimmon pulp.

2. Preheat oven to 325°F. Grease a 9-inch square baking pan. In a large bowl, combine persimmon pulp, eggs, milk, oil or butter, and sugar.

3. Sift flour, baking powder, baking soda, salt, cinnamon, ginger, and nutmeg together and add to persimmon mixture. Add raisins and nuts, if using.

4. Pour mixture into prepared pan and bake until firm but still with a pudding consistency, about 1 hour. Serve with whipped cream.

Cardamom Cake

Serve this dense, rich cake in thin slices, with fresh fruit or a fruit compote.

1. Preheat oven to 300°F. Grease and dust with flour a 10-inch Bundt or tube pan. In a large bowl, beat the 24 tablespoons butter until creamy. Add confectioners' sugar and beat until fluffy. Beat in eggs one at a time.

2. Stir in the 2¾ cups flour. Mix in cardamom, orange zest, lemon zest, and vanilla. Pour mixture into pan.

3. Bake for 1 hour or until cake springs back when touched and begins to pull away from the sides. Cool 10 minutes. Unmold onto a serving plate. Serve warm or at room temperature.

servings: 8 to 10

24 tablespoons (3 sticks) unsalted butter at room temperature, plus more for greasing

2¾ cups sifted cake flour, plus more for dusting pan

1 pound confectioners' sugar

6 large eggs

½ teaspoon hulled cardamom seeds, crushed

½ teaspoon grated orange zest

½ teaspoon grated lemon zest

1½ teaspoon vanilla extract

1880s Gingerbread

servings: 8

16 tablespoons (2 sticks) unsalted
   butter, softened

½ cup dark brown sugar

2 cups molasses

1 cup milk

1 tablespoon ground gingerroot

1 teaspoon ground cinnamon

3 large eggs, separated

4 cups sifted all-purpose flour

1 teaspoon baking soda dissolved in
   1 teaspoon water

This recipe originated with a UNIS student's great-great-grandfather, who was a slave in Washington, D.C. He was literate, which was extremely rare, as slaves were forbidden to learn how to read or write. After being freed by President Lincoln, he joined a Massachusetts regiment and fought for the Union during the Civil War. After the war, he was hired as scrivener by the Federal government. This recipe comes from a cookbook he began in 1889.

1. Preheat oven to 350°F. Line two 8-inch square pans with parchment or waxed paper.

2. In a large bowl, using an electric mixer, cream butter and sugar until fluffy. Add molasses, milk, ginger, and cinnamon. Beat well.

3. In a medium bowl, beat egg whites until stiff. In a separate bowl, beat egg yolks. Add the egg whites, egg yolks, 2 cups of the flour, and the baking soda in water to the butter mixture. Beat in remaining 2 cups flour.

4. Divide mixture evenly between the 2 pans. Bake about 35 minutes, or until cake springs back if lightly touched and just begins to come away from the sides. Serve with whipped cream.

UNITED STATES

Carrot Cake

An American classic with many variations, including this one, which includes crushed pineapple.

1. Preheat oven to 350°F. Grease a 9 x 13 x 2-inch baking pan.

2. In a large bowl, combine oil, sugar, eggs, vanilla, and salt and mix well. Add carrots, walnuts, and pineapple.

3. In a separate bowl, combine flour, cinnamon, and baking soda and stir to mix. Add to carrot mixture and stir to combine. Pour batter into pan.

4. Bake for 30 to 45 minutes, or until toothpick inserted in center comes out clean. Cool cake in pan on wire rack, then remove from pan.

5. For the frosting, in a medium bowl, combine butter and cream cheese and blend well. Gradually beat in confectioners' sugar. Add vanilla and beat until smooth. Frost cake when completely cool.

servings: 12 to 15

cake

1½ cups corn oil

2 cups sugar

3 large eggs

2 teaspoons pure vanilla extract

1 teaspoon salt

2 cups grated carrots

1 cup chopped walnuts

½ cup crushed pineapple, drained

2 cups all-purpose flour

2 teaspoons ground cinnamon

2 teaspoons baking soda

frosting

10 tablespoons (1¼ sticks) butter or margarine, softened

1 package (8 ounces) cream cheese

1 pound confectioners' sugar, or less, to taste

1 teaspoon pure vanilla extract

Aunt Willodean's Pound Cake

servings: 2 loaves

- 16 tablespoons (2 sticks) butter, at room temperature, plus more for greasing
- 2 cups all-purpose flour, sifted 3 times before measuring, plus more for dusting
- 2 cups sugar
- 6 large eggs
- 1 tablespoon pure vanilla extract

Aunt Willodean grew up in a little town in southwest Georgia, where fanciful names are commonplace. She learned to make this cake in the early 1930s from her mother, Lilliebelle, with eggs that came from Lilliebelle's chickens, and butter from the milk of her cow, Prettyface. This recipe may seem rich by today's standards, but when Willo was a child, her mother used the formula of a pound of eggs, a pound of butter, a pound of sugar and a pound of flour to make "pound" cake.

1. Preheat oven to 350°F. Butter and flour two 9 x 5-inch loaf pans, or one 10-inch Bundt pan.

2. Cream the 16 tablespoons butter and the sugar together, in a large mixing bowl, using an electric mixer.

3. Add the eggs, one at a time, and the vanilla. Slowly add the 2 cups flour while mixer is beating. Beat for 3 minutes. Pour batter into the prepared pans or Bundt pan.

4. If using two loaf pans, bake 45 minutes to 1 hour or until tooth-pick inserted in cakes comes out clean. If using a Bundt pan, bake for up to 90 minutes, checking with a toothpick for doneness after 70 minutes.

5. Remove pans from oven and cool completely. Remove cake from pans and wrap tightly with plastic wrap. This cake tastes best the day after baking. It keeps 1 week in an airtight container at room temperature or 3 months if frozen.

UNITED STATES

Holiday Cake

Fresh bing cherries or frozen pitted cherries can be substituted for the sweet maraschino cherries in this festive and fruity cake. Garnish with pecan halves and stemmed whole cherries.

1. Preheat oven to 325°F. Butter a 10-inch tube pan. In a large bowl, combine sugar, cream cheese, the 16 tablespoons butter, and the vanilla. Mix well to blend.

2. Add eggs, one at a time, mixing well after each addition.

3. Sift flour together with baking powder. Gradually add 2 cups of the flour to batter, mixing well after each addition. Toss remaining ¼ cup flour with cherries and the ½ cup chopped pecans. Fold into batter.

4. Sprinkle tube pan with the ½ cup finely chopped pecans and pour in batter.

5. Bake for 1 hour and 20 minutes, or until a toothpick inserted in the center comes out clean. Remove from oven and let cool on a rack for 5 minutes.

6. Run a thin knife around the edge of the pan. Remove cake from pan.

7. Combine confectioners' sugar and milk. Mix well. Drizzle over cake. Garnish with additional cherries and nuts. The cake may be frozen for 3 months wrapped in an airtight container. Thaw for 24 hours at room temperature before serving.

---

servings: 12

- 16 tablespoons (2 sticks) unsalted butter, softened, plus more for greasing
- 1½ cups sugar
- 1 package (8 ounces) cream cheese, softened
- 1½ teaspoons pure vanilla extract
- 4 large eggs
- 2¼ cups all-purpose flour
- 1½ teaspoons baking powder
- ½ cup well-drained maraschino cherries, chopped, plus more for garnish
- ½ cup chopped pecans, plus more for garnish
- ½ cup finely chopped pecans
- 1½ cups sifted confectioners' sugar
- 2 tablespoons milk

Allegretti Chiffon Cake

servings: 10

cake

2¼ cups all-purpose flour

1¾ cups sugar

3 teaspoons baking powder

1 teaspoon salt

½ cup vegetable oil

4 egg yolks, unbeaten

¾ cup cold water

2 teaspoons pure vanilla extract

3 tablespoons grated orange rind

8 egg whites

½ teaspoon cream of tartar

3 squares unsweetened
chocolate, grated

icing

6 tablespoons butter

4 tablespoons heavy cream

4 cups sifted confectioners' sugar

2 teaspoons vanilla extract

3 squares unsweetened chocolate

½ teaspoon vegetable oil

Many decades ago, the great-grandmother of a UNIS alumna discovered this recipe in a women's magazine. It has become a family favorite, especially for birthdays. As for the name Allegretti, it is most probably the name of the woman who first submitted the recipe to the magazine.

1. Preheat oven to 325°F. In a large mixing bowl, sift together flour, sugar, baking powder, and salt.

2. Make a well in the dry ingredients and add vegetable oil, egg yolks, the water, vanilla, and orange rind. Stir to blend.

3. In a large bowl, beat egg whites and cream of tartar until very stiff peaks form. Gently fold egg whites into flour mixture until blended. Fold in grated chocolate. Pour batter into two ungreased 9 x 5-inch loaf pans or one 10-inch tube, angel-food-cake or Bundt pan.

4. Bake for 45 to 60 minutes, or until toothpick inserted in center comes out clean. Remove from oven. Invert cakes on racks and let cool upside down in pans. When cool, run a sharp knife around edges to loosen cakes.

5. Meanwhile, prepare icing. Beat butter until fluffy. Stir in cream, confectioners' sugar, and vanilla. Melt chocolate with the oil in the top of a double boiler set over hot water. Frost the cake with the white icing. Drizzle melted chocolate over white icing.

Twila's Apple Nut Cake

Wonderful hot or cold, this cake can be served with homemade whipped cream or ice cream.

1. Preheat oven to 375°F. Grease a 9 x 13-inch pan.

2. Sift together flour, baking soda, cinnamon, salt, and nutmeg in a large bowl.

3. In a separate large bowl, beat eggs and sugar. Add oil and beat 1 minute.

4. Gradually add flour mixture to egg mixture and stir well. Add apples and nuts.

5. Pour batter into pan and bake for 35 to 40 minutes, or until toothpick inserted in center comes out clean. Let cool on a rack.

6. Sift confectioners' sugar over top.

servings: 12

2 cups all-purpose flour

1 teaspoon baking soda

1 teaspoon ground cinnamon

1 teaspoon salt

Sprinkling of ground or grated nutmeg

3 large eggs

1¾ cups sugar

1 cup vegetable oil

2 cups apples, cored, peeled, and thinly sliced

½ cup chopped nuts

Confectioners' sugar

Strawberry Glazed Cheesecake

servings: 8 to 10

crust

1¾ cups fine graham cracker crumbs

¼ cup finely chopped walnuts

½ teaspoon ground cinnamon

8 tablespoons (1 stick) butter or margarine, melted

filling

3 eggs, well beaten

2 packages (8 ounces each) cream cheese, softened

1 cup sugar

¼ teaspoon salt

2 teaspoons pure vanilla extract

½ teaspoon almond extract

3 cups sour cream

glaze

2 cups (1 pint) fresh strawberries, washed and hulled

1 cup water

1½ tablespoons cornstarch

½ cup sugar

Red food coloring (optional)

In her first attempt at baking this dish, the contributor, a UNIS teacher, mistakenly used a French triple crème cheese Although she later discovered that using Philadelphia-style cream cheese makes this a light yet rich-tasting cheesecake, she still remembers her delicious mistake.

1. Preheat oven to 375°F.

2. For the crust, thoroughly combine graham cracker crumbs, walnuts, cinnamon, and melted butter. Press on bottom and sides of a 9-inch springform pan. Sides should be about 1¾ inches high. Refrigerate until ready to fill.

3. For the filling, combine eggs, cream cheese, sugar, salt, vanilla, and almond extract. Beat until smooth. Blend in sour cream. Pour into crust.

4. Bake cake about 40 minutes or just until set. To cool, turn off oven, prop oven door open, and leave cake inside for 30 minutes. Remove cake to a wire rack to cool completely. Refrigerate for 4 to 5 hours before glazing.

5. To make glaze, crush 1 cup of the strawberries and place in a small saucepan. Add the water and boil for 2 minutes. Strain into a separate saucepan. Mix the cornstarch and sugar and stir into the strawberry mixture. Bring to a boil, stirring constantly. Cook, stirring, until mixture is thick and clear. Add a few drops of food coloring, if desired. Let cool to room temperature. Arrange remaining 1 cup strawberries on top of chilled cake. Top with glaze. Chill about 2 hours before serving.

UNITED STATES

Apple Crisp

From colonial times, just about every American household had a favorite simple, crunchy apple dessert. This is one of them.

1. Preheat oven to 350°F. Rub apple slices with lemon juice. Combine sugar, cinnamon, cloves, and nutmeg. Sprinkle over apples and toss gently. Place apple mixture and raisins in a 1½-quart ovenproof casserole or pie dish.

2. For the topping, blend oats, flour, sugar, salt, and butter until mixture reaches a crumbly consistency. Add nuts, if using, and sprinkle over apple mixture.

3. Bake for 45 minutes, or until apples are tender and topping is crisp and brown. Serve with whipped cream, ice cream, or wedges of Cheddar cheese.

servings: 6

filling

5 to 6 tart apples, such as Granny Smith, Cortlandt, or winesap, peeled, cored, and sliced

2 teaspoons fresh lemon juice

½ cup sugar

1 teaspoon cinnamon

¼ teaspoon ground cloves

½ teaspoon ground nutmeg

⅔ cup golden raisins (optional)

topping

½ cup rolled oats (oatmeal)

½ cup all-purpose flour

½ cup dark brown sugar

¼ teaspoon salt

8 tablespoons (1 stick) butter

½ cup chopped walnuts, almonds, or pecans (optional)

New York State Apple Pie

---

servings: 8

pastry

1½ cups vegetable shortening

3 cups all-purpose flour

1 teaspoon salt

1 large egg, beaten

5 tablespoons water

1 tablespoon vinegar

filling

11 to 12 medium apples, peeled and cored, each cut into 8 sections

3 tablespoons sugar

1 tablespoon ground cinnamon

Juice of ½ lemon

½ cup New York State maple syrup

New York State sharp Cheddar cheese, sliced

This recipe comes from the family of Nelson Rockefeller, a former New York State governor and Vice-President of the United States.

1. In a large bowl, cut shortening into flour, using two kitchen knives or a pastry cutter, and add salt.

2. Combine the egg, water, and vinegar and blend with a slotted spoon until moistened. Pour into flour mixture and mix well.

3. Form dough into a ball and, with the heel of a hand, knead by pushing down once or twice. Reform dough into a ball and flatten. Wrap dough and refrigerate for at least 30 minutes. Dough can be frozen for up to 2 weeks.

4. Preheat oven to 450°F. Place dough in 9 x 13 x 2-inch pan. Press dough out to the edges of the pan with fingertips.

5. For the filling, arrange apples in one layer on the dough.

6. In a small bowl, mix sugar and cinnamon. Sprinkle evenly over apples. Sprinkle with lemon juice.

7. Place in the oven and bake for 20 minutes. Reduce heat to 350°F and bake 30 minutes.

8. Remove from oven, pour on maple syrup, and serve with cheese slices.

UNITED STATES

Pumpkin Pie

Pumpkin has been a part of the American diet since the time of the Pilgrims, and a filling for pies ever since. It's no wonder that pumpkin pie has long been the traditional dessert at Thanksgiving and is often served at Christmas as well. The spices used in this 100-year-old family recipe are the same ones used during the 18th century. Fresh pumpkin will yield the best results.

1. Preheat oven to 400°F. Stir brown sugar into beaten eggs in a large bowl. Blend until thick and creamy.

2. Add salt, cinnamon, nutmeg, cloves, allspice, ginger, and milk or half-and half and stir well. Stir in pumpkin.

3. Pour mixture into pie shell and bake for 15 minutes. Reduce heat to 350°F and cook for another 40 to 45 minutes. When done, the tip of a sharp knife inserted into the center of the pie will come out clean.

Note: Boiling, roasting, or microwaving pieces of fresh pumpkin (after removing the seeds and stringy parts and cutting the pumpkin into 4-inch chunks) is well worth the trouble. Cook pieces until the inner pulp is tender; scrape the soft pulp from the shell, and mash. Extra mashed pumpkin can be frozen for up to 6 months. Small pumpkins are easier to work with and are sweeter.

servings: 6 to 8

1 cup firmly packed brown sugar

2 large eggs, lightly beaten

½ to 1 teaspoon salt

1 teaspoon cinnamon

1 teaspoon ground nutmeg

½ teaspoon ground cloves

½ teaspoon ground allspice

¼ teaspoon ground ginger

1 cup milk or half-and-half

1¼ cups cooked and mashed pumpkin, or 1 can (12 ounces) unseasoned pumpkin

1 8-inch pie shell, unbaked

Sweet Potato Pie

Another pie with origins in colonial America is sweet potato pie, a delicacy traditionally served in the South as part of a Thanksgiving feast or Christmas dinner.

servings: 8

- 3 pounds sweet potatoes (about 4 large potatoes)
- 4 large eggs
- 8 tablespoons (1 stick) butter, melted
- ⅓ cup evaporated milk
- 1 tablespoon all-purpose flour
- 2 tablespoons pure vanilla extract
- 1½ cups sugar
- 2 tablespoons ground nutmeg
- 2 9-inch pie shells

1. Boil sweet potatoes for 30 minutes, or until easily pierced with a fork. Drain, rinse under cold water, and then peel.

2. Preheat oven to 375°F. Put potatoes into a large mixing bowl. Add eggs and beat well. Add butter, evaporated milk, flour, vanilla, sugar, and nutmeg. Beat with an electric mixer for about 5 minutes, until smooth, or by hand for 15 minutes.

3. Spoon mixture into pie shells and bake in the center of the oven for about 50 minutes or until tops are brown and filling has set. Remove from oven and let cool on racks. Serve warm or cold.

UNITED STATES

Easy Pie

Seasonal fruit, such as apples or peaches may be substituted, but plums work best in this simply delicious pie.

1. Preheat oven to 350°F. Place fruit and nuts, if using, in a deep 8-inch pie pan.

2. Sprinkle fruit with ¼ cup of the sugar and toss together.

3. In a large bowl, combine eggs, butter, the remaining ¾ cup sugar, the flour, and vanilla. Mix until smooth and pour over fruit mixture.

4. Bake for 40 minutes. Serve warm with ice cream.

servings: 8

2 cups chopped plums or other fresh, seasonal fruit, such as peaches

½ cup chopped almonds or walnuts (optional)

1 cup sugar

2 eggs

11 tablespoons melted butter

1 cup all-purpose flour

1 teaspoon pure vanilla extract

Pecan Pie

servings: 6 to 8

1¼ cups dark corn syrup

1 cup sugar

4 large eggs

4 tablespoons (½ stick) unsalted butter, melted

1½ cups whole pecans

1 teaspoon pure vanilla extract

1 tablespoon dark rum

½ teaspoon salt

9-inch pie shell

Pecans are an American nut, produced by a variety of the hickory tree. Early explorers observed that they were an important source of food for the native peoples in Texas and around the Mississippi River, where the best pecans are still grown today. This classic Southern recipe is heavenly when served with vanilla ice cream or whipped cream.

1. Preheat oven to 350°F. Combine corn syrup and sugar in a saucepan and bring to a boil. Cook, stirring until sugar dissolves. Remove from heat and let cool slightly.

2. In a medium bowl, beat eggs and gradually add syrup, beating continuously. Add butter, pecans, vanilla, rum, and salt, and pour mixture into pie shell.

3. Bake 50 minutes or until pie is set. Remove from oven. Let cool on a rack.

UNITED STATES

Orange Slices in Champagne Sauce

An easy and elegant dessert, especially good in winter when navel oranges are at their best.

1. Slice oranges into ¼-inch rounds and place in layers in an attractive glass bowl.

2. In a blender or a food processor fitted with a steel blade, combine ginger marmalade, stem ginger, sugar, and Champagne. Blend until smooth.

3. Pour mixture over oranges, cover with plastic wrap, and refrigerate overnight. Turn oranges occasionally.

4. Before serving, lightly toast almonds with oil in a 350°F oven on a baking sheet or in a skillet over moderate heat, shaking the pan often. Sprinkle oranges with toasted almonds.

*Available at specialty food markets; see list of suppliers (page 319).

servings: 6 to 8

8 large navel oranges, peeled, pith removed

1 cup ginger marmalade*

1 cup candied ginger

½ cup superfine sugar

2 cups dry Champagne

½ cup slivered almonds, toasted

1 teaspoon vegetable oil

Fresh Berry Gratin

servings: 2

- 1 pint raspberries, washed and hulled
- 1 pint strawberries, washed, hulled, and sliced
- 1 cup heavy cream
- 2 tablespoons confectioners' sugar
- 1 teaspoon pure vanilla extract
- 4 tablespoons sour cream
- 4 tablespoons light brown sugar

Luscious berries with cream make a simple yet refined ending to a meal. Peaches or blueberries may also be used.

1. Place berries in an 8-inch ovenproof dish.

2. Whip cream with confectioners' sugar and vanilla. Fold in sour cream. Spread mixture over berries. (Can be made ahead to this point and refrigerated; it's best if cooked directly after removing from refrigerator.)

3. Preheat broiler for 15 minutes.

4. Just before broiling, press brown sugar through a strainer to form a thin, even layer over the cream.

5. Place under broiler, 4 inches from the flame, and broil until sugar has burnt, about 2 minutes. Serve immediately.

Frozen Peach Dessert

A refreshing frozen dessert, sometimes called a frappé, that is similar to ice cream.

1. Combine all ingredients, except mint, and pour into a 4-cup mold or ice cube tray. Freeze several hours. Using a food processor fitted with a steel blade, mix to clear ice crystals.

2. Spoon into sherbet or wine glasses and garnish with mint.

servings: 3 to 4

4 ripe peaches, pitted, peeled, and puréed

1¼ cups sugar

1¼ cups sour cream

1¼ cup fresh lemon juice

¾ teaspoon pure vanilla extract

Mint leaves, for garnish

Peanut Blossom Cookies

servings: 48 cookies

1¾ cups all-purpose flour

½ cup sugar, plus 2 tablespoons for rolling cookies

½ cup brown sugar

1 teaspoon baking soda

½ teaspoon salt

½ cup vegetable shortening

½ cup peanut butter

1 large egg

2 tablespoons milk

1 teaspoon pure vanilla extract

48 chocolate kisses, unwrapped

A parent's kisses can do magic when it comes to curing a cut finger or skinned knee. With 48 chocolate kisses, this recipe can also cure an empty stomach!

1. Preheat oven to 350°F. In a mixing bowl, combine all ingredients except chocolate kisses and 2 tablespoons of the sugar. Blend well with an electric mixer at low speed. Dough will be stiff but manageable.

2. Shape into balls about ¾ inches in diameter, using a rounded teaspoon of dough for each ball. Roll balls in the remaining 2 tablespoons sugar and place on ungreased baking sheet. Bake for 10 minutes, 5 minutes on upper rack, 5 minutes on lower rack, or bake in the middle of the oven for 15 minutes.

3. Remove from oven and immediately top each cookie with a chocolate kiss, pressing down firmly so cookie cracks around edges. Let cool on rack.

Uncle Herman's Potato Chip Cookies

When Uncle Herman arrived in the United States from Romania, a lady friend introduced him to these all-American cookies, which he immediately fell in love with.

1. Preheat oven to 350°F. Combine thoroughly flour, butter or margarine, sugar, walnuts or pistachios, vanilla, and potato chips. You may need to use fingers to mix, as the dough gets quite thick.

2. Place teaspoon-size balls of cookie dough on a very lightly greased baking sheet. Press balls down with a fork or fingertips.

3. Bake for 10 to 15 minutes, or until edges are golden brown. Let cool on rack.

servings: 40 cookies

- 2 cups sifted all-purpose flour
- 16 tablespoons (2 sticks) butter or margarine, softened
- ½ cup sugar
- ½ cup walnuts or pistachios, finely ground
- 1 teaspoon pure vanilla extract
- ½ cup finely crushed potato chips
- Vegetable oil, for greasing baking sheet

breakfast, brunch & afternoon tea

Danish Doughnuts

Aebleskiver

A traditional Danish favorite, these luscious doughnuts are made in an aebleskiver pan* or "monk's pan,"—a round skillet with six molded hemispherical cups. In Denmark, knitting needles are used to flip the doughnuts.

1. Whisk milk, egg yolks, and sugar together in a medium bowl.

2. In a separate large bowl, sift flour, baking powder, cardamom, and salt together. Add to yolk mixture. Stir in melted butter.

3. Beat egg whites until stiff, in a small bowl with an electric mixer. Gently fold egg whites into batter. *Do not stir after adding egg whites!*

4. Butter the cups of the *aebleskiver* pan and heat on medium heat. Fill cups of heated and buttered *aebleskiver* pan with batter. When edges begin to brown and a good deal of the batter in the center of each cup remains liquid, flip with small knitting needles or pointed chopsticks. Flip again, until a golden-brown sphere is formed.

5. Remove from pan and sprinkle lightly with confectioners' sugar. Serve with jam and applesauce.

Note: These doughnuts can be made in an ordinary skillet. They will taste the same, but will be shaped like pancakes.

*Available at specialty cookware stores; see list of suppliers (page 319).

---

servings: 6 to 8

2 cups milk

2 large eggs, separated

2 tablespoons sugar

2 cups all-purpose flour

2 teaspoons baking powder

Pinch of freshly ground cardamom (optional)

½ teaspoon salt

2 tablespoons butter, melted, plus more, unmelted for greasing

Confectioners' sugar, for dusting

Grandma Blaize's Buttermilk Scones

servings: 25

5 cups unbleached all-purpose flour plus 2 teaspoons flour, for dusting

1½ cups sugar

1 teaspoon salt

2 tablespoons baking powder

12 tablespoons (1½ sticks) unsalted butter, cut into small pieces

2 tablespoons vegetable shortening

2 large eggs

1½ cups buttermilk

1½ cups raisins or currants

glaze

1 egg white

1 teaspoon water

1 teaspoon cinnamon

1 teaspoon sugar

Years ago, Grandma Blaize emigrated from Grenada to the United States with her 12 children. She brought with her many of the customs of colonial life in the West Indies, including a fondness for rose gardening and traditional English tea. Serve these scones warm with clotted cream or whipped cream and strawberry jam or apple butter.

1. Preheat oven to 400°F.

2. In a large bowl, sift together 5 cups of the flour, the 1½ cups sugar, salt, and baking powder.

3. With a pastry cutter or in a food processor fitted with a steel blade, cut butter and shortening into flour until mixture resembles fine bread crumbs. Transfer to mixing bowl.

4. Add eggs, one at a time, mixing well. Add buttermilk. Mix until dough forms a ball.

5. In a small bowl, mix raisins or currants lightly with remaining 2 teaspoons flour. Remove dough from bowl and place on lightly floured surface. If dough is too sticky to knead, add a small amount of flour. Knead in raisins or currants, gently pushing dough ball down and out twice using the heel of a hand.

6. Sprinkle a bit of flour on work surface and gently roll dough to 1- to 1½-inch thickness. Cut into rounds, no larger than 2-inches. Place rounds on baking sheet. Press remaining dough together. Roll again gently and cut into rounds.

7. For the glaze, beat egg white with the water, cinnamon, and 1 teaspoon sugar. Brush on each scone.

8. Bake 15 to 20 minutes, until golden brown. Let cool before serving.

Note: Coconut milk can be substituted for buttermilk; ½ cup shredded coconut can be added to dough at step 5.

Thirty-Day Muffins

A practical, everyday recipe from Lesotho in southern Africa, this is a most efficient way to make muffins. A big batch of batter, kept in the refrigerator, will last for a month. Just add a bit of milk each time before baking fresh muffins.

1. Beat eggs and sugar in a large bowl, until fluffy. Add the oil, vanilla, and bran. Mix well.

2. In a separate large bowl, sift the flour, salt, and baking soda. Gradually add milk, stirring well after each addition. Add egg mixture and raisins.

3. Place batter in a bowl, cover tightly, and refrigerate for at least 24 hours.

4. Preheat oven to 350°F. Grease medium-size muffin tins. Fill each muffin cup one-third full. Bake for 20 to 25 minutes, or until golden brown. Cook only as many muffins as needed immediately. Batter keeps refrigerated for 30 days. Bake muffins fresh as desired.

---

servings: 4 to 5 dozen muffins

4 eggs

3¼ cups brown sugar

¾ cup vegetable oil

1 teaspoon vanilla extract

4 cups bran

5 cups all-purpose flour

1 teaspoon salt

5 teaspoons baking soda

1 quart milk

½ cup raisins

Savory Sticky Rice

Loh Mai Fun

servings: 8 to 10

5 cups sticky rice,* soaked overnight in water to cover and drained

1 tablespoon five-spice powder*

2 tablespoons plus ¼ cup vegetable oil

4 shallots, peeled and sliced

1 to 2 tablespoons minced garlic

½ cup dried shrimp,* soaked in warm water for 30 minutes and drained

8 dried shiitake mushrooms, soaked in warm water for 30 minutes, drained and water squeezed out

1 can (5.3 ounces or 1 cup) braised peanuts*

2 sweet Chinese sausages,* thinly sliced

1 tablespoon dark soy sauce

2 teaspoons Asian sesame oil

2 tablespoons light soy sauce

2 tablespoons oyster sauce

2 cups chicken broth

2 scallions, trimmed and chopped

Dash of pepper

A filling dish, usually served for breakfast or brunch with dim sum. Serve with sliced fresh red chili peppers or sweet chili sauce.

1. Mix sticky rice with five-spice powder.

2. In a wok or large skillet, stir-fry rice over moderate heat in 2 tablespoons of the oil for about 7 minutes. Set aside.

3. In another large pot, stir-fry shallots over high heat in remaining ¼ cup oil until golden brown, stirring often. Remove shallots from pan and set aside.

4. Stir-fry garlic in same oil for 30 seconds, stirring. Add shrimp, mushrooms, peanuts, and sausages and stir-fry for 5 minutes.

5. Add dark soy sauce, sesame oil, light soy sauce, and oyster sauce and stir-fry 2 minutes more.

6. Add chicken broth and simmer for 5 minutes. Remove from heat and mix in the sticky rice.

7. Place rice mixture into a large bamboo steamer, or a metal steamer, set over a pot of simmering water, and cover. Steam until soft, about 35 minutes in bamboo steamer and 45 minutes in the metal steamer. Add additional chicken broth to rice, if needed, during steaming to prevent dryness. Add additional water to wok or pot during steaming, if necessary.

8. Mound rice in bowl shapes on a serving platter. Garnish with shallots, scallions, and pepper.

Available at Asian food markets; see list of suppliers (page 319).

RUSSIA

Cheese Blintzes/Potato Blintzes

A Russian-Romanian grandmother cooked these blintzes instinctively, adding "a little of this and a little of that." The old-country recipe was preserved and written down by her daughter and granddaughters, who watched closely, measured carefully, and then wrote everything down. Serve with sour cream, applesauce, or fresh fruit.

1. For blintzes, add salt and the water to egg in a medium bowl. Stir in flour and mix until smooth.

2. In a small frying pan, heat 1 tablespoon of the oil over moderate heat. When hot, spoon about 3 to 4 tablespoons of batter and tilt the pan to form a thin, even layer.

3. Cook 1 to 2 minutes until the sides curl and the blintz moves freely when the pan is shaken. Cook only on one side.

4. Turn the blintz out of pan onto a paper towel. Repeat procedure until all batter is used, adding more oil as needed. The batter should yield about 17 blintzes.

5. Mix all cheese filling ingredients in a bowl. Place about 2 tablespoons of cheese mixture in the middle of the cooked side of a blintz. Roll bottom up over cheese, fold in both sides and roll up to the top. Sauté filled blintzes in a small amount of oil, turning, until golden brown.

6. For the potato filling, cook potatoes in boiling water with the 2 teaspoons salt for about 10 minutes, or until soft but not falling apart. Drain potatoes and return to pot.

7. In a skillet, heat oil over medium heat and sauté onion until soft and translucent, stirring often, about 10 minutes. Mash onion into cooked potatoes.

8. Follow procedure for cheese blintzes to assemble and cook potato blintzes.

servings: 4 to 6

blintzes

½ teaspoon salt

1 cup water

1 large egg, beaten

1 cup all-purpose flour

⅓ cup oil

cheese filling

1½ pounds salted farmers' cheese

1 egg yolk

3 tablespoons sugar

½ teaspoon salt

¼ teaspoon vanilla extract

potato filling

2½ pounds all-purpose potatoes, peeled and cut into quarters (4 to 5 potatoes)

2 teaspoons salt

2 tablespoons vegetable oil

1 large onion, finely chopped

RUSSIA

Sour Cream Coffee Cake
Oladyi

servings: 10

- 8 tablespoons (1 stick) unsalted butter or margarine
- 1¼ cups sugar
- 3 large eggs
- 1 cup sour cream
- 1 teaspoon pure vanilla extract
- 2 cups sifted all-purpose flour
- 1 teaspoon baking powder
- 1 teaspoon baking soda
- ⅛ teaspoon salt
- ⅓ cup brown sugar
- 1 teaspoon ground cinnamon
- 1 cup chopped nuts (optional)

Sweet, rich pastries made with generous amounts of butter, sour cream and eggs have always been a much-loved and extravagant pleasure in Russia.

1. Preheat oven to 325°F and grease a 10-inch tube pan.

2. In a large bowl, beat butter and 1 cup of the sugar until light and fluffy, about 5 minutes. Add eggs, sour cream, and vanilla. Continue to beat for 3 minutes, or until ingredients are well blended.

3. Combine flour, baking powder, baking soda, and salt. Add to egg mixture and beat 30 seconds, or until thoroughly combined.

4. For the topping, mix together brown sugar, the remaining ¼ cup sugar, cinnamon, and nuts, if using.

5. Pour half of the batter into greased pan. Spread two-thirds of the topping mixture over batter. Cover with remaining batter, then sprinkle on remaining topping mixture.

6. Bake for 60 minutes, or until toothpick inserted into cake comes out clean.

SWITZERLAND

Muësli

Named for Dr. Bircher Muësli, who devised this tasty and nutritious mix for his patients, this combination of oats, nuts, and dried fruits has been adopted across Switzerland, where every family has its own freshly made version. Muësli is also eaten for lunch or as a snack.

1. In a large glass bowl, soak oats and raisins in the milk until softened, about 30 minutes.

2. Add nuts, sugar, banana, grapes, pear, apples, and oranges.

3. Add whipped cream for texture. Garnish with additional nuts.

Note: This is a basic recipe that may be varied by adding yogurt or seasonal fruit. In summer, use blackberries, strawberries, blueberries, raspberries, peaches, or nectarines; in the fall, use plums, persimmons, or pomegranates. For a tropical flavor, use pineapples, coconuts, mangoes, or bananas.

servings: 6

¾ cup rolled oats

¼ cup dried raisins

1 cup milk

¼ cup each ground almonds and hazelnuts, plus more for garnish

¼ cup white or brown sugar

1 medium banana, sliced

12 seedless grapes

1 unpeeled pear, grated

2 unpeeled apples, grated

2 oranges, peeled, pith and seeds removed, flesh cut from membranes

2 tablespoons whipped cream

Munchkin Cakes

servings: 16

8 tablespoons (1 stick) butter

½ cup sugar

1 large egg, beaten

Grated rind and juice of ½ orange

1¾ cups self-rising flour

½ cup milk

6 tablespoons apricot jam

3 ounces semi-sweet chocolate, melted

Crystallized orange and lemon slices, for garnish

Named for the charming, diminutive residents of Oz, these lovely cakes are perfect with a hot cup of coffee or as part of an elegant afternoon tea.

1. Preheat oven to 350°F. In a pan over low heat, melt butter and add sugar. Cook for 2 minutes, stirring occasionally.

2. In a large bowl, mix egg and orange rind and gradually add butter mixture, beating well. Fold in flour, alternating with milk and orange juice.

3. Spoon batter into paper cupcake wrappers placed in metal cupcake pan. Bake for 25 to 30 minutes, until well risen and golden brown.

4. When cakes are cool, slice off tops, scoop out some cake from the center and place a spoonful of jam in the hollow.

5. Replace the lid and ice with melted chocolate. Top each with an orange or lemon slice.

UNITED KINGDOM

Tea Time Scones

Although scones originated centuries ago in Scotland, they have long since been adopted throughout the British Isles, where they are omnipresent at breakfast and afternoon tea. Strong feelings are expressed about whether to include raisins or currants. And in Devon and Cornwall, famous for clotted cream, a debate continues about whether the cream should be atop the jam, or the jam atop the cream.

1. Preheat oven to 450°F. Sift together flour, salt, and baking powder into a bowl or food processor and add sugar. Cut in the butter, using a pastry blender, a food processor fitted with a steel blade, or two kitchen knives, until mixture resembles fine bread crumbs.

2. Sprinkle milk over flour mixture and gently stir to form a ball. If using a food processor, pulse, stopping as soon as dough comes together into a ball. Remove ball from bowl. Push down and out with the heel of a hand once or twice to knead.

3. Preheat baking sheet, roll out dough to about ½-inch thickness. Cut out 2-inch rounds with a cookie cutter. Collect scraps and form a ball, re-roll and cut dough until it is all used. Handle mixture as little as possible. Arrange scones on preheated baking sheet and brush tops with milk.

4. Bake 10 to 12 minutes, until golden brown and well risen. Remove from oven and wrap in a cloth.

5. Whip cream until stiff. Split scones while still warm and fill with butter, strawberry jam, and whipped cream.

servings: 18 to 24 scones

3 cups self-rising flour

1 teaspoon salt

2 teaspoons baking powder

2 teaspoons superfine sugar

6 tablespoons (¾ stick) cold butter

¾ cup milk

½ cup heavy cream

Poor Knights of Windsor Pudding

servings: 8

1¼ cups milk

8 tablespoons superfine sugar

2 tablespoons sweet sherry

8 slices white bread, crusts removed, each slice cut diagonally into 2 triangles

2 egg yolks

8 tablespoons (1 stick) butter, or less

½ teaspoon ground cinnamon

1 cup heavy cream, whipped

This dish is named for the Poor Knights of Windsor, an order of military veterans founded in 1349.

1. Pour ½ cup plus 2 tablespoons of the milk into a shallow dish. Add 2 tablespoons of the sugar and the sherry. Stir well.

2. Dip bread triangles into sherry mixture, soaking each completely. Drain on a wire rack.

3. Beat egg yolks and remaining ½ cup plus 2 tablespoons milk together and dip bread triangles into egg mixture.

4. Heat butter in a large skillet and, in batches, sauté bread slices until golden. Place on a warmed serving dish.

5. Mix remaining 6 tablespoons sugar with cinnamon and sprinkle over bread. Serve with whipped cream.

UNITED KINGDOM

Date and Walnut Cake

This recipe was given to the mother of a member of the UNIS community by a member of the British royal family. For years, the contributor begged her mother for the recipe. Finally her mother relented. The contributor grabbed the nearest napkin and wrote furiously. She still has the napkin.

1. Preheat oven to 400°F. Grease and line a 9x12-inch pan with parchment. Pour the boiling water over dates and let stand until softened, about 15 minutes.

2. In a large bowl, mix flour, baking powder, and salt.

3. In a separate bowl, beat sugar and 8 tablespoons of the butter until light and fluffy. Beat in the egg and vanilla. Fold in flour mixture and walnuts.

4. Drain the dates, add to the batter and mix well.

5. Pour batter into pan and bake for 15 minutes. Reduce oven temperature to 300°F and bake for 40 minutes more. Let cake cool on a rack before icing.

6. For the icing, place the brown sugar, the remaining 2 tablespoons of butter, and cream or milk in a small saucepan over moderately high heat. Boil for 3 minutes, stirring often. Remove from heat. Beat icing, using an electric mixer on high speed, until it cools and reaches a fudge-like consistency.

7. Spread icing on cake. Sprinkle with chopped walnuts.

servings: 8

1 cup boiling water

1 cup chopped, pitted dates

2½ cups all-purpose flour

1 teaspoon baking powder

½ teaspoon salt

1 cup sugar

10 tablespoons (1¼ sticks) unsalted butter or margarine, softened

1 large egg, beaten

1 teaspoon pure vanilla extract

½ cup chopped walnuts

5 tablespoons soft light brown sugar

2 tablespoons light cream or milk

½ cup chopped walnuts

Maids of Honour Tartlets

servings: 12

filling

½ cup milk

⅓ cup white cake crumbs

4 tablespoons (½ stick) unsalted butter, cut into small pieces

⅓ cup superfine sugar

⅓ cup ground almonds

1 egg, beaten

Grated rind of 1 lemon

3 drops almond extract

dough

2 cups all-purpose flour

Pinch of salt

8 tablespoons (1 stick) unsalted butter, cut into small pieces, plus more for greasing

3 to 4 tablespoons cold milk

½ cup apricot jam

These tartlets were devised by a baker in Richmond, Surrey, whose shop was near King Henry VIII's royal palace. The king was fond of them, and tradition has it that the tartlets are named after the ladies-in-waiting who carried them to the palace.

1. For the filling, scald milk by heating it in a saucepan almost to boiling and remove from heat. Stir in cake crumbs, 4 tablespoons butter, the sugar, ground almonds, egg, lemon rind, and almond extract. Stir well and let stand for 5 minutes.

2. For the dough, mix flour and salt together in a medium bowl. Cut 8 tablespoons butter into flour using a pastry cutter, a food processor fitted with a steel blade, or two kitchen knives, until mixture resembles fine bread crumbs.

3. Sprinkle cold milk over the flour mixture. Blend with kitchen knives until mixture holds together and forms a ball, or in food processor, pulse, stopping the motor when the dough begins to come together. Do not wait until it forms a complete ball.

4. Remove dough from the bowl, adding any loose bits. On a work surface, press down and out on the ball with the heel of a hand once or twice to knead. Re-form into a ball, flatten slightly. Cover tightly and refrigerate for at least 30 minutes.

5. Preheat oven to 425°F. On a lightly floured work surface, roll out pastry and cut rounds, using a fluted 3-inch pastry cutter.

6. Place in buttered tart shells or shallow cupcake pans, and spread jam in the base of each. Divide the filling equally. Bake for 15 to 20 minutes.

UNITED STATES

Sunday Brunch Soufflé

Despite its French-sounding name, this is an all-American breakfast invention—a twist on the classic sausage and eggs.

1. In a large skillet, sauté sausages until almost cooked, about 15 minutes. Drain on paper towels. When cool, slice into 1-inch rounds.

2. Beat eggs with milk, salt, and mustard.

3. In a greased 9 x 13-inch baking dish, arrange bread cubes, sausages, and cheese. Pour in egg mixture and refrigerate overnight.

4. Preheat oven to 350°F. Bake uncovered for 45 minutes, until the top is golden brown and the egg mixture has a soufflé-like appearance.

servings: 4 to 5

1 pound spicy Italian or pork breakfast sausage

6 eggs, beaten

2 cups milk

1 teaspoon salt

1 teaspoon mustard, preferably Dijon

2 slices white bread, cubed

1½ cups grated Cheddar cheese, about ⅓ pound

Pepper to taste

Vegetable oil, for greasing

Chili Cheese Puff

servings: 8 to 10

Vegetable oil, for pan

10 eggs

½ cup all-purpose flour

1 teaspoon baking powder

1 pint small-curd cottage cheese

2 cups (1 pound) grated Monterey Jack and sharp Cheddar cheeses, combined

8 tablespoons (1 stick) butter, melted

1 can (8 ounces) diced green chili peppers

A dish discovered by a UNIS family in a Santa Monica bed-and-breakfast. It represents a typical California-style fusion of Latin ingredients with a baked-egg dish from the American heartland.

1. Preheat oven to 350°F. Lightly coat a 9 x 13-inch pan with vegetable oil.

2. In a large bowl, beat eggs and add all ingredients except chili peppers. Mix well. Pour into pan.

3. Sprinkle chili peppers over top.

4. Bake 35 to 45 minutes. Top should be lightly brown and the center should be firm.

UNITED STATES

Blintz Soufflé

Often identified with Jewish cooking, blintzes, pancakes of Russian-Polish origin, are similar to French crêpes. This easy but impressive casserole-style dish is ideal for a weekend brunch.

1. Preheat oven to 350°F. In large bowl or blender, mix half of the cream cheese, 2 cups of the cottage cheese, the 6 eggs plus 2 of the yolks, ⅓ cup plus 1 tablespoon of the sugar, 1 teaspoon of the vanilla, butter, sour cream, orange juice, flour, and baking powder.

2. Pour half of the batter into a greased 9 x 13-inch baking dish.

3. To prepare blintz filling, mix remaining cream cheese, remaining 2 cups cottage cheese, remaining 2 egg yolks, remaining 1 tablespoon sugar, and remaining 1 teaspoon vanilla in a large bowl. Ingredients should be mixed well, but consistency should remain thick and lumpy.

4. Drop filling by heaping tablespoonfuls over batter in baking dish. Spread evenly with a knife. Filling will mix slightly with batter.

5. Pour remaining batter evenly over filling.

6. Bake uncovered 50 to 60 minutes, or until puffed and golden.

servings: 8 to 10

soufflé

- **2 packages (8 ounces each) cream cheese, cut into small chunks**
- **4 cups small-curd cottage cheese**
- **6 eggs, plus 4 egg yolks**
- **2 tablespoons plus ⅓ cup sugar**
- **2 teaspoons pure vanilla extract**
- **8 tablespoons (1 stick) butter or margarine, softened**
- **1½ cups sour cream**
- **½ cup orange juice**
- **1 cup all-purpose flour**
- **2 heaping teaspoons baking powder**

Catherine Mott's 1907 Waffles

Waffles, introduced by the Dutch of Nieuw Amsterdam in the early 1600s, have been popular in America ever since. This recipe is a classic, discovered by the great-grandmother of a UNIS student in her favorite cookbook, published in 1907.

servings: 4

2 cups all-purpose flour

2 teaspoons baking powder

1 teaspoon salt

1½ cups milk

3 eggs, separated

3 tablespoons butter, melted

1. In a medium bowl, sift flour, baking powder, and salt.

2. In a separate medium bowl, beat milk and egg yolks together. Stir into dry ingredients. Stir in butter.

3. In a separate bowl, beat egg whites until stiff; gently fold into batter.

4. Spoon batter onto a prepared preheated waffle iron. Serve hot with maple syrup.

Maple Pear Pancake

Since 1796, when the first cookbook published in America featured a recipe for pancakes, creative cooks have been adapting the basic recipe.

1. Preheat oven to 350°F. In a medium bowl, combine milk, egg, and melted butter.

2. Into a large bowl, sift flour, sugar, salt, and baking powder. Stir in milk mixture. Let stand for 10 minutes.

3. Cook pears over moderately high heat with the maple syrup until caramelized in a large cast-iron skillet, about 5 minutes.

4. Arrange pears in a nonstick or lightly oiled 9 x 13-inch or 10-inch baking pan. Pour batter over pears. Place in oven and bake 15 to 20 minutes, or until toothpick inserted in center comes out clean.

5. Invert onto a platter and serve with additional maple syrup.

servings: 2 to 4

1 cup milk

1 egg

2 tablespoons butter, melted

1 cup all-purpose flour

2 tablespoons sugar

½ teaspoon salt

2 teaspoons baking powder

2 to 3 pears, peeled, cored, and thinly sliced

¼ cup maple syrup

contributors

Judy Abrams
B. J. Adler
Katherine Adler
Zachary Adler
Rawya Agha
Hilary Ainger
Marcia Alexander
Mass Ruhaiza Ali
Audre Allen
Francesca Altamura
Steve Alter
Harumi Aoto Donoyan
Katya Arnold
Michael Arricale
Wendy Bachman
Nathalie Barrie
The Bauza Family
Annette Becker
Janett Beswick
Susan Bolotin
Rebecca Bondor
Barrin Bonet
Sumie Tanaka-Bonet
Judy Boomer
Merle Brenner
Françoise Brodsky
Lisa Lacher Bryan
Laura Butler

Gina Buttafoco
Martha Byrum
Marcia Callender
Judith King-Calnek
Terrence Calnek
Barrington Alexander Calvert
Delia Leon Cameo
Joanne Canary
Harriet Canepa
Luciana Capretti
Coleen Carol
Robert Caron
Karen Cavanagh
Teresita V. Centenara
Sha-Mayne Chan
Nora Chanko
Josseline Charas
Stephanie Cheah
Victoria Cheah
Junghwa Choi
Alexander Claes
Irene Clark
Mara McCauley-Clemenza
Jayne Cohen
Natalie R. Cohen
John Cole
Sachiko Dahoui
Baerbel Dainard

Lena K. Datwani
Leslie Davenport
Muriel Davis
Marie DeLaune
Elizabeth De Oliveira e Silva
Amy DeRosa
Cassandra Dick
April Dillon
Molly Alger Dirnberger
Henrietta di Domenico
Harumi Donoyan
Cynthia Dubensky
Marie Laure DuCamp
Robin Gadsden-Dupree
Yvette Duran
Paul Ehrman
Engin Ansalone Elal
Vivian Ellner
Rebecca Lao Emerson
Suzi Epstein
Erla Erlingsdotter
Honey Essman
David Evans
Sara Evans
Nimati Jaouni Fahmawi
Douglas Fairchild
Emily Fano
Zina Favuzza

Sue Felsher

Marian Ferrara

Kay Finch

Mariam Wiernik-Findakly

Donna Fleming

Ellen Forti

Susan Fraga

Brigitte Francois

Alma Frank

Helen W. Gadsden

Leslie Hunter-Gadsden

David Galst

Joann Paley Galst

Sadica Garcia

Jill Garrity

Stephanie Gelb

Karina Gerlach

Brenda Barnes-George

Marie Gibson

George Gilbert

Susanne Hollander Gilbert

Grandmother of Jennie Gilbert

Debbie Glick

Toby Glickman

Mia Goldman

Sarina Goldstein

Maria Dudin Goodwin

Chantal Gouy

Judy Granger

Deborah Green

Jocelyn Greene

Katherine Greene

Richard Greene

Ilene Greenman

Bernice Haber

Defne Halman

Kuniko Hamada

Nezhat Hashemi

Angela Heung

M. Hilmi

Laurinda Liang Ho

Valerie Hobbs

Agnes F. Holland

Susan Horton

Jennifer Hughes

Catherine Hunter

Lloyd B. Hunter

Patricia Huyghue

Shil Hwang

Anne-Khemari Hy

Bonita Insanally

Carolyn Isles

Saloua Jendoubi

Teresa Jouany

Wan Zainin Wan Jusoh

Sam Sabine Kamenitzer

Josiane Kamler

Candy Karcher

Magumi Kasuga

Vibha Kaushal

Jan Kawamura Kay

Liz Kennedy

Aleem Khan

Sylviane Khanna

Maxine L. Kibble

Margaret Salameh King

Brigitte Kinniburgh

Eva Klein

Gladys Meier-Klodt

Taesun Kocjan

Ann Santacroce Kolsun

Barbara A. Kolsun

William J. Kolsun

Guenter Kopcke

Gray Kunz

Nicole Kunz

Martha La Cava

Benedetta Ladisa

Louise Laheurte

Susan Lang

Robert Lascaro

Allyson Lazar

Debbie Lazar

Deirdre Leber

Dan Leigh
Susan Gammie Leigh
Carol Leonard
Connie Leuenberger
Laurie Levin
Alan Levy
Kathy Lichter
Nancy Lichter
Lily Liew
Lenore R. S. Lim
Anne Locke
Wiebeke Loewe
Nancy S. F. Llow
Louisa Lopez
Anne Lowenstein
Susan Lyons
Bruce MacDonald
John Mallios
Mary Mallios
Demetra Manaris
Nancy Manter
Roberta Markel
Susan Markham
Barbara Marsh
Flaminia Martini
Amy Mass
Sue Mathews
Myo Maung
Stacy Mavidis
Anne Ferril McCaffrey
Maggie McCaffrey
Philip McCaffrey
Jean McGavin
William McGilvray
Andrew Enloe McIntyre
Apsara Mehta
Julia Melcher
Leslie Melcher
Nancy Melcher

Paris Melcher
Cheri Melone
Frances Merkler
Richard Merkler
Pnina Michelson
Dr. Paul Mider
Joette Mindlin
Parveen Mirza
Mary Mochochoko
Rosemary Mollon
Belinda Muniz
Miki Murata
Claire Murphy
Rebecca Murry
Joshua Muscat
Amir Nikravesh
Valerie Neal
Yerka Nobilo
Sachiko Noguchi
Marjorie Nunnelly
Mrs. Gordon M. Nunnellly
Anne O'Brien
Paola Oliva
Anne Cunningham O'Neill
Liliane Menin-Opsomer
Patricia Orfanos
Maureen Overall
Mi Sun Park
Jyoti Patel
Nermin Pekin
Michèle Piper
Antonia Pocock
Joyce Poolman
Manju Lata Prasad
Phuong L. Quach
Suzanne Randolph
Gladys Rasheed
Franca Rawitz
Eric Rayman

Joan Reibman
Elizabeth Reis
Leah Rangel-Ribeiro
Victor Rangel-Ribeiro
Alice Richardson
Erif Rison
Carolyn Rispo
Maude Robertson
Margaret Romairone
Carl Rosenmann
Gina Ross
John Rothman
Randee Rubin
Josef S. Ruetzel
Pat Russac
Arlene Sahraie
Nidal Said
Debbie Sala
Ellen Salant
Elizabeth Ritter Samuelson
Connie Sanchez
Alexis Santoro
Brian Santoro
C. H. Saw
Karl Scharf
Neil Schickner
Cheryl Schneider
Emily S. Schneider
Rachel Schneider
Susan Greenberg Schneider
Luthel Sealy
Moulay Seghrouchni
Barbara Sehgal
Gauri Shah
Susan Shapiro
Rajul Sheth
Donna Shirreffs
Pat Shimonov
Charles A. Shorter, Jr.

Danielle Shteynfeld

Olga Shumikhin

J. F. Simelane

Karen Simon

Rema Singh

Rosemary Cipriani-Sklar

Dorothy Small

Mary Smith

Patricia L. Smith

Ann Sobotka

Isabelle Soudrie

Frank Spinelli

Lucea Spinelli

Linda Stein

David Stern

Pamela Stevens

Deborah Straubinger

Amy Stravitz

Geetha Raman Subramanyam

Alicia Svenson

Enrico Taffone

Mary Taveras

Anne Pike-Tay

Barbara Taylor

George Taylor

Jane Taylor

Rosalind Teo

Marjorie Teplitz

Stephanie Teuwen

Otto Thav

Aurelia Cline-Thomas

Ransford Cline-Thomas

Melani Maslow Tice

Susana Torino

Dody Tsiantar

Cecelia Tsien

Nicole Tsien

Elaine Unkeless

Frederick Lim Uy

Carla Valdivia

Frederika Van Eyndhoven

Viviane Dewachter-Van Haecke

Carola Van Kampen

Abel Villacorta

Ana Carola Villacorta

Violeta Villacorta

Christian Wadsack

Gabrielle Kraatz-Wadsack

Eleanor Waldner

Stewart Waltzer

Caroline W. Wanene

Meredith Warshaw

Suzanne Wasserman

Elizabeth Watt

Richard E. Weisberg

Jay Weiser

Margaret Weiss

Lesley Wellott

Joan Lumpkin Wheeler

Elaine K. Whitehouse

Virginia Whitelaw

Valerie Williams

Lotus Wong

Jenny Woo

Lin Xu

Atsushi Yoneda

Naoko Yoneda

Susan Youngman

Sandy Yulke

Anne Zacharia

Gail Hall Zarr

Daniel Zimmer

Mary Ann Zimmer

Catherine Zito

Oranit Zuckerman

equivalents

The exact equivalents in the following tables have been rounded for convenience.

LIQUIDS

US

3 teaspoons	1 tablespoon
2 tablespoons	1 ounce
8 ounces	1 cup
16 ounces/2 cups	1 pint
32 ounces/2 pints	1 quart
128 ounces/4 quarts	1 gallon

UK

3 teaspoons	1 tablespoon
2 tablespoons	1 ounce
10 ounces	1 cup
20 ounces/2 cups	1 pint
40 ounces/2 pints	1 quart
160 ounces/4 quarts	1 gallon

Metric

1 US teaspoon	5 milliliters
1 US tablespoon	15 milliliters
1 US cup	¼ liter
1 US pint	½ liter
1 US quart	1 liter

WEIGHTS

US/UK	Metric
1 ounce	30 grams
3.5 ounces	100 grams
16 ounces/1 pound	450 grams
2.2 pounds	1,000 grams/1 kilogram

OVEN TEMPERATURES

Fahrenheit	Celsius	Gas Mark
325–350°F	165–175°C	2½–3
350°F	180°C	4
375°F	190°C	5
400°F	205°C	6

suppliers

Asian foods

Asian Market Corporation
71½ Mulberry Street, New York, NY 10013
212.962.2028

Han Ah Reum
25 West 32 Street, New York, NY 10001
212.695.3283

Kam Kuo Food Corporation
7 Mott Street, New York, NY 10013
212.349.3097

Kam Man Food Products, Inc.
200 Canal Street, New York, NY 10013
212.571.0171 or 212.571.0330
Mail order available.

Tan Al Hoa Supermarket
81-81½ Bowery, New York, NY 10013
212.219.0893

Brazilian foods

Plataforma
316 West 49 Street, New York, NY 10019
212.245.0505

Indian and Middle Eastern foods

Kalustyan's
123 Lexington Avenue, New York, NY 10016
212.685.3451
Mail order available.

Japanese foods

Sunrise Mart
4 Stuyvesant Street, New York, NY 10003
212.598.3040; fax 212.598.9033 for deliveries
Mail order available.

Yaohan
595 River Road, Edgewater, NJ 07020
201.941.9113

Latin American foods

Mexicano Lindo
2265 Second Avenue, New York, NY 10035
212.410.4728

Specialty foods

Balducci's
424 Avenue of the Americas, New York, NY 10011
800.225.3822
Mail order available.

Citarella's
2135 Broadway, New York, NY 10023
212.874.0383; 24-hour line: 800.588.0383

Esposito's Meat Shop
500 Ninth Avenue, New York, NY 10018
212.279.3298

Specialty cookware

Broadway Panhandler
477 Broome Street, New York, NY 10013
212.966.3434
Mail order available.

Kam Kuo Food Corporation
See Asian food markets.

Kam Man Food Products, Inc.
See Asian food markets.

Sunrise Mart
See Japanese food markets.

Zabar's
2245 Broadway, New York, NY 10024
212.787.2000

index

index by country